MINNESOTA
HIGH SCHOOL MATHEMATICS (5-12)

By: Sharon Wynne, M.S.

XAMonline, INC.
Boston

Library of Congress Cataloging-in-Publication Data

Wynne, Sharon A.
　　Minnesota High School Mathematics (5-12) / Sharon A. Wynne 1st ed.
　　ISBN 978-1-60787-077-7
　　1. High School Mathematics (5-12)
　　2. Study Guides
　　3. Minnesota
　　4. Teachers' Certification & Licensure
　　5. Careers

Disclaimer:

The opinions expressed in this publication are the sole works of XAMonline and were created independently from the National Education Association, Educational Testing Service, or any State Department of Education, National Evaluation Systems or other testing affiliates.

Between the time of publication and printing, state specific standards as well as testing formats and Web site information may change and therefore would not be included in part or in whole within this product. Sample test questions are developed by XAMonline and reflect content similar to that on real tests; however, they are not former test questions. XAMonline assembles content that aligns with state standards but makes no claims nor guarantees teacher candidates a passing score. Numerical scores are determined by testing companies such as NES or ETS and then are compared with individual state standards. A passing score varies from state to state.

Printed in the United States of America　　　　　　　　　　　　　　　　œ-1

Minnesota High School Mathematics (5-12)
ISBN: 978-1-60787-077-7

Table of Contents

DOMAIN I
NUMBER SENSE 1

COMPETENCY 1
UNDERSTAND NUMBERS AND NUMBER SYSTEMS 3

Skill 1.1: Demonstrating knowledge of magnitude, mental mathematics, place value, and the reasonableness of results 3

Skill 1.2: Demonstrating knowledge of the properties and relations of number systems *(e.g., integer, rational, complex)* 4

Skill 1.3: Translating between equivalent representations of algebraic and transcendental numbers 6

Skill 1.4: Translating between geometric and polar representations of complex numbers 7

Skill 1.5: Interpreting complex solutions to equations 11

COMPETENCY 2
UNDERSTAND NUMBER THEORY AND OPERATIONS ON NUMBERS 12

Skill 2.1: Applying basic properties of number theory *(e.g., LCM, GCF, divisibility, prime and composite numbers, Euclidean algorithm)* to solve mathematical and real-world problems 12

Skill 2.2: Demonstrating knowledge of number operations, including alternative computational algorithms 17

Skill 2.3: Applying the properties *(e.g., associative, distributive)* of number operations 22

COMPETENCY 3
APPLY PRINCIPLES OF PROBLEM SOLVING 25

Skill 3.1: Analyzing methods of estimation and the reasonableness of estimates 25

Skill 3.2: Selecting the best problem-solving approach to apply in a particular situation 27

Skill 3.3: Solving problems using different strategies and representations *(e.g., ratio and proportions, percents, scientific notation)* 29

DOMAIN II
FUNCTIONS, ALGEBRA, AND CALCULUS 33

COMPETENCY 4
UNDERSTAND THE PROPERTIES AND REPRESENTATIONS OF FUNCTIONS 35

Skill 4.1: Applying the concept of patterns *(e.g., series and sequences, iteration and recursion, induction, finite differences)* **to model situations, make predictions, and solve problems**... 35

Skill 4.2: Analyzing the characteristics of functions 39

Skill 4.3: Recognizing different representations of relations and functions *(e.g., verbal descriptions, ordered pairs, graphs)*............... 43

Skill 4.4: Applying the concepts of inverse and composite functions to solve problems... 48

COMPETENCY 5
APPLY ALGEBRAIC TECHNIQUES 51

Skill 5.1: Applying properties of group and field structures to algebraic expressions... 51

Skill 5.2: Solving problems that involve variable quantities *(e.g., simplifying algebraic expressions, factoring)*............................. 52

Skill 5.3: Applying the laws of exponents and logarithms 60

Skill 5.4: Demonstrating knowledge of linear algebra, including vectors and matrix operations on vectors 63

COMPETENCY 6
ANALYZE LINEAR AND NONLINEAR FUNCTIONS AND THEIR APPLICATIONS 67

Skill 6.1: Analyzing linear and nonlinear functions *(e.g., slope, intercept, roots, asymptotes)*..................................... 67

Skill 6.2: Identifying the effects of algebraic transformations on the graph of a function... 82

Skill 6.3: Demonstrating knowledge of the use of technology *(e.g., graphing utilities, spreadsheets)* **to analyze relationships between different representations** *(e.g., equations, graphs)* **of functions and inequalities** 85

Skill 6.4: Applying linear and nonlinear functions to model real-world situations and solve problems using a variety of graphic and algebraic methods 86

COMPETENCY 7
APPLY KNOWLEDGE OF TRIGONOMETRY AND CALCULUS.. 95

Skill 7.1: Demonstrating knowledge of the concepts of limits and continuity... 95

Skill 7.2: Applying unit circle trigonometry, identities, and equations to solve problems and model real-world situations 101

Skill 7.3: Demonstrating knowledge of the definition of the derivative and its relationship to rate of change 109

Skill 7.4: Demonstrating knowledge of the definite integral, area under the curve, and techniques of numerical integration 115

Skill 7.5: Applying the fundamental theorem of calculus to solve mathematical and real-world problems 122

DOMAIN III
MEASUREMENT AND GEOMETRY

.... 129

COMPETENCY 8
APPLY PRINCIPLES OF MEASUREMENT AND GEOMETRY TO SOLVE PROBLEMS

.... 131

Skill 8.1: Solving problems involving conversions within and between different systems of measurement, including dimensional analysis 131

Skill 8.2: Solving mathematical and real-world problems involving measurable attributes of simple or composite figures and shapes *(e.g., length, capacity, angle measure)* 139

Skill 8.3: Solving mathematical and real-world problems involving indirect measurement *(e.g., proportional reasoning, Pythagorean theorem, trigonometric ratios, unit circle trigonometry)* 148

Skill 8.4: Solving problems involving the effects of changing the dimensions of a figure or shape on its area and volume 153

COMPETENCY 9
ANALYZE FIGURES AND SHAPES IN TWO AND THREE DIMENSIONS

.... 154

Skill 9.1: Applying the properties of polygons and circles to solve mathematical and real-world problems 154

Skill 9.2: Applying the properties of two- and three-dimensional shapes to solve mathematical and real-world problems 165

Skill 9.3: Analyzing formal and informal arguments and proofs 172

Skill 9.4: Evaluating arguments, reasoning, and the validity of conclusions 173

Skill 9.5: Analyzing systems of geometry, including Euclidean, non-Euclidean, and projective geometries 175

COMPETENCY 10
ANALYZE FIGURES AND SHAPES USING COORDINATE AND TRANSFORMATIONAL GEOMETRY

.... 177

Skill 10.1: Analyzing two- and three-dimensional figures and shapes in the coordinate plane 177

Skill 10.2: Applying geometric properties and the concepts of distance, midpoint, and slope in coordinate systems to solve mathematical and real-world problems 180

Skill 10.3: Applying transformations *(e.g., rotations, reflections, translations)* to figures in the coordinate plane, and analyzing topological properties and transformations..182

Skill 10.4: Analyzing the use of the techniques of coordinate geometry in geometric proofs 191

Skill 10.5: Applying vectors and polar and parametric equations to solve problems...194

DOMAIN IV
DATA, PROBABILITY, AND DISCRETE MATH 201

COMPETENCY 11
APPLY KNOWLEDGE OF THE COLLECTION, PRESENTATION, AND ANALYSIS OF DATA 203

Skill 11.1: Devising a plan for collecting data using appropriate sampling techniques......................................**203**

Skill 11.2: Selecting an effective format for organizing and describing data distributions **205**

Skill 11.3: Interpreting data presented in a variety of formats **209**

Skill 11.4: Applying descriptive statistics *(e.g., measures of central tendency, variation)* **to data** **209**

Skill 11.5: Applying inferential statistics *(e.g., confidence intervals, statistical significance)* **and concepts of validity and reliability** **214**

COMPETENCY 12
UNDERSTAND THE PRINCIPLES OF PROBABILITY 218

Skill 12.1: Analyzing the relationship between randomness and sampling methods in making statistical claims about populations..**218**

Skill 12.2: Determining the probabilities of simple and compound events using counting principles and the concept of sample space **219**

Skill 12.3: Estimating probabilities based on data collection, experiments, and simulations **225**

Skill 12.4: Applying discrete and continuous probability distributions *(e.g., uniform, binomial, normal)* **to make inferences about a population** **226**

COMPETENCY 13
UNDERSTAND THE PROCESSES AND APPLICATIONS OF DISCRETE MATHEMATICS 229

Skill 13.1: Applying systematic counting techniques **229**

Skill 13.2: Applying symbolic logic **233**

Skill 13.3: Performing operations on matrices..**240**

Skill 13.4: Applying a variety of models *(e.g., vertex-edge graphs, trees, arrays)* **to solve problems** **244**

DOMAIN V
MATHEMATICAL PROCESSES

.... 247

COMPETENCY 14
UNDERSTAND MATHEMATICAL CONNECTIONS AND COMMUNICATION

.... 249

Skill 14.1: Identifying connections between concepts and procedures in mathematics...249

Skill 14.2: Identifying connections between mathematics and other disciplines...250

Skill 14.3: Expressing mathematical ideas in a variety of formats *(e.g., verbally, graphically, symbolically)* 251

Skill 14.4: Representing word problems algebraically 254

Skill 14.5: Identifying contributions to mathematics made by different individuals and cultures and the type of societal problems that gave rise to mathematical systems...254

COMPETENCY 15
UNDERSTAND THE CONTENT AND METHODS FOR DEVELOPING STUDENTS' CONTENT-AREA READING SKILLS TO SUPPORT THEIR READING AND LEARNING IN MATHEMATICS

.... 257

Skill 15.1: Demonstrating knowledge of key components and processes involved in reading *(e.g., vocabulary knowledge, including orthographic and morphological knowledge; background knowledge; knowledge of academic discourse, including the syntactic and organizational structures used in print and digital academic texts; print processing abilities, including decoding skills; use of cognitive and metacognitive skills and strategies)* 257

Skill 15.2: Demonstrating ability to plan instruction and select strategies to support all students' content-area reading *(e.g., differentiating instruction to meet the needs of students with varying reading proficiency levels and linguistic backgrounds, identifying and addressing gaps in students' background knowledge, scaffolding reading tasks for students who experience comprehension difficulties)* 259

Skill 15.3: Demonstrating knowledge of explicit strategies for facilitating students' comprehension before, during, and after reading content-area texts and for promoting their use of comprehension strategies 263

Skill 15.4: Demonstrating knowledge of explicit strategies for promoting students' academic language and vocabulary development, including their knowledge of domain-specific vocabulary words 265

Skill 15.5: Demonstrating ability to plan instruction and select strategies that support students' reading and understanding of mathematics texts *(e.g., asking students to translate between different mathematical representations, asking students to describe in words or sentences the relationship between symbols and the situation being modeled, matching mathematical representations to differences in learning styles)* 267

SAMPLE TEST

Sample Test 271

Answer Key 289

Rigor Table 290

Sample Test with Rationales...291

MINNESOTA
HIGH SCHOOL
MATHEMATICS (5-12)

SECTION 1
ABOUT XAMONLINE

XAMonline—A Specialty Teacher Certification Company

Created in 1996, XAMonline was the first company to publish study guides for state-specific teacher certification examinations. Founder Sharon Wynne found it frustrating that materials were not available for teacher certification preparation and decided to create the first single, state-specific guide. XAMonline has grown into a company of over 1,800 contributors and writers and offers over 300 titles for the entire PRAXIS series and every state examination. No matter what state you plan on teaching in, XAMonline has a unique teacher certification study guide just for you.

XAMonline—Value and Innovation

We are committed to providing value and innovation. Our print-on-demand technology allows us to be the first in the market to reflect changes in test standards and user feedback as they occur. Our guides are written by experienced teachers who are experts in their fields. And our content reflects the highest standards of quality. Comprehensive practice tests with varied levels of rigor means that your study experience will closely match the actual in-test experience.

To date, XAMonline has helped nearly 600,000 teachers pass their certification or licensing exams. Our commitment to preparation exceeds simply providing the proper material for study—it extends to helping teachers **gain mastery** of the subject matter, giving them the **tools** to become the most effective classroom leaders possible, and ushering today's students toward a **successful future**.

SECTION 2
ABOUT THIS STUDY GUIDE

Purpose of This Guide

Is there a little voice inside of you saying, "Am I ready?" Our goal is to replace that little voice and remove all doubt with a new voice that says, "I AM READY. **Bring it on!**" by offering the highest quality of teacher certification study guides.

Organization of Content

You will see that while every test may start with overlapping general topics, each is very unique in the skills they wish to test. Only XAMonline presents custom content that analyzes deeper than a title, a subarea, or an objective. Only XAMonline presents content and sample test assessments along with **focus statements**, the deepest-level rationale and interpretation of the skills that are unique to the exam.

Title and field number of test

→Each exam has its own name and number. XAMonline's guides are written to give you the content you need to know for the specific exam you are taking. You can be confident when you buy our guide that it contains the information you need to study for the specific test you are taking.

Subareas

→These are the major content categories found on the exam. XAMonline's guides are written to cover all of the subareas found in the test frameworks developed for the exam.

Objectives

→These are standards that are unique to the exam and represent the main subcategories of the subareas/content categories. XAMonline's guides are written to address every specific objective required to pass the exam.

Focus statements

→These are examples and interpretations of the objectives. You find them in parenthesis directly following the objective. They provide detailed examples of the range, type, and level of content that appear on the test questions. **Only XAMonline's guides drill down to this level.**

How Do We Compare with Our Competitors?

XAMonline—drills down to the focus statement level.
CliffsNotes and REA—organized at the objective level
Kaplan—provides only links to content
MoMedia—content not specific to the state test

Each subarea is divided into manageable sections that cover the specific skill areas. Explanations are easy to understand and thorough. You'll find that every test answer contains a rejoinder so if you need a refresher or further review after taking the test, you'll know exactly to which section you must return.

How to Use This Book

Our informal polls show that most people begin studying up to eight weeks prior to the test date, so start early. Then ask yourself some questions: How much do you really know? Are you coming to the test straight from your teacher-education program or are you having to review subjects you haven't considered in ten years? Either way, take a **diagnostic or assessment test** first. Also, spend time on sample tests so that you become accustomed to the way the actual test will appear.

This guide comes with an online diagnostic test of 30 questions found online at *www.XAMonline.com*. It is a little boot camp to get you up for the task and reveal things about your compendium of knowledge in general. Although this guide is structured to follow the order of the test, you are not required to study in that order. By finding a time-management and study plan that fits your life you will be more effective. The results of your diagnostic or self-assessment test can be a guide for how to manage your time and point you toward an area that needs more attention.

After taking the diagnostic exam, fill out the **Personalized Study Plan** page at the beginning of each chapter. Review the competencies and skills covered in that chapter and check the boxes that apply to your study needs. If there are sections you already know you can skip, check the "skip it" box. Taking this step will give you a study plan for each chapter.

Week	Activity
8 weeks prior to test	Take a diagnostic test found at www.XAMonline.com
7 weeks prior to test	Build your Personalized Study Plan for each chapter. Check the "skip it" box for sections you feel you are already strong in. ✗ SKIP IT ☐
6-3 weeks prior to test	For each of these four weeks, choose a content area to study. You don't have to go in the order of the book. It may be that you start with the content that needs the most review. Alternately, you may want to ease yourself into plan by starting with the most familiar material.
2 weeks prior to test	Take the sample test, score it, and create a review plan for the final week before the test.
1 week prior to test	Following your plan (which will likely be aligned with the areas that need the most review) go back and study the sections that align with the questions you may have gotten wrong. Then go back and study the sections related to the questions you answered correctly. If need be, create flashcards and drill yourself on any area that you makes you anxious.

SECTION 3
ABOUT THE MINNESOTA HIGH SCHOOL MATHEMATICS (5-12) EXAM

What is the Minnesota High School Mathematics (5-12) Exam?

The Minnesota High School Mathematics (5-12) exam is meant to assess mastery of the content knowledge required to teach high school mathematics in Minnesota public schools.

Often **your own state's requirements** determine whether or not you should take any particular test. The most reliable source of information regarding this is your state's Department of Education. This resource should have a complete list of testing centers and dates. Test dates vary by subject area and not all test dates necessarily include your particular test, so be sure to check carefully.

If you are in a teacher-education program, check with the Education Department or the Certification Officer for specific information for testing and testing timelines. The Certification Office should have most of the information you need.

If you choose an alternative route to certification you can either rely on our website at *www.XAMonline.com* or on the resources provided by an alternative certification program. Many states now have specific agencies devoted to alternative certification and there are some national organizations as well, for example:
National Association for Alternative Certification
http://www.alt-teachercert.org/index.asp

Interpreting Test Results

Contrary to what you may have heard, the results of the Minnesota High School Mathematics (5-12) test are not based on time. More accurately, your score will be based on the raw number of points you earn in each section, the proportion of that section to the entire subtest, and the scaling of the raw score. Raw scores are converted to a scale of 100 to 300. It is likely to your benefit to complete as many questions in the time allotted, but it will not necessarily work to your advantage if you hurry through the test.

Scores are available by email if you request this when you register. Score reports are available 21 days after the testing window and posted to your account for 45 days as PDFs. Scores will also be sent to your chosen institution(s).

What's on the Test?

The Minnesota High School Mathematics (5-12) exam is a computer-based test and consists of two subtests, each lasting one hour. You can take one or both subtests at one testing appointment. A scientific calculator and a formulas page are provided with your test. The breakdown of the questions is as follows:

Category	Approximate Number of Questions	Approximate Percentage of the Test
SUBTEST 1	48	
I: Number Sense		43%
II: Functions, Algebra, and Calculus		57%
SUBTEST 2	48	
I: Measurement and Geometry		38%
II: Data, Probability, and Discrete Math		37%
III: Mathematical Processes		25%

Question Types

You're probably thinking, enough already, I want to study! Indulge us a little longer while we explain that there is actually more than one type of multiple-choice question. You can thank us later after you realize how well prepared you are for your exam.

1. Complete the Statement. The name says it all. In this question type you'll be asked to choose the correct completion of a given statement. For example:

> **The Dolch Basic Sight Words consist of a relatively short list of words that children should be able to:**
>
> A. Sound out
>
> B. Know the meaning of
>
> C. Recognize on sight
>
> D. Use in a sentence

The correct answer is C. In order to check your answer, test out the statement by adding the choices to the end of it.

2. **Which of the Following.** One way to test your answer choice for this type of question is to replace the phrase "which of the following" with your selection. Use this example:

> **Which of the following words is one of the twelve most frequently used in children's reading texts:**
>
> A. There
>
> B. This
>
> C. The
>
> D. An

Don't look! Test your answer. _____ is one of the twelve most frequently used in children's reading texts. Did you guess C? Then you guessed correctly.

3. **Roman Numeral Choices.** This question type is used when there is more than one possible correct answer. For example:

> **Which of the following two arguments accurately supports the use of cooperative learning as an effective method of instruction?**
> I. Cooperative learning groups facilitate healthy competition between individuals in the group.
> II. Cooperative learning groups allow academic achievers to carry or cover for academic underachievers.
> III. Cooperative learning groups make each student in the group accountable for the success of the group.
> IV. Cooperative learning groups make it possible for students to reward other group members for achieving.
>
> A. I and II
>
> B. II and III
>
> C. I and III
>
> D. III and IV

Notice that the question states there are **two** possible answers. It's best to read all the possibilities first before looking at the answer choices. In this case, the correct answer is D.

4. Negative Questions. This type of question contains words such as "not," "least," and "except." Each correct answer will be the statement that does **not** fit the situation described in the question. Such as:

> **Multicultural education is not**
>
> A. An idea or concept
>
> B. A "tack-on" to the school curriculum
>
> C. An educational reform movement
>
> D. A process

Think to yourself that the statement could be anything but the correct answer. This question form is more open to interpretation than other types, so read carefully and don't forget that you're answering a negative statement.

5. Questions that Include Graphs, Tables, or Reading Passages. As always, read the question carefully. It likely asks for a very specific answer and not a broad interpretation of the visual. Here is a simple (though not statistically accurate) example of a graph question:

> **In the following graph in how many years did more men take the NYSTCE exam than women?**
>
>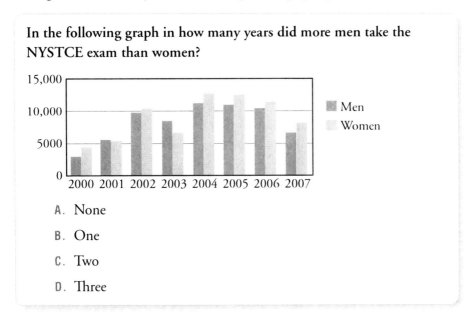
>
> A. None
>
> B. One
>
> C. Two
>
> D. Three

It may help you to simply circle the two years that answer the question. Make sure you've read the question thoroughly and once you've made your determination, double check your work. The correct answer is C.

SECTION 4
HELPFUL HINTS

Study Tips

1. **You are what you eat.** Certain foods aid the learning process by releasing natural memory enhancers called CCKs (cholecystokinin) composed of tryptophan, choline, and phenylalanine. All of these chemicals enhance the neurotransmitters associated with memory and certain foods release memory enhancing chemicals. A light meal or snacks of one of the following foods fall into this category:

   • Milk   • Rice   • Eggs   • Fish

   • Nuts and seeds   • Oats   • Turkey

   The better the connections, the more you comprehend!

2. **See the forest for the trees.** In other words, get the concept before you look at the details. One way to do this is to take notes as you read, paraphrasing or summarizing in your own words. Putting the concept in terms that are comfortable and familiar may increase retention.

3. **Question authority.** Ask why, why, why? Pull apart written material paragraph by paragraph and don't forget the captions under the illustrations. For example, if a heading reads *Stream Erosion* put it in the form of a question (Why do streams erode? What is stream erosion?) then find the answer within the material. If you train your mind to think in this manner you will learn more and prepare yourself for answering test questions.

4. **Play mind games.** Using your brain for reading or puzzles keeps it flexible. Even with a limited amount of time your brain can take in data (much like a computer) and store it for later use. In ten minutes you can: read two paragraphs (at least), quiz yourself with flash cards, or review notes. Even if you don't fully understand something on the first pass, your mind stores it for recall, which is why frequent reading or review increases chances of retention and comprehension.

5. **Get pointed in the right direction.** Use arrows to point to important passages or pieces of information. It's easier to read than a page full of yellow highlights. Highlighting can be used sparingly, but add an arrow to the margin to call attention to it.

6. **The pen is mightier than the sword.** Learn to take great notes. A by-product of our modern culture is that we have grown accustomed to getting our information in short doses. We've subconsciously trained ourselves to assimilate information into neat little packages. Messy notes fragment the flow of information. Your notes can be much clearer with proper formatting. *The Cornell Method* is one such format. This method was popularized in *How to Study in College*, Ninth Edition, by Walter Pauk. You can benefit from the method without purchasing an additional book by simply looking up the method online. Below is a sample of how *The Cornell Method* can be adapted for use with this guide.

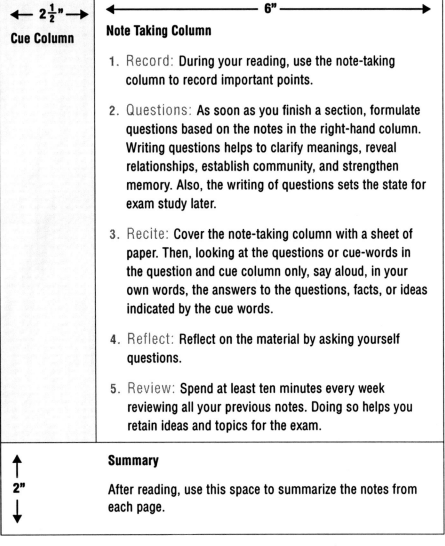

$\leftarrow 2\frac{1}{2}" \rightarrow$ Cue Column	$\longleftarrow$ 6" $\longrightarrow$ Note Taking Column
	1. Record: During your reading, use the note-taking column to record important points.
	2. Questions: As soon as you finish a section, formulate questions based on the notes in the right-hand column. Writing questions helps to clarify meanings, reveal relationships, establish community, and strengthen memory. Also, the writing of questions sets the state for exam study later.
	3. Recite: Cover the note-taking column with a sheet of paper. Then, looking at the questions or cue-words in the question and cue column only, say aloud, in your own words, the answers to the questions, facts, or ideas indicated by the cue words.
	4. Reflect: Reflect on the material by asking yourself questions.
	5. Review: Spend at least ten minutes every week reviewing all your previous notes. Doing so helps you retain ideas and topics for the exam.
$\uparrow$ 2" $\downarrow$	**Summary** After reading, use this space to summarize the notes from each page.

Adapted from How to Study in College, Ninth Edition, by Walter Pauk, ©2008 Wadsworth

The proctor will write the start time where it can be seen and then, later, provide the time remaining, typically fifteen minutes before the end of the test.

7. Place yourself in exile and set the mood. Set aside a particular place and time to study that best suits your personal needs and biorhythms. If you're a night person, burn the midnight oil. If you're a morning person set yourself up with some coffee and get to it. Make your study time and place as free from distraction as possible and surround yourself with what you need, be it silence or music. Studies have shown that music can aid in concentration, absorption, and retrieval of information. Not all music, though. Classical music is said to work best

8. Check your budget. You should at least review all the content material before your test, but allocate the most amount of time to the areas that need the most refreshing. It sounds obvious, but it's easy to forget. You can use the study rubric above to balance your study budget.

Testing Tips

1. Get smart, play dumb. Sometimes a question is just a question. No one is out to trick you, so don't assume that the test writer is looking for something other than what was asked. Stick to the question as written and don't overanalyze.

2. Do a double take. Read test questions and answer choices at least twice because it's easy to miss something, to transpose a word or some letters. If you have no idea what the correct answer is, skip it and come back later if there's time. If you're still clueless, it's okay to guess. Remember, you're scored on the number of questions you answer correctly and you're not penalized for wrong answers. The worst case scenario is that you miss a point from a good guess.

3. Turn it on its ear. The syntax of a question can often provide a clue, so make things interesting and turn the question into a statement to see if it changes the meaning or relates better (or worse) to the answer choices.

4. Get out your magnifying glass. Look for hidden clues in the questions because it's difficult to write a multiple-choice question without giving away part of the answer in the options presented. In most questions you can readily eliminate one or two potential answers, increasing your chances of answering correctly to 50/50, which will help out if you've skipped a question and gone back to it (see tip #2).

5. Call it intuition. Often your first instinct is correct. If you've been studying the content you've likely absorbed something and have subconsciously retained the knowledge. On questions you're not sure about trust your instincts because a first impression is usually correct.

6. Graffiti. Sometimes it's a good idea to mark your answers directly on the test booklet and go back to fill in the optical scan sheet later. You don't get extra points for perfectly blackened ovals. If you choose to manage your test this way, be sure not to mismark your answers when you transcribe to the scan sheet.

7. Become a clock-watcher. You have a set amount of time to answer the questions. Don't get bogged down laboring over a question you're not sure about when there are ten others you could answer more readily. If you choose to follow the advice of tip #6, be sure you leave time near the end to go back and fill in the scan sheet.

Do the Drill

No matter how prepared you feel it's sometimes a good idea to apply Murphy's Law. So the following tips might seem silly, mundane, or obvious, but we're including them anyway.

1. Remember, you are what you eat, so bring a snack. Choose from the list of energizing foods that appear earlier in the introduction.

2. You're not too sexy for your test. Wear comfortable clothes. You'll be distracted if your belt is too tight or if you're too cold or too hot.

3. Lie to yourself. Even if you think you're a prompt person, pretend you're not and leave plenty of time to get to the testing center. Map it out ahead of time and do a dry run if you have to. There's no need to add road rage to your list of anxieties.

4. Bring sharp number 2 pencils. It may seem impossible to forget this need from your school days, but you might. And make sure the erasers are intact, too.

5. No ticket, no test. Bring your admission ticket as well as **two** forms of identification, including one with a picture and signature. You will not be admitted to the test without these things.

6. You can't take it with you. Leave any study aids, dictionaries, notebooks, computers, and the like at home. Certain tests **do** allow a scientific or four-function calculator, so check ahead of time to see if your test does.

7. Prepare for the desert. Any time spent on a bathroom break **cannot** be made up later, so use your judgment on the amount you eat or drink.

8. Quiet, Please! Keeping your own time is a good idea, but not with a timepiece that has a loud ticker. If you use a watch, take it off and place it nearby but not so that it distracts you. And **silence your cell phone.**

To the best of our ability, we have compiled the content you need to know in this book and in the accompanying online resources. The rest is up to you. You can use the study and testing tips or you can follow your own methods. Either way, you can be confident that there aren't any missing pieces of information and there shouldn't be any surprises in the content on the test.

If you have questions about test fees, registration, electronic testing, or other content verification issues please visit *www.mtle.nesinc.com.*

Good luck!

Sharon Wynne
Founder, XAMonline

DOMAIN I
NUMBER SENSE

PERSONALIZED STUDY PLAN

KNOWN MATERIAL/ SKIP IT

PAGE	COMPETENCY AND SKILL	
3	**1:**	**Understand numbers and number systems**	☐
	1.1:	Demonstrating knowledge of magnitude, mental mathematics, place value, and the reasonableness of results	☐
	1.2:	Demonstrating knowledge of the properties and relations of number systems	☐
	1.3:	Translating between equivalent representations of algebraic and transcendental numbers	☐
	1.4:	Translating between geometric and polar representations of complex numbers	☐
	1.5:	Interpreting complex solutions to equations	☐
12	**2:**	**Understand number theory and operations on numbers**	☐
	2.1:	Applying basic properties of number theory to solve mathematical and real-world problems	☐
	2.2:	Demonstrating knowledge of number operations, including alternative computational algorithms	☐
	2.3:	Applying the properties of number operations	☐
25	**3:**	**Apply principles of problem solving**	☐
	3.1:	Analyzing methods of estimation and the reasonableness of estimates	☐
	3.2:	Selecting the best problem-solving approach to apply in a particular situation	☐
	3.3:	Solving problems using different strategies and representations	☐

COMPETENCY 1
UNDERSTAND NUMBERS AND NUMBER SYSTEMS

SKILL 1.1 Demonstrating knowledge of magnitude, mental mathematics, place value, and the reasonableness of results

Place Value

In a number, every digit has a face value and a place value. The face values of the digits in the number 3467 are 3, 4, 6, and 7. The place value of a digit depends on its position in the number.

Whole number place value is determined by the relative positions of the digits to the left of the decimal point. Consider the number 792: reading from left to right, the first digit (7) represents the hundreds place. Thus, there are seven sets of 100 in the number 792. The second digit (9) represents the tens place, i. e., nine sets of ten. The last digit (2) represents the ones place.

Decimal place value is determined by the relative positions of the digits to the right of the decimal point. Consider the number 4.873: reading from left to right, the first digit (4) is in the ones place. The first digit after the decimal (8) is in the tenths place and indicates that the number contains eight tenths. The next digit (7) is in the hundredths' place and tells us the number contains seven hundredths. The same pattern applies to the rest of the number, with each successive digit to the right of the decimal point decreasing progressively by powers of ten.

Example: The positions of the digits in the number 12345.6789 indicate the following powers of ten:

10^4	10^3	10^2	10^1	10^0		10^{-1}	10^{-2}	10^{-3}	10^{-4}
1	2	3	4	5	.	6	7	8	9

Mental Math and Estimates of Magnitude

Mental calculations may be used to estimate and check the reasonableness of answers. The highest place value in a number can be used to make a mental estimate of its "order of magnitude." For instance, if the highest place value of a number is 10^6, one can say that the number is in the millions. This will place the estimate within a factor of 10 of the exact answer. Although this is a very rough estimate, it can be useful in many situations. This is particularly important when calculators are used. Students need to be able to verify that the answer they are getting by punching in numbers is in the correct range and makes sense in the given context. Another simple check for reasonableness is to ask whether the answer expected is more or less than a given number. It is astonishing how many errors of computation can be avoided using this method. For instance, when converting 20 Km to meters, asking whether the expected answer is greater than or less than 20 will help decide whether one should multiply or divide by 1,000 (a common point of confusion in conversion problems).

For further discussion of estimation methods and reasonableness of estimates, see Skill 3.1.

> ### SKILL 1.2 Demonstrating knowledge of the properties and relations of number systems *(e.g., integer, rational, complex)*

Real Numbers

The following chart shows the relationships among the subsets of the real numbers.

Real Numbers

REAL NUMBERS:
numbers that can be represented by an infinite decimal representation

REAL NUMBERS are denoted by $\mathbb{R}$ and are numbers that can be shown by an infinite decimal representation such as 3.286275347 . . . . Real numbers include rational numbers, such as 242 and $\frac{-23}{129}$, and irrational numbers, such as $\sqrt{2}$ and π, and can be represented as points along an infinite number line. Real numbers are also known as "the unique complete Archimedean *ordered field*." Real numbers are to be distinguished from imaginary numbers, which involve a factor of $\sqrt{-1}$.

Real numbers are classified as follows:

CLASSIFICATIONS OF REAL NUMBERS	
Natural Numbers Denoted by $\mathbb{N}$	The counting numbers. 1, 2, 3, . . .
Whole Numbers	The counting numbers along with zero. 0, 1, 2, 3, . . .
Integers, Denoted by $\mathbb{Z}$	The counting numbers, their negatives, and zero. . . . , -2, -1, 0, 1, 2, . . .
Rationals, Denoted by $\mathbb{Q}$	All of the fractions that can be formed using whole numbers. Zero cannot be the denominator. In decimal form, these numbers will be either terminating or repeating decimals. Simplify square roots to determine if the number can be written as a fraction.
Irrationals	Real numbers that cannot be written as a fraction. The decimal forms of these numbers neither terminate nor repeat. Examples include π, e, and $\sqrt{2}$.

Complex Numbers

The set of complex numbers is denoted by $\mathbb{C}$. The set $\mathbb{C}$ is defined as $\{a + bi : a, b \in \mathbb{R}\}$ ($\in$ means "element of"). In other words, complex numbers are an extension of real numbers made by attaching an imaginary number i, which satisfies the equality $i^2 = -1$. COMPLEX NUMBERS are of the form $a + bi$, where a and b are real numbers and $i = \sqrt{-1}$. Thus, a is the real part of the number and b is the imaginary part of the number. When i appears in a fraction, the fraction is usually simplified so that i is not in the denominator. The set of complex numbers includes the set of real numbers, where any real number n can be written in its equivalent complex form as $n + 0i$. In other words, it can be said that $\mathbb{R} \subseteq \mathbb{C}$ (or $\mathbb{R}$ is a subset of $\mathbb{C}$).

> **COMPLEX NUMBERS:** numbers of the form $a + bi$, where a and b are real numbers and $i = \sqrt{-1}$

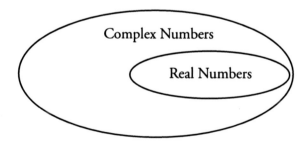

The number $3i$ has a real part 0 and imaginary part 3; the number 4 has a real part 4 and an imaginary part 0. As another way of writing complex numbers, we can express them as ordered pairs:

Complex Number	Ordered Pair
$3 + 2i$	$(3, 2)$
$\sqrt{3} + \sqrt{3}i$	$(\sqrt{3}, \sqrt{3})$
$7i$	$(0, 7)$
$\dfrac{6 + 2i}{7}$	$\left(\dfrac{6}{7}, \dfrac{2}{7}\right)$

The basic operations for complex numbers can be summarized as follows, where $z_1 = a_1 + b_1 i$ and $z_2 = a_2 + b_2 i$. Note that the operations are performed in the standard manner, where i is treated as a standard radical value. The result of each operation is written in the standard form for complex numbers. Also note that the COMPLEX CONJUGATE of a complex number $z = a + bi$ is denoted as $z^* = a - bi$.

> **COMPLEX CONJUGATE:** for a complex number $z = a + bi$, this is denoted as $z^* = a - bi$

$$z_1 + z_2 = (a_1 + a_2) + (b_1 + b_2)i$$
$$z_1 - z_2 = (a_1 - a_2) + (b_1 - b_2)i$$
$$z_1 z_2 = (a_1 a_2 - b_1 b_2) + (a_1 b_2 - a_2 b_1)i$$
$$\frac{z_1}{z_2} = \frac{z_1}{z_2}\frac{z_2^*}{z_2^*} = \frac{a_1 a_2 + b_1 b_2}{a_2^2 + b_2^2} + \frac{a_2 b_1 - a_1 b_2}{a_2^2 + b_2^2}i$$

Note that, because the division operation above is defined, the multiplicative inverse of any complex number $z \neq 0$ is also defined (where z_1 is 1 and z_2 is z) in the set of complex numbers.

In addition to these operations, the absolute value of a complex number, $z = a + bi$ (written $|z|$ or $|a + bi|$), is also defined. (The absolute value may also be termed the "magnitude" or the "modulus" of the number.)
$$|z| = \sqrt{zz^*} = \sqrt{a^2 + b^2}$$

SKILL 1.3 Translating between equivalent representations of algebraic and transcendental numbers

Real and complex numbers can be divided into two sets, algebraic and transcendental. Algebraic numbers are those that are solutions of polynomial equations with rational coefficients. Such solutions may be rational or irrational. For instance, $\sqrt{2}$ is the irrational solution of the polynomial equation $x^2 - 2 = 0$ and is an algebraic number. Transcendental numbers are those that are not solutions of polynomial equations and are always irrational. Since a polynomial equation has a finite number of solutions, the set of algebraic numbers is countable.

The set of transcendental numbers, on the other hand, is uncountable. The quantities π and e are two familiar transcendental numbers.

Since algebraic and transcendental numbers belong to mutually exclusive sets, there cannot be an exact algebraic representation of a transcendental number. This is the source of the ancient problem of "squaring the circle", i.e. constructing a square with the same area as a given circle. Since π is a transcendental number, it is impossible to find the exact length of the side of the desired square. It is, however, possible to make approximations that are extremely close to the actual value.

Even though no exact algebraic representation can be found for quantities such as π and e, mathematicians through the ages have developed representations using continued fractions or infinite series that converge, i.e., get closer to a particular sum as more terms are included. An example is given below:

$$\pi = 4 \sum_{k=0}^{\infty} \frac{(-1)^k}{2k+1} = \frac{4}{1} - \frac{4}{3} + \frac{4}{5} - \frac{4}{7} + \frac{4}{9} + \dots$$

SKILL 1.4 Translating between geometric and polar representations of complex numbers

As mentioned above, complex numbers can be written as ordered pairs. Thus, complex numbers can be plotted graphically in a Cartesian complex plane, where the x-axis represents real numbers and the y-axis represents imaginary numbers. An equivalent representation, following a graphical approach, is to use polar coordinates (a magnitude and an angle). These two representations are shown below for the example of $2 + 3i$.

Complex numbers can be plotted graphically in a Cartesian complex plane, where the x-axis represents real numbers and the y-axis represents imaginary numbers.

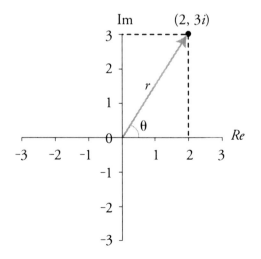

Thus, a complex number $a + bi$ can be represented using a vector of length r and an angle θ, measured in the counterclockwise direction from the x-axis. Using trigonometry, the complex number $a + bi$ can be written as follows (for more on trigonometry, see Competency 7).

$$a + bi = r(\cos\theta + i\sin\theta)$$

Note that

$$r = \sqrt{a^2 + b^2}$$
$$\theta = \arctan\frac{b}{a}.$$

Because complex numbers can be written as ordered pairs, they can also be treated as vectors in the two-dimensional (complex) plane. (For more on vectors, see Competency 10.) For instance, the sum (or difference) of two complex numbers is the same as the sum (difference) of two vectors corresponding to the same ordered pairs. Thus, $(1 - 2i) + (2 + 2i)$ can be found graphically.

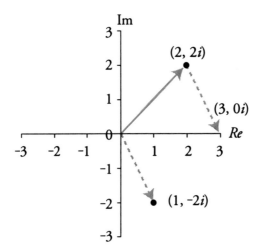

The result, found in the graph above using vector addition, is $3 + 0i$.

In addition to the use of trigonometric functions for a polar representation, complex numbers can also be represented in polar form using exponentials. To derive Euler's formula, define z as follows.

$$z = \cos\theta + i\sin\theta$$

Differentiate z with respect to θ and form a differential equation (for more on differential and integral calculus, see Competency 7).

$$\frac{dz}{d\theta} = \frac{d}{d\theta}(\cos\theta + i\sin\theta)$$
$$\frac{dz}{d\theta} = -\sin\theta + i\cos\theta$$
$$dz = (-\sin\theta + i\cos\theta)d\theta$$

Note that dz can be rewritten as follows using the definition of i.

$$dz = (i^2\sin\theta + i\cos\theta)d\theta$$
$$dz = i(\cos\theta + i\sin\theta)d\theta = iz\,d\theta$$
$$\frac{dz}{z} = id\theta$$

Integrate the result.

$$\int \frac{dz}{z} = \int i\, d\theta$$
$$\ln z = i\theta$$

Use the rules of exponentials to find z.

$$e^{\ln z} = e^{i\theta}$$
$$z = \cos\theta + i\sin\theta = e^{i\theta}$$

This is Euler's formula. Thus, complex numbers can be written in either trigonometric or exponential polar form.

$$a + bi = r(\cos\theta + i\sin\theta) = re^{i\theta}$$

This exponential polar form is particularly beneficial for fast multiplication and division of complex numbers, because these operations simply involve multiplying or dividing the multiplicative factors (r) and adding or subtracting the exponents ($i\theta$). In addition, the square root operation becomes more lucid when this representation is used, since

$$\sqrt{a + bi} = \sqrt{re^{i\theta}} = \sqrt{r}\, e^{i\frac{\theta}{2}}.$$

Example: Write $2 - 5i$ in polar form.

This complex number can be written either in terms of sine and cosine or in terms of an exponential. In either case, first calculate r and θ.

$$r = \sqrt{2^2 + (-5)^2} = \sqrt{4 + 25} = \sqrt{29} \approx 5.385$$
$$\theta = \arctan\left(-\frac{5}{2}\right) \approx -1.190$$

Thus,

$$2 - 5i \approx 5.385[\cos(-1.190) + i\sin(-1.190)]$$
$$= 5.385[\cos 1.190 - i\sin 1.190]$$

or

$$2 - 5i \approx 5.385e^{-1.190i}.$$

In the first case, the result can be checked by evaluating the trigonometric functions and multiplying.

$$5.385[\cos 1.190 - i\sin 1.190] \approx 5.385[0.372 - i\,0.928]$$
$$5.385[\cos 1.190 - i\sin 1.190] \approx 2.003 - i\,4.998$$

Although a lack of numerical accuracy yields a result that is not exact, it is close enough to assume that it is correct. To be more certain, simply use greater numerical accuracy throughout the problem.

Example: Express x + ix tan x in polar form.

Calculate r and θ, noting that the real and imaginary parts of this complex number are functions instead of numbers.

$$r = \sqrt{x^2 + (x \tan x)^2} = \sqrt{x^2 + x^2 \tan^2 x} = \sqrt{x^2 (1 + \tan^2 x)}$$
$$r = \sqrt{x^2 \sec^2 x} = x \sec x$$
$$\theta = \arctan\left(\tfrac{x \tan x}{x}\right) = \arctan (\tan x) = x$$

Write the polar form.

$$x + i \tan x = x \sec x (\cos x + i \sin x)$$
$$x + i \tan x = (x \sec x)e^{ix}$$

Expand the trigonometric polar form to test the result.

$$x \sec x (\cos x + i \sin x) = x \sec x \cos x + ix \sec x \sin x$$
$$x \sec x (\cos x + i \sin x) = x \frac{\cos x}{\cos x} + ix \frac{\sin x}{\cos x} = x + ix \tan x$$

The result is confirmed.

Example: Find the imaginary part of the expression $\dfrac{\sqrt{3 + 2i}}{-1 + 5i}$.

The imaginary part of this expression can be found by reducing it to the form $a + bi$. To do so, first evaluate the square root using the polar form.

$$3 + 2i = |3 + 2i|\, e^{i\arctan\frac{2}{3}} \approx \sqrt{(3 + 2i)(3 - 2i)}\, e^{0.588i}$$
$$3 + 2i \approx \sqrt{(3 + 2i)(3 - 2i)}\, e^{0.588i} = \sqrt{9 + 4}\, e^{0.588i} = \sqrt{13}\, e^{0.588i}$$

Evaluate the square root of this value.

$$\sqrt{3 + 2i} \approx \sqrt{3.606 e^{0.588i}} \approx 1.899 e^{0.294i}$$

Return this result to $a + bi$ form.

$$\sqrt{3 + 2i} \approx 1.899 e^{0.294i} = 1.899 \cos 0.294 + i1.899 \sin 0.294$$
$$\sqrt{3 + 2i} \approx 1.818 + 0.550i$$

Next, use the complex conjugate to eliminate the denominator of the original fraction given in the question.

$$\frac{\sqrt{3 + 2i}}{-1 + 5i} \approx \frac{1.818 + 0.550i}{-1 + 5i}\left(\frac{-1 - 5i}{-1 - 5i}\right)$$
$$\frac{\sqrt{3 + 2i}}{-1 + 5i} \approx \frac{-1.818 - 9.09i - 0.550i + 2.75}{1 + 25} = \frac{0.932 - 964i}{26}$$

Thus, the imaginary part of the expression is approximately $-\frac{9.64}{26}$, or about -0.371.

Numerous problems do not have solutions that are contained in the set of real numbers. In such cases, complex solutions may be required. Consider the following canonical example.

$$x^2 + 1 = 0$$

This equation cannot be solved for x in the real domain.

$$x^2 = -1$$
$$x = \pm\sqrt{-1}$$

Since there is no real number whose square is -1, there is no real solution for x. The imaginary number i is a solution, however; thus, this equation can be solved in the complex domain.

$$x = \pm i$$

More generally, the Fundamental Theorem of Algebra states that any polynomial of degree n must have n solutions (or roots), which may include real, complex, or nondistinct roots (or some combination thereof).

Other operations can likewise lead to imaginary results. Consider, for instance, the natural logarithm of a negative numbers (for more on logarithms, see Competency 5).

$$\ln(-1) = ?$$

In the real domain, this expression is undefined, because there is no real exponent of e that results in a negative number. If Euler's formula is applied, however, a solution from the set of complex numbers becomes apparent.

$$\ln(-1) = \ln(\cos \pi + i \sin \pi) = \ln(e^{i\pi})$$
$$\ln(-1) = i \pi \ln(e) = i \pi$$

Thus, the expression has an equivalent numerical expression from the set of complex numbers. (For precision, it is noteworthy that the general result is in π, where n is an integer.)

Example: Find all the roots of the polynomial $x^3 - x^2 + 3x - 3$.

This problem can be tackled in any of several ways. First, note that the Fundamental Theorem of Algebra requires that the polynomial must have three solutions. In this case, the polynomial can be factored. By inspection, it appears that $x = 1$ might be a solution:

$$(1)^3 - (1)^2 + 3(1) - 3 = 1 - 1 + 3 - 3 = 0$$

Thus, $(x - 1)$ must be a factor in the expression. The remaining factor must be a polynomial of degree two.

$$x^3 - x^2 + 3x - 3 = (x - 1)(ax^2 + bx + c)$$

Obviously, a must be equal to 1. Likewise, c must be equal to 3.

$$(x - 1)(x^2 + bx + 3) = x^3 - x^2 + bx^2 - bx + 3x - 3$$
$$x^3 - x^2 + 3x - 3 = x^3 - (1 - b)\,x^2 - (b - 3)\,x - 3$$

Thus, $b = 0$.

$$x^3 - x^2 + 3x - 3 = (x - 1)(x^2 + 3)$$

Factoring once more yields

$$0 = (x - 1)(x + i\sqrt{3})(x - i\sqrt{3}).$$

The roots are 1, $i\sqrt{3}$, and $-i\sqrt{3}$.

COMPETENCY 2
UNDERSTAND NUMBER THEORY AND OPERATIONS ON NUMBERS

> **SKILL 2.1** **Applying basic properties of number theory** *(e.g., LCM, GCF, divisibility, prime and composite numbers, Euclidean algorithm)* **to solve mathematical and real-world problems**

Divisibility Rules

1. A number is *divisible by 2* if that number is an even number (i.e., the last digit is 0, 2, 4, 6, or 8).

   Consider a number *abcd* defined by the digits *a*, *b*, *c*, and *d* (for instance, 1,234). Rewrite the number as follows.

   $$10abc + d = abcd$$

   Note that $10abc$ is divisible by 2. Thus, the number *abcd* is only divisible by 2 if *d* is divisible by two; in other words, *abcd* is divisible by two only if it is an even number. For example, the last digit of 1,354 is 4, so it is divisible by 2. On the other hand, the last digit of 240,685 is 5, so it is not divisible by 2.

2. A number is *divisible by 3* if the sum of its digits is evenly divisible by 3.

Consider a number *abcd* defined by the digits *a*, *b*, *c*, and *d*. The number can be written as

$$abcd - 1000a + 100b - 10c + d$$

The number can also be rewritten as

$$abcd = (999 + 1)a + (99 + 1)b + (9 + 1)c + d$$
$$abcd = 999a + 99b + 9c + (a + b + c + d)$$

Note that the first three terms in the above expression are all divisible by 3. Thus, the number is evenly divisible by 3 only if $a + b + c + d$ is divisible by 3. The same logic applies regardless of the size of the number. This proves the rules for divisibility by 3.

The sum of the digits of 964 is $9 + 6 + 4 = 19$. Since 19 is not divisible by 3, neither is 964. The digits of 86,514 are $8 + 6 + 5 + 1 + 4 = 24$. Since 24 is divisible by 3, 86,514 is also divisible by 3.

3. A number is *divisible by 4* if the number formed by its last two digits is evenly divisible by 4.

Let a number *abcd* be defined by the digits *a*, *b*, *c*, and *d*.

$$ab(100) + cd = abcd$$

Since 100 is divisible by 4, 100*ab* is also divisible by 4. Thus, *abcd* is divisible by 4 only if *cd* is divisible by 4.

$$25ab + \frac{cd}{4} = \frac{abcd}{4}$$

The number 113,336 ends with the number 36 for the last two digits. Since 36 is divisible by 4, 113,336 is also divisible by 4. The number 135,627 ends with the number 27. Since 27 is not evenly divisible by 4, the number 135,627 is not divisible by 4.

4. A number is *divisible by 5* if the number ends in either a 5 or a 0.

Use the same number *abcd*.

$$100ab + cd = abcd$$

The first term is evenly divisible by 5, but the second term is only evenly divisible by 5 if it is 0, 5, 10, 15, . . . , 95. In other words, *abcd* is divisible by 5 only if it ends in a 0 or a 5. For instance, 225 ends with a 5, so it is divisible by 5. The number 470 is also divisible by 5 because its last digit is a 0. The number 2,358 is not divisible by 5 because its last digit is an 8.

5. A number is *divisible by 6* if the number is even and the sum of its digits is evenly divisible by 3 or 6.

Let a number *efgh* be defined by the digits *e*, *f*, *g*, and *h*. If *efgh* is even, then it is divisible by 2. Write *abcd* as follows.

$$\frac{efgh}{2} = abcd = 999a + 99b + 9c + (a + b + c + d)$$
$$efgh = 2abcd = 2(999)a + 2(99)b + 2(9)c + 2(a + b + c + d)$$

Then divide *efgh* by 6.

$$\frac{efgh}{6} = \frac{2(999)}{6}a + \frac{2(99)}{6}b + \frac{2(9)}{6}c + \frac{2}{6}(a + b + c + d)$$
$$\frac{efgh}{6} = 333a + 33b + 3c + \frac{2}{6}(a + b + c + d)$$

Notice that *efgh* is divisible by 6 only if the sum of the digits is divisible by 3 or by 6. The number *efgh* must also be even, since 2 is a factor of 6. For instance, 4,950 is an even number and its digits add to 18 ($4 + 9 + 5 + 0 = 18$). Since the number is even and the sum of its digits is 18 (which is divisible by 3 and 6), then 4,950 is divisible by 6. On the other hand, 326 is an even number, but its digits add up to 11. Since 11 is not divisible by 3 or 6, then 326 is not divisible by 6.

6. A number is *divisible by 8* if the number formed by its last three digits is evenly divisible by 8.

   The logic for the proof of this case follows that of numbers divisible by 2 and 4. The number 113,336 ends with the 3-digit number 336 in the last three places. Since 336 is divisible by 8, then 113,336 is also divisible by 8. The number 465,627 ends with the number 627 in the last three places. Since 627 is not evenly divisible by 8, then 465,627 is also not divisible by 8.

7. A number is *divisible by 9* if the sum of its digits is evenly divisible by 9.

   The logic for the proof of this case follows that for the case of numbers that are divisible by 3 and 6. The sum of the digits of 874, for example, is $8 + 7 + 4 = 19$. Since 19 is not divisible by 9, neither is 874. The sum of the digits of 116,514 is $1 + 1 + 6 + 5 + 1 + 4 = 18$. Since 18 is divisible by 9, 116,514 is also divisible by 9.

The Fundamental Theorem of Arithmetic

Every integer greater than 1 can be written uniquely in the form

$$p_1^{e_1} p_2^{e_2} \cdots p_k^{e_k}.$$

The p_i are distinct prime numbers and the e_i are positive integers.

Greatest common factor

GCF is the abbreviation for the GREATEST COMMON FACTOR. The GCF is the largest number that is a factor of all the numbers given in a problem. The GCF can

> **GREATEST COMMON FACTOR:** the largest number that is a factor of all the numbers given in a problem

be no larger than the smallest number given in the problem. If no other number is a common factor, then the GCF will be the number 1. To find the GCF, list all possible factors of the smallest number given (include the number itself). Starting with the largest factor (which is the number itself), determine if it is also a factor of all the other given numbers. If so, that is the GCF. If that factor does not work, try the same method on the next smaller factor. Continue until a common factor is found. This is the GCF. Note: There can be other common factors besides the GCF.

The GCF can be no larger than the smallest number given in the problem.

Example: Find the GCF of 12, 20, and 36.

The smallest number in the problem is 12. The factors of 12 are 1, 2, 3, 4, 6, and 12. 12 is the largest factor, but it does not divide evenly into 20. Neither does 6, but 4 will divide into both 20 and 36 evenly. Therefore, 4 is the GCF.

Example: Find the GCF of 14 and 15.

Factors of 14 are 1, 2, 7, and 14. 14 is the largest factor, but it does not divide evenly into 15. Neither does 7 or 2. Therefore, the only factor common to both 14 and 15 is the number 1, which is the GCF.

The Euclidean Algorithm is a formal method for determining the greatest common divisor (GCD, another name for GCF) of two positive integers. The algorithm can be formulated in a recursive manner that simply involves repetition of a few steps until a terminating point is reached. The algorithm can be summarized as follows, where a and b are the two integers for which determination of the GCD is to be undertaken. (Assign a and b such that $a > b$.)

1. If $b = 0$, a is the GCD

2. Calculate $c = a \bmod b$

3. If $c = 0$, b is the GCD

4. Go back to step 2, replacing a with b and b with c

Note that the mod operator in this case is simply a remainder operator. Thus, $a \bmod b$ is the remainder of division of a by b.

Example: Find the GCD of 299 and 351.

To find the GCD, first let $a = 351$ and $b = 299$. Begin the algorithm as follows.
    Step 1: $b \neq 0$
    Step 2: $c = 351 \bmod 299 = 52$
    Step 3: $c \neq 0$

Perform the next iteration, starting with step 2.

Step 2: $c = 299 \bmod 52 = 39$
Step 3: $c \neq 0$

Continue to iterate recursively until a solution is found.

Step 2: $c = 52 \bmod 39 = 13$
Step 3: $c \neq 0$

Step 2: $c = 39 \bmod 13 = 0$
Step 3: $c = 0$: GCD $= 13$

Thus, the GCD of 299 and 351 is 13.

Least common multiple

LCM is the abbreviation for LEAST COMMON MULTIPLE. The least common multiple of a group of numbers is the smallest number that all of the given numbers will divide into. The least common multiple will always be the largest of the given set of numbers or a multiple of the largest number.

Example: Find the LCM of 20, 30 and 40.
The largest number given is 40, but 30 will not divide evenly into 40. The next multiple of 40 is 80 (2×40), but 30 will not divide evenly into 80 either. The next multiple of 40 is 120. 120 is divisible by both 20 and 30, so 120 is the LCM (least common multiple).

Example: Find the LCM of 96, 16 and 24.
The largest number is 96. 96 is divisible by both 16 and 24, so 96 is the LCM.

> **LEAST COMMON MULTIPLE:** the smallest number that all of the given numbers will divide into

> *The least common multiple will always be the largest of the given set of numbers or a multiple of the largest number.*

Modular Arithmetic

MODULAR ARITHMETIC involves numbers and operations that have a circular or wrap-around characteristic, such as that shown by a clock or even the odometer of an automobile. Given a set of integers from 0 to n (or, identically, 1 to $n + 1$), any result of an operation is actually the remainder of the quotient of the result divided by $n + 1$. Thus, in terms of a clock, which involves "modulo 12" arithmetic,

$$7 + 10 = 5.$$

Alternatively, this operation can be expressed

$$7 + 10 \equiv 5 \ (\bmod \ 12).$$

In other words, ten hours after 7 o'clock is 5 o'clock (in the context of time on a standard twelve-hour clock). The number 12 in this case is called the modulus.

> **MODULAR ARITHMETIC:** involves numbers and operations that have a circular or wrap-around characteristic, such as that shown by a clock or even the odometer of an automobile

The symbol ≡ indicates congruence. Generally, for any value c and arbitrary integer i in modulo n arithmetic, the following statement is always true:

$c + ni \equiv c \pmod{n}$.

This rule is useful when a negative number is encountered. Simply add any multiple of the modulus to find the correct result of the operation.

Likewise,

$ni \equiv 0 \pmod{n}$.

The case of modulo 2 arithmetic (which involves the integers 0 and 1) has particular application to binary and Boolean systems.

Example: Calculate the following in modulo 5 arithmetic:
3 + 8, (4)(7), 7 − 8.
In each case, use the remainder of the result divided by the modulus to find the correct answer.

$\text{remainder}\left(\frac{3+8}{5}\right) = 1 \qquad 3 + 8 \equiv \pmod{5}$

$\text{remainder}\left(\frac{4 \times 7}{5}\right) = 3 \qquad 4 \times 7 \equiv \pmod{5}$

For the last operation, use the rule $c + ni \equiv c \pmod{n}$ to find the answer.

$\text{remainder}\left(\frac{7-8}{5}\right) = \text{-}1 \qquad (7 - 8) + 5 \equiv 4 \pmod{5}$

Example: A bicycle has a simple odometer that goes up to 999 miles. If the current odometer reading is 431 miles, what will it read 1500 miles later?
The odometer has readings that range from 0 to 999. Upon reaching 999, the odometer returns to 0 after the next mile. Thus, use modulo 1000 (or 999 + 1) arithmetic to solve this problem.

$431 + 1500 \equiv 931 \pmod{1000}$

The odometer will read 931.

SKILL Demonstrating knowledge of number operations, including
2.2 alternative computational algorithms

Operations on Whole Numbers

Mathematical operations include addition, subtraction, multiplication, and division. Addition can be indicated by these expressions: *sum, greater than, and, more than, increased by, added to.* Subtraction can be expressed by the phrases *difference, fewer than, minus, less than, and decreased by.* Multiplication is shown by *product, times, multiplied by,* and *twice.* Division is indicated by *quotient, divided by,* and *ratio.*

Addition and subtraction

There are two main procedures used in addition and subtraction: adding or subtracting single digits and "carrying" or "borrowing."

Example: Find the sum of 346 + 225 using place value.

PLACE VALUE		
100	**10**	**1**
3	4	6
2	2	5
5	6	11
5	7	1

Standard algorithm for addition check:

```
   3 ¹4 6
 + 2  2 5
   5  7 1
```

Example: Find the difference 234 − 46 using place value.

PLACE VALUE		
100	**10**	**1**
1	13	4
	4	6

PLACE VALUE		
100	**10**	**1**
1	12	14
	4	6
1	**8**	**8**

Standard algorithm for subtraction check:

```
   2 3 4
 −   4 6
   1 8 8
```

Multiplication and division

Multiplication is one of the four basic number operations. In simple terms, multiplication is the addition of a number to itself a certain number of times. For example, 4 multiplied by 3 is the equal to 4 + 4 + 4 or 3 + 3 + 3 + 3. Another way of conceptualizing multiplication is to think in terms of groups. For example, if we have 4 groups of 3 students, the total number of students is 4 multiplied by 3. We call the solution to a multiplication problem the PRODUCT.

PRODUCT: a solution to a multiplication problem

Example: A student buys 4 boxes of crayons. Each box contains 16 crayons. How many total crayons does the student have?

The number of crayons is 16 × 4.

$$\begin{array}{r} 16 \\ \times\ \ 4 \\ \hline 64 \end{array}$$ Total number of crayons equals 64 crayons.

Division, the inverse of multiplication, is another of the four basic number operations. When we divide one number by another, we determine how many times we can multiply the divisor (number divided by) before we exceed the number we are dividing (dividend). For example, 8 divided by 2 equals 4 because we can multiply 2 four times to reach 8 (2 × 4 = 8 or 2 + 2 + 2 + 2 = 8). Using the grouping conceptualization we used with multiplication, we can divide 8 into 4 groups of 2 or 2 groups of 4. We call the answer to a division problem the QUOTIENT.

QUOTIENT: the answer to a division problem

If the divisor does not divide evenly into the dividend, we express the leftover amount either as a remainder or as a fraction with the divisor as the denominator. For example, 9 divided by 2 equals 4 with a remainder of 1 or $4\frac{1}{2}$.

Example: Each box of apples contains 24 apples. How many boxes must a grocer purchase to supply a group of 252 people with one apple each?

The grocer needs 252 apples. Because he must buy apples in groups of 24, we divide 252 by 24 to determine how many boxes he needs to buy.

$$\begin{array}{r} 10 \\ 24\overline{)252} \\ -\ 24 \\ \hline 12 \\ -\ \ 0 \\ \hline 12 \end{array}$$ → The quotient is 10 with a remainder of 12.

Thus, the grocer needs 10 full boxes plus 12 more apples. Therefore, the minimum number of boxes the grocer must purchase is 11 boxes.

Adding and Subtracting Decimals

When adding and subtracting decimals, we align the numbers by place value as we do with whole numbers. After adding or subtracting each column, we bring the decimal down, placing it in the same location as in the numbers added or subtracted.

Example: Find the sum of 152.3 and 36.342.

```
  152.300
+  36.342
  188.642
```

Note that we placed two zeroes after the final place value in 152.3 to clarify the column addition.

Example: Find the difference of 152.3 and 36.342.

```
    2 9 10            (4)11(12)
  152.300           152.300
 −  36.342          −  36.342
       58           115.958
```

Note how we borrowed to subtract from the zeros in the hundredths and thousandths place of 152.300.

Operations with Signed Numbers

When adding and subtracting numbers with the same sign, the result will also have the same sign. When adding numbers that have different signs, subtract the smaller number from the larger number (ignoring the sign) and then use the sign of the larger number. When subtracting a negative number, change the sign of the number to a positive sign and then add it (i.e., replace the two negative signs by a positive sign).

Examples:

$$(3) + (4) = 7$$
$$(-8) + (-4) = -12$$
$$(6) - (5) = 1$$
$$(3) - (6) = -3$$
$$(-4) - (2) = -6$$
$$(-6) - (-10) = 4$$

When we multiply two numbers with the same sign, the result is positive. If the two numbers have different signs, the result is negative. The same rule follows for division.

Examples:

$(5)(5) = 25$

$(5)(-6) = -30$

$(-19)(-2) = 38$

$16 \div 4 = 4$

$(-34) \div 2 = -17$

$(-18) \div (-2) = 9$

$27 \div (-3) = -9$

Order of Operations

The Order of Operations is to be followed when evaluating expressions with multiple operations. Remember the mnemonic PEMDAS (Please Excuse My Dear Aunt Sally) to follow these steps in order:

1. Simplify inside grouping characters such as parentheses, brackets, radicals, fraction bars, etc.

2. Multiply out expressions with exponents.

3. Do multiplication or division from left to right.

   Note: Multiplication and division are equivalent even though multiplication is mentioned before division in the mnemonic PEMDAS.

4. Do addition or subtraction from left to right.

   Note: Addition and subtraction are equivalent even though addition is mentioned before subtraction in the mnemonic PEMDAS.

Example:

Evaluate: $\dfrac{12(9 - 7) + 4 \times 5}{3^4 + 2^3}$

$\dfrac{12(9 - 7) + 4 \times 5}{3^4 + 2^3}$

$= \dfrac{12(2) + 4 \times 5}{3^4 + 2^3}$ Simplify within parentheses.

$= \dfrac{12(2) + 4 \times 5}{81 + 8}$ Multiply out exponent expressions.

$= \dfrac{24 + 20}{81 + 8}$ Do multiplication and division.

$= \dfrac{44}{89}$ Do addition and substraction.

Fields and Rings

Any set that includes at least two nonzero elements that satisfies the field axioms for addition and multiplication is a FIELD. The real numbers, $\mathbb{R}$, as well as the complex numbers, $\mathbb{C}$, are each a field, with the real numbers being a subset of the complex numbers. The field axioms are summarized below.

FIELD: any set that includes at least two nonzero elements that satisfies the field axioms for addition and multiplication

FIELD AXIOMS	
ADDITION	
Commutativity	$a + b = b + a$
Associativity	$a + (b + c) = (a + b) + c$
Identity	$a + 0 = a$
Inverse	$a + (-a) = 0$
MULTIPLICATION	
Commutativity	$ab = ba$
Associativity	$a(bc) = (ab)c$
Identity	$a \times 1 = a$
Inverse	$a \times \frac{1}{a} = 1 \qquad (a \neq 0)$
ADDITION AND MULTIPLICATION	
Distributivity	$a(b + c) = (b + c)a = ab + ac$

Note that both the real numbers and the complex numbers satisfy the axioms summarized above.

RING: an integral domain with two binary operations (addition and multiplication) where, for every nonzero element a and b in the domain, the product ab is nonzero

A RING is an integral domain with two binary operations (addition and multiplication) where, for every nonzero element a and b in the domain, the product ab is nonzero. A field is a ring in which multiplication is commutative, or $a \times b = b \times a$, and all nonzero elements have a multiplicative inverse. The set $\mathbb{Z}$ (integers) is a ring that is not a field in that it does not have the multiplicative inverse;

therefore, integers are not a field. A polynomial ring is also not a field, as it also has no multiplicative inverse. Furthermore, matrix rings do not constitute fields because matrix multiplication is not generally commutative.

Note: Multiplication is implied when there is no symbol between two variables. Thus, a $\times$ b can be written ab. Multiplication can also be indicated by a raised dot ($\cdot$).

Real numbers are an ordered field and can be ordered

As such, an ordered field F must contain a subset P (such as the positive numbers) such that if a and b are elements of P, then both $a + b$ and ab are also elements of P. (In other words, the set P is closed under addition and multiplication.) Furthermore, it must be the case that for any element c contained in F, exactly one of the following conditions is true: c is an element of P, $-c$ is an element of P, or $c = 0$.

The rational numbers also constitute an ordered field

The set P can be defined as the positive rational numbers. For each a and b that are elements of the set $\mathbb{Q}$ (the rational numbers), $a + b$ is also an element of P, as is ab. (The sum $a + b$ and the product ab are both rational if a and b are rational.) Since P is closed under addition and multiplication, $\mathbb{Q}$ constitutes an ordered field.

Complex numbers, unlike real numbers, cannot be ordered

Consider the number $i = \sqrt{-1}$ contained in the set $\mathbb{C}$ of complex numbers. Assume that $\mathbb{C}$ has a subset P (positive numbers) that is closed under both addition and multiplication. Assume that $i > 0$. A difficulty arises in that $i^2 = -1 < 0$, so i cannot be included in the set P. Likewise, assume $i < 0$. The problem once again arises that $i^4 = 1 > 0$, so i cannot be included in P. It is clearly the case that $i \neq 0$, so there is no place for i in an ordered field. Thus, the complex numbers cannot be ordered.

Example: Prove that for every integer y, if y is an even number, then y^2 is even.

The definition of *even* implies that for each integer y there is at least one integer x such that $y = 2x$.

$$y = 2x$$
$$y^2 = 4x^2$$

Since $4x^2$ is always evenly divisible by two ($2x^2$ is an integer), y^2 is even for all values of y.

Example: *If a, b, and c are positive real numbers, prove that c(a + b) = (b + a)c.*

Use the properties of the set of real numbers.

$$c(a + b) = c(b + a) \quad \text{Additive commutativity}$$
$$= cb + ca \quad \text{Distributivity}$$
$$= bc + ac \quad \text{Multiplicative commutativity}$$
$$= (b + a)c \quad \text{Distributivity}$$

Example: *Given real numbers a, b, c, and d, where ad = −bc, prove that (a + bi)(c + di) is real.*

Expand the product of the complex numbers.

$$(a + bi)(c + di) = ac + bci + adi + bdi^2$$

Use the definition of i^2.

$$(a + bi)(c + di) = ac - bd + bci + adi$$

Apply the fact that ad = −bc.

$$(a + bi)(c + di) = ac - bd + bci - bci = ac - bd$$

Since a, b, c and d are all real, $ac - bd$ must also be real.

Closure

Another useful property that can describe arbitrary sets of numbers (including fields and rings) is CLOSURE. A set is closed under an operation if the operation performed on any given elements of the set always yields a result that is likewise an element of the set. For instance, the set of real numbers is closed under multiplication, because for any two real numbers a and b, the product ab is also a real number.

> **CLOSURE:** a set is closed under an operation if the operation performed on any given elements of the set always yields a result that is likewise an element of the set

Example: *Determine if the set of integers is closed under division.*

For the set of integers to be closed under division, it must be the case that $\frac{a}{b}$ is an integer for any integers a and b. Consider $a = 2$ and $b = 3$.

$$\frac{a}{b} = \frac{2}{3}$$

This result is not an integer. Therefore, the set of integers is not closed under division.

COMPETENCY 3
APPLY PRINCIPLES OF PROBLEM SOLVING

SKILL 3.1 Analyzing methods of estimation and the reasonableness of estimates

There are several different ways of estimating. A common estimation strategy involves replacing numbers with simpler numbers that make for simpler computations. These methods include rounding, front-end digit estimation, and compensation.

Front-End Estimation

Although rounding is done to a specific place value (e.g., the nearest ten or hundred), front-end estimation involves rounding or truncating to the place value of the first digit in the number. The following example uses front-end estimation.

Example: Estimate the result of the calculation $\frac{58 \times 810}{1989}$.

To simplify the calculation, round each number to the highest place value. Thus, the calculation becomes

$$\frac{58 \times 810}{1989} \approx \frac{60 \times 800}{2000} = \frac{48000}{2000} = 24.$$

A more-precise result is 23.62. In this case, the estimated value is close to the exact result.

Compensation

Another estimation technique, compensation, involves replacing different numbers in different ways so that one change can more or less compensate for the other.

Example: Calculate 32 + 53.

Although this example is simple, it is noteworthy that compensation can make the numbers easier to handle mentally.

$$32 + 53 = 30 + 55 = 85$$

Here both numbers are replaced in a way that minimizes the change; one number is increased and the other is decreased. This technique can also be applied

> Estimation and approximation can be used to check the reasonableness of answers or to speed up a calculation where exact answers are not required. Estimation can be particularly important when calculators are used. Estimation also requires good mental math skills.

to algebraic expressions. In such cases, compensation or other similar forms of reorganization of numbers can drastically simplify certain operations.

Calculating a Range

A third estimation strategy calculates a range for the result.

Example: Estimate 458 + 873.

Again, this is a very simple example, but the principle can be applied to a range of different calculations. A simple range containing the answer can be found as follows.

$$458 + 873 > 400 + 800 = 1200$$
$$458 + 873 < 500 + 900 = 1400$$

Thus, the correct answer is in the following range:

$$1200 < 458 + 873 < 1400.$$

Various other estimation techniques can be applied as well, depending on the problem being solved.

Reasonableness

> The reasonableness of an estimate can be judged in various ways, depending on the context of the problem. For instance, if the exact result of a calculation or the exact solution to a problem is known, then the estimated value can be considered reasonable if it varies from the exact value by a sufficiently small percentage.

The reasonableness of an estimate can be judged in various ways, depending on the context of the problem. For instance, if the exact result of a calculation or the exact solution to a problem is known, then the estimated value can be considered reasonable if it varies from the exact value by a sufficiently small percentage. Often, a variation of a few percent is acceptable; in some contexts, up to 10% variation is likewise acceptable. Large variations, however, may indicate that the estimate is not reasonable.

If the exact result or solution is not known, the reasonableness of an estimate can be judged to some extent by the expected effect of the procedure used in the estimate. For example, if a number is rounded in a calculation and the process of rounding has a small effect on the value of the number (only a percent or two, for instance), it may be likely that the estimate is reasonable.

The particular operations involved in a calculation are important to making a good judgment, however. Consider the calculation $10.4929 - 10.5103$. If these numbers are rounded to the nearest one, or even to the nearest tenth, then the estimated result is zero instead of -0.0174. In some contexts, this difference may be negligible, but in other contexts, it may be very important. Thus, estimating the reasonableness of an estimate requires consideration of not only the numbers and the operations involved in the problem but also the context of the problem.

SKILL 3.2 Selecting the best problem-solving approach to apply in a particular situation

The process of problem solving in mathematics is similar to that in other disciplines. One of the first steps is to identify what is known about the problem. Each problem for which a solution can be found should provide enough information to form a starting point from which a valid sequence of reasoning leads to the desired conclusion: a solution to the problem. Between identification of known information and identification of a solution to the problem is a gray area that, depending on the problem, could potentially involve a myriad of different approaches. Two potential approaches that do not involve a "direct" solution method are discussed below.

Each problem for which a solution can be found should provide enough information to form a starting point from which a valid sequence of reasoning leads to the desired conclusion: a solution to the problem.

Guess-and-Check

The guess-and-check strategy calls for making an initial guess of the solution, checking the answer, and using the outcome of this check to inform the next guess. With each successive guess, one should get closer to the correct answer. Constructing a table from the guesses can help organize the data.

Example: There are 100 coins in a jar: 10 are dimes, and the rest are pennies and nickels. If there are twice as many pennies as nickels, how many pennies and nickels are in the jar?

Based on the given information, there are 90 total nickels and pennies in the jar (100 coins − 10 dimes = 90 nickels and pennies). Also, there are twice as many pennies as nickels. Using this information, guess results that fulfill the criteria and then adjust the guess in accordance with the result. Continue this iterative process until the correct answer is found: 60 pennies and 30 nickels. The table below illustrates this process.

NUMBER OF PENNIES	NUMBER OF NICKELS	TOTAL NUMBER OF PENNIES AND NICKELS
40	20	60
80	40	120
70	35	105
60	30	90

Working Backward

Another non-direct approach to problem solving is working backwards. If the result of a problem is known (for example, in problems that involve proving a particular result), it is sometimes helpful to begin from the conclusion and attempt to work backwards to a particular known starting point. A slight variation of this approach involves both working backwards and working forwards until a common point is reached somewhere in the middle. The following example from trigonometry illustrates this process.

Example: Prove that $\sin^2 \theta = \frac{1}{2} - \frac{1}{2}\cos2\theta$.

If the method for proving this result is not clear, one approach is to work backwards and forwards simultaneously. The following two-column approach organizes the process. Judging from the form of the result, it is apparent that the Pythagorean identity is a potential starting point.

<table>
<tr><td>

$\sin^2 \theta + \cos^2 \theta = 1$

$\sin^2 \theta = 1 - \cos^2 \theta$

</td><td>

$\sin^2 \theta = \frac{1}{2} - \frac{1}{2}\cos2\,\theta$

$\sin^2 \theta = \frac{1}{2} - \frac{1}{2}(2\cos^2 \theta - 1)$

$\sin^2 \theta = \frac{1}{2} - \cos^2 \theta + \frac{1}{2}$

$\sin^2 \theta = 1 - \cos^2 \theta$

</td></tr>
</table>

Thus, a proof is apparent based on the combination of the reasoning in these two columns.

Reasonableness

When solving any problem, it is helpful to evaluate the reasonableness of the solution. Often, errors in the solution lead to final results that do not make any sense in the context of the problem. Thus, checking the reasonableness of the solution can be a fast way to help determine if an error was made at some point in the process. Although such checks help to raise confidence in a solution, they do not necessarily guarantee that a solution is correct.

For instance, an error can result in a relatively small deviation in a numerical result; although the answer may still seem reasonable, it could still be incorrect. Thus, the reasonableness of a solution is a necessary but not sufficient check of its correctness.

Two characteristics of a numerical answer that can be quickly evaluated are sign and magnitude. If a problem calls for determining the length of a side of some geometric figure, for example, then a negative number should indicate an error at

Selection of an appropriate problem-solving strategy depends largely on the type of problem being solved and the particular area of mathematics with which the problem deals. For instance, problems that involve proving a specific result often require different approaches than do problems that involve finding a numerical result.

Two characteristics of a numerical answer that can be quickly evaluated are sign and magnitude.

some point in the solution. Similarly, a result that is magnitudes larger than would seem appropriate to the other aspects of the problem (such as the lengths of other measurements) could also indicate an error.

Additionally, the problem may provide information that limits the answer to a certain range. For example, if a problem asks for the average speed of an automobile over some distance and range of speeds, it is clear that the average speed should not exceed the maximum speed, nor should it be less than the minimum speed. Again, although this type of evaluation does not necessarily help to judge answers that fall within this range, it does help rule out results containing particularly egregious errors. On the other hand, if a speed distribution is shown that is weighted heavily toward faster speeds than slower speeds, it would then be reasonable to assume that the correct solution should be at the higher end of the speed range of the car. Similar types of qualitative evaluation or rough estimation for judging the reasonableness of a solution can be applied to other problems as well.

SKILL 3.3 Solving problems using different strategies and representations
(e.g., ratio and proportions, percents, scientific notation)

Consumer Applications

The UNIT RATE when purchasing an item is its price divided by the number of units of measure (pounds, ounces, etc.) in the item. The item with the lower unit rate has the lower price.

> **UNIT RATE:** when purchasing an item, the price of that item divided by the number of units of measure

Example: Find the item with the best unit price.
    $1.79 for 10 ounces
    $1.89 for 12 ounces
    $5.49 for 32 ounces

$\frac{1.79}{10} = 0.179$ per ounce $\frac{1.89}{12} = 0.1575$ per ounce $\frac{5.49}{32} = 0.172$ per ounce

The best price is $1.89 for 12 ounces.

A second way to find the better buy is to make a proportion with the price over the number of ounces (or whatever). Cross-multiply the proportion, writing the products above the numerator that is used. The better price will have the smaller product.

Example: Find the better buy: $8.19 for forty pounds or $4.89 for twenty-two pounds. Find the unit costs.

$$\frac{40}{8.19} = \frac{1}{x}$$
$$40x = 8.19$$
$$x = 0.20475$$

$$\frac{22}{4.89} = \frac{1}{x}$$
$$22x = 4.89$$
$$x = 0.222\overline{27}$$

Since $0.20475 < 0.222\overline{27}$, $8.19 is the lower price and a better buy.

To find the amount of sales tax on an item, change the percent of sales tax into an equivalent decimal number. Then multiply the decimal number times the price of the object to find the sales tax. The total cost of an item will be the price of the item plus the sales tax.

Example: A guitar costs $120.00 plus 7% sales tax. How much are the sales tax and the total cost?

$7\% = .07$ as a decimal
$(.07)(120) = \$8.40$ sales tax
$\$120.00 + \$8.40 = \$128.40 \leftarrow$ total price

An alternative method to find the total cost is to multiply the price times the factor 1.07 (price + sales tax).

$\$120 \times 1.07 = \$8.40$

This gives you the total cost in fewer steps.

Example: A suit costs $450.00 plus $6\frac{1}{2}$% sales tax. How much are the sales tax and the total cost?

$6\frac{1}{2}\% = .065$ as a decimal
$(.065)(450) = \$29.25$ sales tax
$\$450.00 + \$29.25 = \$479.25 \leftarrow$ total price

An alternative method to find the total cost is to multiply the price times the factor 1.065 (price + sales tax).

$\$450 \times 1.065 = \$479.25$

This gives you the total cost in fewer steps.

Ratios

A RATIO is a comparison of two numbers. If a class has 11 boys and 14 girls, the ratio of boys to girls could be written one of three ways:

11:14   or   11 to 14   or $\frac{11}{14}$

> **RATIO:** a comparison of two numbers

The ratio of girls to boys is

14:11   or   14 to 11   or $\frac{14}{11}$

Ratios can be reduced when possible. A ratio of 12 cats to 18 dogs would reduce to 2:3, 2 to 3, or $\frac{2}{3}$.

Note: Read ratio questions carefully. Given a group of 6 adults and 5 children, the ratio of children to the entire group would be 5:11.

Proportions

A PROPORTION is an equation in which a fraction is set equal to another. To solve the proportion, multiply each numerator times the other fraction's denominator. Set these two products equal to each other and solve the resulting equation. This is called CROSS-MULTIPLYING the proportion.

Example: $\frac{4}{15} = \frac{x}{60}$ *is a proportion.*
To solve this, cross-multiply:

$(4)(60) = (15)(x)$

$240 = 15x$

$16 = x$

Example: $\frac{x + 3}{3x + 4} = \frac{2}{5}$ *is a proportion.*
To solve, cross-multiply:

$5(x + 3) = 2(3x + 4)$

$5x + 15 = 6x + 8$

$7 = x$

Example: $\frac{x + 2}{8} = \frac{2}{x - 4}$ *is another proportion.*
To solve, cross-multiply:

$(x + 2)(x - 4) = 8(2)$

$x^2 - 2x - 8 = 16$

$x^2 - 2x - 24 = 0$

$(x - 6)(x + 4) = 0$

$x = 6 \text{ or } x = -4$

Both answers work.

Fractions, decimals, and percents can be used interchangeably in problems.

- To change a percent into a decimal, move the decimal point two places to the left and drop the percent sign.

> **PROPORTION:** an equation in which a fraction is set equal to another

> **CROSS-MULTIPLYING:** multiplying each fraction's numerator times the other fraction's denominator

- To change a decimal into a percent, move the decimal two places to the right and add a percent sign.

- To change a fraction into a decimal, divide the numerator by the denominator.

- To change a decimal number into an equivalent fraction, write the decimal part of the number as the fraction's numerator. As the fraction's denominator, use the place value of the last column of the decimal. Reduce the resulting fraction as far as possible.

Example: J.C. Nickels has Hunch jeans for sale at $\frac{1}{4}$ off the usual price of $36.00. Shears and Roadster have the same jeans for sale at 30% off their regular price of $40. Find the cheaper price.

$\frac{1}{4}$ = .25 so .25(36) = $9.00 off; $36 − 9 = $27 sale price

30% = .30 so .30(40) = $12 off; $40 − 12 = $28 sale price

The price at J.C Nickels is actually $1 lower.

> **SCIENTIFIC NOTATION:**
> a method for writing very large and very small numbers

SCIENTIFIC NOTATION is a convenient method for writing very large and very small numbers. It employs two factors: The first factor is a number greater than zero and less than 10, and the second factor is a power of 10. This notation is a shorthand way to express large numbers (like the weight in kilograms of 100 freight cars) or small numbers (like the weight in grams of an atom).

Example: 356.73 can be written in various forms:

$$356.73 = 3567.3 \times 10^{-1} \quad (1)$$
$$= 35673 \times 10^{0} \quad (2)$$
$$= 35.673 \times 10^{1} \quad (3)$$
$$= 3.5673 \times 10^{2} \quad (4)$$
$$= 0.35673 \times 10^{3} \quad (5)$$

Only (4) is written in proper scientific notation format.

Example: A particular material has a mass of 0.01 grams in one liter. What is the material's density in grams per milliliter?

A cursory examination of this problem shows that it will be necessary to divide a small number (0.01 grams) by a large number (1000 milliliters = 1 liter) to get the density. Thus, scientific notation is a helpful representation of the numbers in the problem. The density d is

$$d = \frac{1 \times 10^{-2}\,\text{g}}{1 \times 10^{3}\,\text{mL}} = 1 \times 10^{-5}\,\frac{\text{g}}{\text{mL}}.$$

The calculation and the result in this case are simplified considerably through the use of scientific notation. The solution is in a much neater form than 0.00001.

DOMAIN II
FUNCTIONS, ALGEBRA, AND CALCULUS

PERSONALIZED STUDY PLAN

KNOWN MATERIAL/ SKIP IT

PAGE	COMPETENCY AND SKILL	
35	**4:**	**Understand the properties and representations of functions**	☐
	4.1:	Applying the concept of patterns to model situations, make predictions, and solve problems	☐
	4.2:	Analyzing the characteristics of functions	☐
	4.3:	Recognizing different representations of relations and functions	☐
	4.4:	Applying the concepts of inverse and composite functions to solve problems	☐
51	**5:**	**Apply algebraic techniques**	☐
	5.1:	Applying properties of group and field structures to algebraic expressions	☐
	5.2:	Solving problems that involve variable quantities	☐
	5.3:	Applying the laws of exponents and logarithms	☐
	5.4:	Demonstrating knowledge of linear algebra, including vectors and matrix operations on vectors	☐
68	**6:**	**Analyze linear and nonlinear functions and their applications**	☐
	6.1:	Analyzing linear and nonlinear functions	☐
	6.2:	Identifying the effects of algebraic transformations on the graph of a function	☐
	6.3:	Demonstrating knowledge of the use of technology to analyze relationships between different representations of functions and inequalities	☐
	6.4:	Applying linear and nonlinear functions to model real-world situations and solve problems using a variety of graphic and algebraic methods	☐
96	**7:**	**Apply knowledge of trigonometry and calculus**	☐
	7.1:	Demonstrating knowledge of the concepts of limits and continuity	☐
	7.2:	Applying unit circle trigonometry, identities, and equations to solve problems and model real-world situations	☐
	7.3:	Demonstrating knowledge of the definition of the derivative and its relationship to rate of change	☐
	7.4:	Demonstrating knowledge of the definite integral, area under the curve, and techniques of numerical integration	☐
	7.5:	Applying the fundamental theorem of calculus to solve mathematical and real-world problems	☐

COMPETENCY 4
UNDERSTAND THE PROPERTIES AND REPRESENTATIONS OF FUNCTIONS

SKILL 4.1 Applying the concept of patterns *(e.g., series and sequences, iteration and recursion, induction, finite differences)* **to model situations, make predictions, and solve problems**

Sequences

A NUMERICAL SEQUENCE is a pattern of numbers arranged in a particular order. Inspection of a sequence sometimes reveals a particular rule that is followed in creating it. For instance, 1, 4, 9, 16, ... is a series that consists of the squares of the natural numbers. Using this rule, the next term in the series, 25, can be found by squaring the next natural number: 5.

Example: Find the next term in the series 1, 1, 2, 3, 5, 8,....
Inspecting the terms in the series, one finds that this pattern is neither arithmetic nor geometric. Every term in the series is the sum of the previous two terms. Thus, the next term is $5 + 8 = 13$.

This particular sequence is a well-known series named the Fibonacci sequence.

> **NUMERICAL SEQUENCE:** a pattern of numbers arranged in a particular order

> *Tabular, numeric, graphical, symbolic, or even pictorial data sometimes contain inherent patterns and relationships. Identifying these patterns allows one to extend them and make predictions about data outside the given range.*

Tables
Example: Kepler discovered a relationship between the average distance of a planet from the sun and the time it takes the planet to orbit the Sun.

The following table shows the data for the six planets closest to the sun:

	MERCURY	VENUS	EARTH	MARS	JUPITER	SATURN
Average Distance, x	0.387	0.723	1	1.523	5.203	9.541
x^3	0.058	0.378	1	3.533	140.852	868.524
Time, y	0.241	0.615	1	1.881	11.861	29.457
y^2	0.058	0.378	1	3.538	140.683	867.715

Looking at the data in the table, we can assume that $x^3 = y^2$. We can conjecture the following function for Kepler's relationship:

$$y = \sqrt{x^3}.$$

A **RECURRENCE RELATION** is an equation that defines a sequence recursively; in other words, each term of the sequence is defined as a function of the preceding terms. For instance, the formula for the balance of an interest-bearing savings account after t years, which is given above in closed form (that is, explicit form), can be expressed recursively as follows.

$$A_t = A_{t-1}\left(1 + \tfrac{r}{n}\right)^n \text{ where } A_0 = P$$

> **RECURRENCE RELATION:** an equation that defines a sequence recursively; in other words, each term of the sequence is defined as a function of the preceding terms

Here, r is the annual interest rate and n is the number of times the interest is compounded per year. Mortgage and annuity parameters can also be expressed in recursive form. Calculation of a past or future term by applying a recursive formula multiple times is called **ITERATION**.

Sequences of numbers can be defined by iteratively applying a recursive pattern. For instance, the Fibonacci sequence is defined as follows.

$$F_i = F_{i-1} + F_{i-2} \quad \text{where } F_0 = 0 \text{ and } F_1 = 1$$

> **ITERATION:** the process of calculating a past or future term by applying a recursive formula multiple times

Applying this recursive formula gives the sequence $\{0, 1, 1, 2, 3, 5, 8, 13, 21, \ldots\}$.

It is sometimes difficult or impossible to write recursive relations in explicit or closed form. In such cases, especially when computer programming is involved, the recursive form can still be helpful. When the elements of a sequence of numbers or values depend on one or more previous values, then it is possible that a recursive formula could be used to summarize the sequence.

If a value or number from a later point in the sequence (that is, other than the beginning) is known and it is necessary to find previous terms, then the indices of the recursive relation can be adjusted to find previous values instead of later ones. Consider, for instance, the Fibonacci sequence.

$$F_i = F_{i-1} + F_{i-2}$$
$$F_{i+2} = F_{i+1} + F_i$$
$$F_i = F_{i+2} - F_{i+1}$$

Thus, if any two consecutive numbers in the Fibonacci sequence are known, then the previous numbers of the sequence can be found (in addition to the later numbers).

Example: Write a recursive formula for the following sequence: {2, 3, 5, 9, 17, 33, 65, ...}.

By inspection, it can be seen that each number in the sequence is equal to twice the previous number, less 1. If the numbers in the sequence are indexed such that,

for the first number, $i = 1$, and so on, then the recursion relation is the following.
$$N_i = 2N_{i-1} - 1$$

Example: If a recursive relation is defined by $N_i = N_{i-1}^2$ and the fourth term is 65,536, what is the first term?

Adjust the indices of the recursion and then solve for N_i.
$$N_{i+1} = N_i^2$$
$$N_i = \sqrt{N_{i+1}}$$

Use this relationship to backtrack to the first term.
$$N_3 = \sqrt{N_4} = \sqrt{65,536} = 256$$
$$N_2 = \sqrt{N_3} = \sqrt{256} = 16$$
$$N_1 = \sqrt{N_2} = \sqrt{16} = 4$$

The first term of the sequence is thus 4.

Converting Between Recursive and Closed Forms

It helpful in some situations to convert between the recursive form and the closed form of a function. Given a closed-form representation of a function, the recursive form can be found by writing out the corresponding series or sequence and then determining a pattern or formula that accurately represents that series or sequence. Consider, for instance, the mortgage principal formula in recursive form is

$$A_i = A_{i-1}(1 + \tfrac{r}{n}) - M \qquad \text{where } A_0 = P.$$

Here, A_i is the remaining principal on the mortgage after the ith payment, r is the annual interest rate, which is compounded n times annually, and M is the monthly payment. The initial value P is the original loan amount for the mortgage. To obtain a closed-form expression for this recursive formula, first write out the terms of the corresponding sequence.

$$A_0 = P$$
$$A_1 = P(1 + \tfrac{r}{n}) - M$$
$$A_2 = A_1(1 + \tfrac{r}{n}) - M = P(1 + \tfrac{r}{n})^2 - M(1 + \tfrac{r}{n}) - M$$
$$A_3 = A_2(1 + \tfrac{r}{n}) - M = P(1 + \tfrac{r}{n})^3 - M(1 + \tfrac{r}{n})^2 - M(1 + \tfrac{r}{n}) - M$$

This pattern continues until $i = k$, where k is the total number of payments in the mortgage term. Note that the term A_k can be written as follows, where $z = 1 + \tfrac{r}{n}$:
$$A_k = Pz^k - M\{z^{k-1} + z^{k-2} + \dots z^2 + z + 1\}.$$

But the expression in the curly brackets is simply a geometric series, which can be written in closed form as
$$z^{k-1} + z^{k-2} + \dots z^2 + z + 1 = \tfrac{1 - z^k}{1 - z}.$$

Thus, the closed form expression for the principal remaining after k payments on the mortgage is

$$A_k = Pz^k - M\frac{1-z^k}{1-z} \qquad \text{where } z = 1 + \frac{r}{n}.$$

The process for converting from closed form to recursive form is similar (it is essentially the reverse of the process described above). Simply write out the terms, determine the pattern and then write the ith value in terms of the value of $(i-1)$ or $(i+1)$.

Modeling Phenomena with Sequences and Series

Arithmetic and geometric sequences and series can be used to model various phenomena and are especially useful for financial mathematics. Compound interest, annuities, and mortgages can all be modeled using sequences and series. Growth and decay problems, such as those that arise in physics and other sciences, can also be modeled using sequences and series.

Compound interest

Compound interest can be modeled by deriving a general formula for the total amount of money available after a principal deposit P has accrued interest at rate of r (a decimal) compounded n times annually for t years. The same sequence-based approach to modeling compound interest is illustrative and can be applied in a similar manner to the various aspects of annuities and mortgages as well. Interest is compounded n times per year, so, after each interval, the total balance accrues interest at a rate $\frac{r}{n}$. For the first instance,

$$A_1 = P + \frac{r}{n}P = P(1 + \frac{r}{n}).$$

In the second instance,

$$A_2 = A_1 + \frac{r}{n}A_1 = A_1(1 + \frac{r}{n}).$$

The pattern continues. Note that if the expression is written out fully, then

$$A_2 = A_1(1 + \frac{r}{n}) = P(1 + \frac{r}{n})^2.$$

The pattern that emerges from this approach can be expressed generally for a sequence with n terms.

$$A_n = P(1 + \frac{r}{n})^n$$

A_n is the total amount (principal plus accrued interest) after one year. Thus, for t years, the total balance is the following.

$$A = P(1 + \frac{r}{n})^{nt}$$

If the interest is compounded continuously, then the formula becomes the limit of the above expression as n approaches infinity.

$$A = \lim_{n \to \infty} \left[P(1 + \frac{r}{n})^{nt} \right]$$

By rearranging this expression, a simpler form of the limit can be found.

$$A = P \lim_{n \to \infty} [(1+ \tfrac{1}{n/r})^{n/r}]^{rt} = P \lim_{n/r \to \infty} [(1+ \tfrac{1}{n/r})^{n/r}]^{rt}$$

Evaluating the limit reveals the balance after t years with continuously compounded interest.

$$A = Pe^{rt}$$

Example: Calculate the interest accrued after 3 years for $1,000 in a savings account that compounds the interest monthly at an annual rate of 3%.

Use the formula derived above, where $t = 3$, $n = 12$, $P = 1,000$, and $r = 0.03$.

$$A = P(1 + \tfrac{r}{n})^{nt} = \$1000(1 + \tfrac{0.03}{12})^{(12)(3)} = \$1000(1.0025)^{36}$$
$$A = \$1094.05$$

Thus, the total interest accrued is $94.05.

Example: What is the total balance after 5 years in a savings account with an annual continuously compounded interest rate of 1% if the initial deposit is $500?

Use the expression for continuously compounded interest, substituting all the relevant information described in the problem.

$$A = Pe^{rt} = \$500e^{(0.01)(5)} = \$500e^{0.05}$$
$$A = \$525.64$$

SKILL 4.2 Analyzing the characteristics of functions

A RELATION is any set of ordered pairs. The DOMAIN OF A RELATION is the set containing all the first coordinates of the ordered pairs, and the RANGE OF A RELATION is the set containing all the second coordinates of the ordered pairs.

A FUNCTION is a relation in which each value in the domain corresponds to only one value in the range. It is notable, however, that a value in the range may correspond to any number of values in the domain. Thus, although a function is necessarily a relation, not all relations are functions, since a relation is not bound by this rule.

RELATION: any set of ordered pairs

DOMAIN OF A RELATION: the set containing all the first coordinates of the ordered pairs

RANGE OF A RELATION: the set containing all the second coordinates of the ordered pairs

FUNCTION: a relation in which each value in the domain corresponds to only one value in the range

Example: Which set illustrates a function?

A. { (0, 1)   (0, 2)   (0, 3)   (0, 4) }

B. { (3, 9)   (–3, 9)   (4, 16)   (–4, 16) }

C. { (1, 2)   (2, 3)   (3, 4)   (1, 4) }

D. { (2, 4)   (3, 6)   (4, 8)   (4, 16) }

For a relation to be a function, each number in the domain can be matched with only one number in the range. Choice A is not a function because 0 is mapped to 4 different numbers in the range. In choice C, 1 is mapped to two different numbers. In choice D, 4 is also mapped to two different numbers. So the answer is choice B.

A relation can also be described algebraically. An equation such as $y = 3x + 5$ describes a relation between the independent variable x and the dependent variable y. Thus, y is written as $f(x)$ or a "function of x."

On a graph, use the vertical line test to check whether a relation is a function. If any vertical line intersects the graph of a relation in more than one point, then the relation is not a function.

Example: Determine whether the following graph depicts a function.

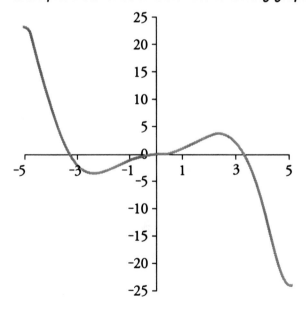

Use the vertical line test on the graph, as shown below. Every vertical line crosses the plotted curve only once. Therefore, the graph depicts a function.

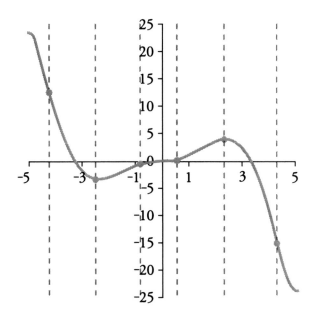

A MAPPING is essentially the same as a function. Mappings (or maps) can be depicted using diagrams with arrows drawn from each element of the domain to the corresponding element (or elements) of the range. If two arrows originate from any single element in the domain, then the mapping is not a function. Likewise, for a function, if each arrow is drawn to a unique value in the range (that is, there are no cases where more than one arrow is drawn to a given value in the range), then the relation is one-to-one.

> **MAPPING:** essentially the same as a function

> *A mapping is essentially the same as a function. Mappings (or maps) can be depicted using diagrams with arrows drawn from each element of the domain to the corresponding element (or elements) of the range.*

Example: Are the mappings shown below true functions?

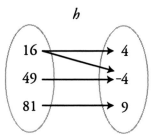

The mapping f is a function, but h is not.

The domain and the range of a function may be determined by inspecting the graph of the function or by analyzing the algebraic formula for the function.

Example: Determine the domain and the range of the following graph:

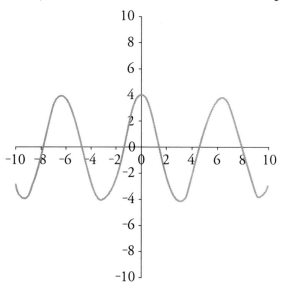

The domain of the function shown in the graph is infinite in both directions. Since the function is periodic and the y values vary between +4 and -4, the range of the function is -4 to +4.

Example: Determine the domain of the function depicted in the following graph.

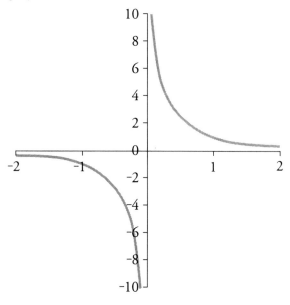

Note that this function is not continuous. It has two asymptotes: one for $y = 0$ and one for $x = 0$. It is apparent that the function is not defined for $x = 0$, but that it has finite values everywhere else. Thus, the domain of the function is all real numbers except 0.

The function plotted here is $y = \frac{1}{x}$; thus, by way of the function, it is clear that the range includes all real values except 0, for which the function goes to either positive or negative infinity in the limit (depending on the direction).

Example: Give the domain for the function over the set of real numbers:
$$y = \frac{3x + 2}{2x^2 - 3}$$
Find the values of x for which the denominator is 0. These values are excluded from the domain.

$$2x^2 - 3 = 0$$
$$2x^2 = 3$$
$$x^2 = \frac{3}{2}$$
$$x = \pm\sqrt{\frac{3}{2}} = \pm\sqrt{\frac{3}{2}} \times \sqrt{\frac{2}{2}} = \pm\frac{\sqrt{6}}{2}$$

Example: Determine the domain and the range of this mapping.

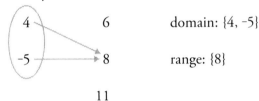

domain: {4, -5}

range: {8}

SKILL 4.3 Recognizing different representations of relations and functions *(e.g., verbal descriptions, ordered pairs, graphs)*

A relationship between two quantities can be represented in a variety of ways, including as a symbolic expression (for instance, $f(x) = 3x^2 + \sin x$), a graph, a table of values, and a common-language expression (for example, "The speed of the car increases linearly from zero to 100 miles per hour in twelve seconds."). In the following example, the rule $y = 9x$ describes the relationship between the total amount earned, y, and the total amount of $9 sunglasses sold, x. In a relationship of this type, one of the quantities (e.g., total amount earned) is dependent on the other (e.g., number of glasses sold). They are known as the dependent and independent variables, respectively.

A table using these data would appear as:

Number of Sunglasses Sold	1	5	10	15
Total Dollars Earned	9	45	90	135

COORDINATE PAIR: the (x, y) relationship between a pair of values

Each (x, y) relationship between a pair of values is called the COORDINATE PAIR that can be plotted on a graph. The coordinate pairs (1, 9), (5, 45), (10, 90), and (15, 135) are plotted on the graph below.

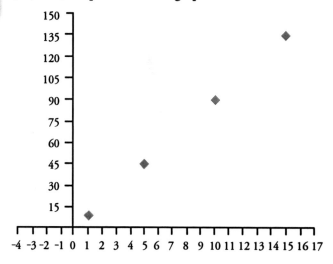

This graph shows a linear relationship. A linear relationship is one in which two quantities are proportional to each other. Doubling x also doubles y. On a graph, a straight line depicts a linear relationship.

The function, or relationship between two quantities, may be analyzed to determine how one quantity depends on the other.

For example, the function above shows a relationship between y and x:
   $y = 2x + 1$.

The relationship between two or more variables can be analyzed using a table, graph, written description, or symbolic rule. The function $y = 2x + 1$ is written as a symbolic rule. The same relationship is also shown in the table below:

x	0	2	3	6	9
y	1	5	7	13	19

This relationship could be written in words by saying that the value of y is equal to two times the value of x, plus one. This relationship could be shown on a graph by plotting given points such as the ones shown in the table above.

The ability to convert among various representations of a function depends on how much information is provided. For instance, although a graph of a function can provide some clues as to its symbolic representation, it is often difficult or impossible to obtain an exact symbolic form based only on a graph. The same difficulty applies to tables.

Converting from a symbolic form to a graph or table, however, is relatively simple, especially if a computer is available. The symbolic expression need simply be evaluated for a representative set of points that can be used to produce a sufficiently detailed graph or table.

It is important to note that the particular symbols used in function notation are not important, as long as they are used consistently. Thus, the following are all the same function with different symbols used to represent the erstwhile x and y notation.

$$f(\alpha) = \alpha^2$$
$$\beta(r) = r^2$$
$$\pi(W) = W^2$$

The fundamental principle for this function notation is to represent that for each x (or other variable) value, the function (be it f, β, or any other symbol) has only one value.

Symmetries in a function can also be described in terms of reflections or "mirror images." A function can be symmetric about the the y-axis (but not about the x-axis, except for the function $f(x) = 0$, since every function must pass the vertical line test). A function is symmetric about the y-axis if, for every point (x, y) that is included on the graph of the function, the point $(-x, y)$ is also included on the graph. Consider the function $f(x) = x^2$. Note that for each point (x, x^2) on the graph, the point $(-x, x^2)$ is also on the graph. The symmetry of the function about the y-axis can also be seen in the graph below.

> A function is symmetric about the y-axis if, for every point (x, y) that is included on the graph of the function, the point (-x, y) is also included on the graph.

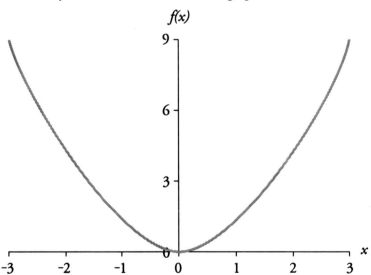

A function that is symmetric about the y-axis is also called an EVEN FUNCTION.

Although functions cannot be symmetric about the x-axis, relations that do not obey the vertical line test can be symmetric in this way. A relation is symmetric

> **EVEN FUNCTION:** a function that is symmetric with respect to the y-axis

A relation is symmetric about the x-axis if for every point (x, y) in the graph of the relation, the point (x, -y) is also in the graph.

about the *x*-axis if, for every point (*x, y*) in the graph of the relation, the point (*x, −y*) is also in the graph.

Consider, for instance, the relation $g(x) = \pm\sqrt{x}$. For every value of *x* in the domain, the points $(x, \sqrt{x})$ and $(x, -\sqrt{x})$ are both in the graph, as shown below.

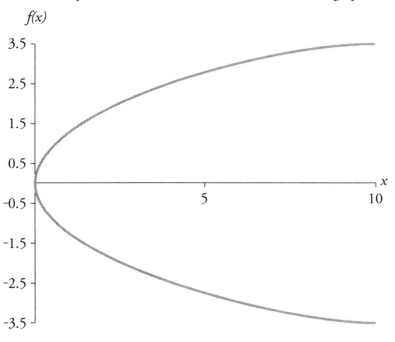

Functions may also be symmetric with respect to the origin. Such functions are called **ODD (OR ANTISYMMETRIC) FUNCTIONS** and are defined by the property that for any point (*x, y*) on the graph of the function, the point (−*x, −y*) is also on the graph of the function. The function $f(x) = x^3$, for instance, is symmetric with respect to the origin, as shown in the graph below.

ODD (OR ANTISYM-METRIC) FUNCTIONS: a function that is symmetric with respect to the origin

A function is symmetric with respect to the origin if for any point (x, y) on the graph of the function, the point (-x, -y) is also on the graph of the function.

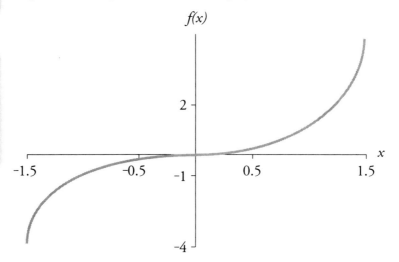

Example: Determine if the given function is even, odd, or neither even nor odd.

1. $f(x) = x^4 - 2x^2 + 7$

   $f(-x) = (-x)^4 - 2(-x)^2 + 7$

   $f(-x) = x^4 - 2x^2 + 7$

   1. Find $f(-x)$.

   2. Replace x with $-x$.

   3. Since $f(-x) = f(x)$, $f(x)$ is an even function.

2. $f(x) = 3x^3 + 2x$

   $f(-x) = 3(-x)^3 + 2(-x)$

   $f(-x) = -3x^3 - 2x$

   $-f(x) = -3x^3 - 2x$

   1. Find $f(-x)$.

   2. Replace x with $-x$.

   3. Since $f(x)$ is not equal to $f(-x)$, $-f(x) = (3x^3 + 2x)$

   4. Try $-f(x)$.

   5. Since $f(-x) = -f(x)$, $f(x)$ is an odd function.

3. $g(x) = 2x^2 - x + 4$

   $g(-x) = 2(-x)^2 - (-x) + 4$

   $g(-x) = 2x^2 + x + 4$

   $g(x) = -2x^2 + x - 4$

   1. First find $g(-x)$.

   2. Replace x with $-x$.

   3. Since $g(-x)$ does not equal $g(-x)$, $-g(x) = -(2x^2 - x + 4)$, $g(x)$ is not an even function

   4. Try $-f(x)$.

   5. Since $-g(x)$ does not equal $g(-x)$, $g(x)$ is not an odd function.

Thus, $g(x)$ is neither an even nor an odd function.

A relation is considered one-to-one if each value in the domain corresponds to only one value in the range and if each value in the range corresponds to only one value in the domain. Thus, a one-to-one relation is also a function, but it adds an additional condition.

In the same way that the graph of a relation can be examined using the vertical line test to determine whether it is a function, the horizontal line test can be used to determine if a function is a one-to-one relation. If no horizontal lines superimposed on the plot intersect the graph of the relation in more than one place, then the relation is one-to-one (assuming it also passes the vertical line test and, therefore, is a function). Inverse functions are discussed in *Skill 4.4*.

Applying the concepts of inverse and composite functions to solve problems

Addition of Functions

$(f + g)(x) = f(x) + g(x)$

To add two functions, add together their solutions.

For example, if $f(x) = x^2 + 1$ and $g(x) = 6x - 1$,
$(f + g)(1) = f(1) + g(1) = 2 + 5 = 7$
$(f + g)(x) = f(x) + g(x) = (x^2 + 1) + (6x - 1) = x^2 + 6x.$

Subtraction of Functions

$(f - g)(x) = f(x) - g(x)$

To subtract two functions, subtract the solution of one from the solution of the other. For example, if $f(x) = 3x - 4$ and $g(x) = 5x + 2$,
$(f - g)(2) = f(2) - g(2) = 2 - 12 = -10.$
$(f - g)(x) = f(x) - g(x) = (3x - 4) - (5x + 2) = -2x - 6.$

Example: Given $f(x) = 3x + 1$ and $g(x) = 4 + 3x$, find $(f + g)(x)$, $(f - g)(x)$, $(f \times g)(x)$, and $(\frac{f}{g})(x)$.

To find the answers, just apply the indicated operations (addition, subtraction, multiplication, and division).

$$(f + g)(x) = f(x) + g(x) = [3x + 1] + [4 + 3x]$$
$$= 3x + 3x + 1 + 4$$
$$= 6x + 5$$
$$(f - g)(x) = f(x) - g(x) = [3x + 1] - [4 + 3x]$$
$$= 3x - 3x + 1 - 4$$
$$= -3$$
$$(f \times g)(x) = [f(x)][g(x)] = (3x + 1)(4 + 3x)$$
$$= 12x + 4 + 9x^2 + 3x$$
$$= 9x^2 + 15x + 4$$
$$\left(\frac{f}{g}\right)x = \frac{f(x)}{g(x)} = \frac{3x + 1}{4 + 3x}$$

Example: Given $f(x) = 2x$, $g(x) = x + 4$, and $h(x) = 5 - x^3$, find $(f + g)(2)$, $(h - g)(2)$, $(f \times h)(2)$, and $(\frac{h}{g})(2)$.

$f(2) = 2(2) = 4$
$g(2) = (2) + 4 = 6$
$h(2) = 5 - (2)^3 = 5 - 8 = -3$

Evaluate the following:

$(f + g)(2) = f(2) + g(2) = 4 + 6 = 10$
$(h - g)(2) = h(2) - g(2) = -3 - 6 = -9$
$(f \times h)(2) = f(2) \times h(2) = (4)(-3) = -12$
$(\frac{h}{g})(2) = h(2) \div g(2) = -3 \div 6 = -0.5$

The addition of functions is commutative and associative:

$f + g = g + f$ and $(f + g) + h = f + (g + h)$.

Composition of Functions

Composition of functions is way of combining functions such that the range of one function is the domain of another. For instance, the composition of functions f and g can be either $f \circ g$ (the composite of f with g) or $g \circ f$ (the composite of g with f). Another way of writing these compositions is $f(g(x))$ and $g(f(x))$. The domain of includes all values x such that $g(x)$ is in the domain of $f(x)$.

Example: What is the composition $f \circ g$ for functions $f(x) = ax$ and $g(x) = bx^2$?

The correct answer can be found by substituting the function $g(x)$ into $g \circ f$.

$f(g(x)) = ag(x) = abx^2$

On the other hand, the composition $g \circ f$ would yield a different answer.

$g(f(x)) = b(f(x))^2 = b(ax)^2 = a^2bx^2$

Example: If $f(x) = sqrt(x)$ and $g(x) = x + 2$, find the composition functions $f \circ g$ and $g \circ f$ and state their domains.

$(f \circ g)(x) = f(g(x)) = f(x + 2) = sqrt(x + 2)$
$(g \circ f)(x) = g(f(x)) = g(sqrt(x)) = sqrt(x) + 2$

The domain of $f(g(x))$ is $x \geq -2$ because $x + 2$ must be nonnegative in order to take the square root.

The domain of $g(f(x))$ is $x \geq 0$ because x must be nonnegative in order to take the square root.

Note that defining the domain of composite functions is important when square roots are involved.

Inverses of Functions

The inverse of a function $f(x)$ is typically labeled $f^{-1}(x)$ and satisfies the following two relations:

$$f(f^{-1}(x)) = x$$
$$f^{-1}(f(x)) = x$$

For a function $f(x)$ to have an inverse, it must be one-to-one. This fact is easily seen, since both $f(x)$ and $f^{-1}(x)$ must satisfy the vertical line test (that is, both must be functions). A function takes each value in a domain and relates it to only one value in the range. Logically, then, the inverse must do the same, only backwards: relate each value in the range to a single value in the domain.

Finding inverses of functions

Finding the inverse of a function can be a difficult or impossible task, but there are some simple approaches that can be followed in many cases. The simplest method for finding the inverse of a function is to interchange the variable and the function symbols and then solve to find the inverse. The approach is summarized in the outline below, given a one-to-one function $f(x)$.

1. Replace the symbol $f(x)$ with x

2. Replace all instances of x in the function definition with $f^{-1}(x)$ (or y or some other symbol)

3. Solve for $f^{-1}(x)$

4. Check the result using $f(f^{-1}(x)) = x$ or $f^{-1}(f(x)) = x$

Example: Determine if the function f(x) = x² has an inverse. If so, find the inverse.

First, determine if $f(x)$ is one-to-one. Note that $f(1) = f(-1) = 1$, so $f(x)$ is not one-to-one, and it therefore has no inverse function.

Example: Determine if the function f(x) = x³ + 1 has an inverse. If so, find the inverse.

The function $f(x) = x^3 + 1$ has an inverse because it increases monotonically for $x > 0$ and decreases monotonically for $x < 0$. As a result, it is one-to-one, and the inverse exists. To calculate the inverse, let y be $f^{-1}(x)$. Replace $f(x)$ with x and replace x with y.

$$f(x) = x^3 + 1 \longrightarrow x = y^3 + 1$$

Solve for y.

$$x - 1 = y^3$$
$$y = \sqrt[3]{x - 1}$$
$$f^{-1}(x) = \sqrt[3]{x - 1}$$

Test the result.

$$f^{-1}(f(x)) = \sqrt[3]{(x^3 + 1) - 1}$$
$$f^{-1}(f(x)) = \sqrt[3]{x^3 + 1 - 1} = \sqrt[3]{x^3} = x$$

The result is correct.

COMPETENCY 5
APPLY ALGEBRAIC TECHNIQUES

SKILL 5.1 **Applying properties of group and field structures to algebraic expressions**

See Skill 2.3 for a discussion of field and ring properties

A GROUP is a set of numbers that obeys certain axioms with respect to a particular binary operation (such as addition). For a set, G, to be a group, the set must be closed under the defined operation, which must obey associativity; the set must contain an identity element; and each element must have an inverse element also in set G. These rules are summarized below for elements a, b, and c in set G for the binary operation $*$.

PROPERTY	NOTATION
Closure	$a * b \in G$
Associativity	$a * (b * c) = (a * b) * c$
Identity	$I \in G$ such that $I * a = a * I = a$
Inverse	$a_{inv} \in G$ such that $a_{inv} * a = a * a_{inv} = I$

GROUP: a set of numbers that obeys certain axioms with respect to a particular binary operation (such as addition)

According to the inverse rule, I is the same as the identity element. An example of a group is the set of integers under addition. For any two integers a and b, the sum $a + b$ is also an integer—thus, the set of integers is closed under addition. Also, associativity applies, since $a + (b + c) = (a + b) + c$ for any integers a, b, and c. The identity element 0 (zero) is also in the set of integers, and $0 + a = a + 0 = a$, for all a. Furthermore, the inverse element $-a$, for all a, leads to $a + (-a) = 0$. Thus, the set of integers also obeys the identity and inverse axioms, meaning that integers are a group under the binary operation of addition.

> ### SKILL 5.2 Solving problems that involve variable quantities *(e.g., simplifying algebraic expressions, factoring)*

Adding Polynomials

We find the sum of two polynomials by grouping the like powers, retaining their signs and adding the coefficients of like powers. There are different ways to add polynomials.

Using the horizontal method to add like terms

Remove the parentheses, and identify like terms. Group the like terms together. Add the like terms.

Example: Add $(2x^2 - 4)$ and $(x^2 + 3x - 3)$.
$$(2x^2 - 4) + (x^2 + 3x - 3) = 2x^2 + x^2 + 3x - 4 - 3$$
$$= 3x^2 + 3x - 7$$

Example: Add $(5x - 1) + (10x^2 + 7x)$.
$$(5x - 1) + (10x^2 + 7x) = 10x^2 + 5x + 7x - 1$$
$$= 10x^2 + 12x - 1$$

Example: Add $(20x^2 + 2) + (15x^2 - 8) + (3x^2 - 4)$.
$$(20x^2 + 2) + (15x^2 - 8) + (3x^2 - 4) = 20x^2 + 15x^2 + 3x^2 + 2 - 8 - 4$$
$$= 38x^2 - 10$$

Using the vertical method to add like terms

Arrange the like terms so they are lined up under one another in vertical columns. Add the like terms in each column, following the rules for adding the signed numbers.

Example: Add $(2x^2 - 4)$ and $(x^2 + 3x - 3)$.

$$2x^2 + 0x - 4$$
$$\underline{x^2 + 3x - 3}$$
$$3x^2 + 3x - 7$$

Example: Add $(x^4 - 3x^3 + 2x + 6)$ and $(x^3 + 2)$.

$$x^4 - 3x^3 + 2x + 6$$
$$\underline{0x^4 + \ x^3 + 0x + 2}$$
$$x^4 - 3x^3 + 2x + 8$$

Example: Add $(3y^7 - 2y^2 + 3)$ and $(y^6 - 3y^4 + y^2 + y)$.

$$3y^7 - 0y^6 + 0y^5 + 0y^4 + 0y^3 - 2y^2 + 0y + 3$$
$$\underline{0y^7 + 1y^6 + 0y^5 - 3y^4 + 0y^3 + 1y^2 + 1y + 0}$$
$$3y^7 + \ y^6 + 0y^5 - 3y^4 + 0y^3 - \ y^2 + \ y + 3$$

The answer is $3y^7 + y^6 - 3y^4 - y^2 + y + 3$.

Subtracting Polynomials

Subtract like terms by changing the signs of the terms being subtracted and following the rules for addition of polynomials.

Example: Subtract $(y^4 + 4y^2 + 5y - 4)$ from $(3y^5 + y^4 - 3y^3 - 2y + 1)$.
First, we change the sign of each term of the polynomial being subtracted. So the polynomial $y^4 + 4y^2 + 5y - 4$ becomes $-y^4 - 4y^2 - 5y + 4$.

$$(3y^5 + y^4 - 3y^3 - 2y + 1) - (y^4 + 4y^2 + 5y - 4)$$
$$= (3y^5 + y^4 - 3y^3 - 2y + 1) + (-y^4 - 4y^2 - 5y + 4)$$
$$= 3y^5 + 0y^4 - 3y^3 - 7y + 5$$
$$= 3y^5 - 3y^3 - 7y + 5$$

Example: Subtract $(p^3 + 4p^2 - 5p - 6)$ from $(7p^3 - 3p + 5)$.
$$(7p^3 - 3p + 5) - (p^3 + 4p^2 - 5p - 6) = 7p^3 - p^3 - 4p^2 - 3p + 5p + 5 + 6$$
$$= 6p^3 - 4p^2 + 2p + 11$$

Using the vertical method to subtract polynomials

We change the sign of each term of the polynomial being subtracted and add with the other polynomial.

Example: Subtract ($t^3 − 5t + 1$) from ($t^4 + 3t^3 − 5t − 1$).

$$t^4 + 3t^3 − 5t − 1$$
$$\underline{0t^4 − \;\; t^3 + 5t − 1}$$
$$t^4 + 2t^3 + 0t − 2$$

The answer is $t^4 + 2t^3 − 2$.

Example: Subtract ($p^3 + 4p^2 − 5p − 6$) from ($7p^3 − 3p + 5$).

After changing the sign of each term of $p^3 + 4p^2 − 5p − 6$, we have to add with $7p^3 + 0p^2 − 3p + 5$.

$$7p^3 + 0p^2 − 3p + \;\; 5$$
$$\underline{−p^3 − 4p^2 + 5p + \;\; 6}$$
$$6p^3 − 4p^2 + 2p + 11$$

Multiplying Polynomials

All of the terms of the second polynomial are to be multiplied by each term of the first polynomial to get the product.

Example: Simplify ($5x$)($2x^3$).

$$(5x^2)(2x^3) = (5 × 2)(x^2 × x^2)$$
$$= 10x^2$$

Example: Simplify ($-3x$)($4x^2 − x + 10$).

$$(−3x)(4x^2 − x + 10) = (−3x × 4x^2) − (−3x × x) + (−3x × 10)$$
$$= −12x^3 − −3x^2 + −30x$$
$$= −12x^3 + 3x^2 − 30x$$

Example: Simplify ($y + 2$)($y − 3$).

$$(y + 2)(y − 3) = (y × y) − (y × 3) + (2 × y) − (2 × 3)$$
$$= y^2 − 3y + 2y − 6$$
$$= y^2 − y − 6$$

Example: Find the product of ($2p + 6$)($2p − 6$).

$$(2p + 6)(2p − 6) = (2p × 2p) − (2p × 6) + (6 × 2p) − (6 × 6)$$
$$= 4p^2 − 12p^2 + 12p − 36$$
$$= 4p^2 − 36$$

Dividing Polynomials

One polynomial can be divided by another using long division that is similar to long division performed with numbers, i.e., start working with the front part of the dividend and bring down one term at a time. The examples given below will clarify the procedure.

Example: Divide $2x^2 + 5x - 1$ by $2x - 1$.

$$
\begin{array}{r}
x \\
2x - 1 \overline{)\,2x^2 + 5x - 1} \\
\underline{-(2x^2 - x)} \\
6x - 1
\end{array}
$$

First, note that $2x$ times x will give $2x^2$
Bring down the -1

$$
\begin{array}{r}
x + 3 \\
2x - 1 \overline{)\,2x^2 + 5x - 1} \\
\underline{-(2x^2 - x)} \\
6x - 1 \\
\underline{-(6x - 3)} \\
2
\end{array}
$$

Note that $2x$ ties 3 gives $6x$

The quotient is $x + 3$ and the remainder is 2.

Example: Divide $2t^3 - 9t^2 + 11t - 3$ by $2t - 3$.

$$
\begin{array}{r}
t^2 - 3t + 1 \\
2t - 3 \overline{)\,2t^3 - 9t^2 + 11t - 3} \\
\underline{-(2t^3 - 3t^2)} \\
-6t^2 + 11t \\
\underline{-(6t^2 + 9t)} \\
2t - 3 \\
\underline{-(2t - 3)} \\
0
\end{array}
$$

The quotient is $t^2 - 3t + 1$ and the remainder is zero.

If the divisor is of the form $x - a$, synthetic division may be used to divide polynomials.

Finding the LCD

Find the LCD for $x^2 - 4$, $x^2 + 5x + 6$, and $x^2 + x - 6$.

$x^2 - 4$	factors into $(x - 2)(x + 2)$
$x^2 + 5x + 6$	factors into $(x + 3)(x + 2)$
$x^2 + x - 6$	factors into $(x + 3)(x + 2)$

The LCD is $(x + 3)(x + 2)(x - 2)$.

Adding Algebraic Fractions

To add algebraic fractions, first express the fractions in terms of their lowest common denominator (LCD), and then add their numerators to obtain the numerator that is divided by the LCD to arrive at the answer.

Example: Add $(\frac{3a}{2})$ and $(\frac{5a}{3})$.

$$(\tfrac{3a}{2}) + (\tfrac{5a}{3}) = (\tfrac{3a \times 3}{6}) + (\tfrac{5a \times 2}{6})$$
$$= \tfrac{9a}{6} + \tfrac{10a}{6}$$
$$= \tfrac{19a}{6} = 3\tfrac{1}{6}a$$

Example: Find the sum of $(\frac{5}{x + y})$ and $(\frac{4}{x - y})$.

$$(\tfrac{5}{x + y}) + (\tfrac{5}{x - y}) = \left[\tfrac{5(x - y)}{(x + y)(x - y)}\right] + \left[\tfrac{4(x + y)}{(x + y)(x - y)}\right]$$
$$= \tfrac{5(x - y) + 4(x + y)}{(x + y)(x - y)}$$
$$= \tfrac{5x - 5y + 4x + 4y}{x^2 - y^2}$$
$$= \tfrac{9x - y}{x^2 - y^2}$$

Example: Find the value of $(\frac{7x}{8}) + 4$.

$$(\tfrac{7x}{8}) + 4 = (\tfrac{7x \times 1}{8}) + (\tfrac{4 \times 8}{8})$$
$$= \tfrac{7x + 32}{8}$$

Example:

$$\frac{5}{6a^3b^2} + \frac{1}{4ab^3} = \frac{5(2b)}{6a^3b^2(2b)} + \frac{1(3a^2)}{4ab^3(3a^2)} = \frac{10a}{12a^3b^3} + \frac{3b^2}{12a^3b^3} = \frac{10a + 3b^2}{12a^3b^3}$$

This will not reduce, since all three terms are not divisible by anything.

Subtracting Algebraic Fractions

To subtract algebraic fractions, first express the fractions in terms of their LCD and then subtract their numerators to obtain the numerator that is divided by the LCD to arrive at the answer.

Example:

$$\frac{2}{x^2 - 4} - \frac{3}{x^2 + 5x + 6} + \frac{7}{x^2 + x - 6} =$$
$$\frac{2}{(x - 2)(x + 2)} - \frac{3}{(x + 3)(x + 2)} + \frac{7}{(x + 3)(x - 2)} =$$
$$\frac{2(x + 3)}{(x - 2)(x + 2)(x + 3)} - \frac{3(x - 2)}{(x + 3)(x + 2)(x - 2)} + \frac{7(x + 2)}{(x + 3)(x - 2)(x + 2)} =$$
$$\frac{2x + 6}{(x - 2)(x + 2)(x + 3)} - \frac{3x - 6}{(x + 3)(x + 2)(x - 2)} + \frac{7x + 14}{(x + 3)(x - 2)(x + 2)} =$$
$$\frac{2x + 6 - (3x - 6) + 7x + 14}{(x + 3)(x - 2)(x + 2)} = \frac{6x + 26}{(x + 3)(x - 2)(x + 2)}$$

This will not reduce.

Multiplying Algebraic Fractions

Factorize the numerators and denominators. Then cancel the factors that are common to each numerator and denominator before applying multiplication to obtain the answer.

Example: Find the product of $(\frac{a}{3})$ and $(\frac{b}{4})$.

$$(\tfrac{a}{3}) \times (\tfrac{b}{4}) = \frac{a \times b}{3 \times 4} = \frac{ab}{12}$$

Example: Simplify $(\frac{5x^2}{2x^2 - 2x})(\frac{x^2 - 1}{x^2 + x})$.

$(\frac{5x^2}{2x^2 - 2x})(\frac{x^2 - 1}{x^2 + x}) = [\frac{5x^2}{2x(x - 1)}][\frac{(x + 1)(x - 1)}{x(x + 1)}] = \frac{5}{2}$, since all of the common factors from the numerator and the denominator are canceled.

Example: Multiply $(\frac{4x^2}{x - 2})(\frac{x^2 - 4}{12})$.

$$(\tfrac{4x^2}{x - 2})(\tfrac{x^2 - 4}{12}) = (\tfrac{4x^2}{x - 2})[\tfrac{(x - 2)(x + 2)}{4 \times 3)}]$$
$$= \frac{x^2(x + 2)}{3}$$

Dividing Algebraic Fractions

To divide the algebraic fractions, invert the second fraction and multiply it by the first fraction. In other words, you must multiply both fractions after taking the reciprocal of the divisor. Then factorize the numerator and denominator and cancel all the common factors.

Example: Simplify $(\frac{x - 3}{4}) \div (\frac{x + 3}{8})$.

$$(\tfrac{x - 3}{4}) \div (\tfrac{x + 3}{8}) = (\tfrac{x - 3}{4})(\tfrac{8}{x + 3})$$
$$= \frac{2(x - 3)}{x + 3}$$

Example: Simplify $(\frac{m^2 + 2m}{3m^3}) \div (\frac{5m + 10}{6})$.

$$(\tfrac{m^2 + 2m}{3m^3}) \div (\tfrac{5m + 10}{6}) = [\tfrac{m(m + 2)}{3m^3}] \div [\tfrac{5(m + 2)}{6}]$$
$$= [\tfrac{m(m + 2)}{3m^3}][\tfrac{6}{5(m + 2)}]$$
$$= \frac{2}{5m^2}$$

Example: Find $(\frac{12y + 24}{36}) \div (\frac{y^2 + 3y + 2}{2})$.

$$(\tfrac{12y + 24}{36}) \div (\tfrac{y^2 + 3y + 2}{2}) = [\tfrac{12(y + 2)}{12 \times 3}] \div [\tfrac{(y + 2)(y + 1)}{2}]$$
$$= (\tfrac{y + 2}{3})[\tfrac{2}{(y + 2)(y + 1)}]$$
$$= \frac{2}{3(y + 1)}$$

Applications

Some problems can be solved using equations with rational expressions. First, write the equation. To solve it, multiply each term by the LCD of all of the fractions. This will cancel out all of the denominators and give an equivalent algebraic equation that can be solved.

Example: The denominator of a fraction is two less than three times the numerator. If 3 is added to both the numerator and the denominator, the new fraction equals $\frac{1}{2}$.

original fraction: $\dfrac{x}{3x-2}$ revised fraction: $\dfrac{x+3}{3x+1}$

$$\frac{x+3}{3x+1} = \frac{1}{2}$$

$$2x + 6 = 3x + 1$$

$$x = 5$$

So the original fraction is $\dfrac{5}{13}$.

Example: Elly Mae can feed the animals in 15 minutes. Jethro can feed them in 10 minutes. How long will it take them if they work together?

If Elly Mae can feed the animals in 15 minutes, then she could feed $\frac{1}{15}$ of them in 1 minute, $\frac{2}{15}$ of them in 2 minutes, and $\frac{x}{15}$ of them in x minutes. In the same fashion, Jethro could feed $\frac{x}{10}$ of them in x minutes. Together they complete 1 job. The equation is:

$$\frac{x}{15} + \frac{x}{10} = 1$$

Multiply each term by the LCD (least common denominator) of 30:

$$2x + 3x = 30$$

$$x = 6 \text{ minutes}$$

Example: A salesman drove 480 miles from Pittsburgh to Hartford. The next day he returned the same distance to Pittsburgh in half an hour less time than his original trip took, because he increased his average speed by 4 mph. Find his original speed.

Since distance = rate $\times$ time, then time $= \frac{\text{distance}}{\text{rate}}$

original time $- \frac{1}{2}$ hour = shorter return time

$$\frac{480}{x} - \frac{1}{2} = \frac{480}{x+4}$$

Multiplying by the LCD of $2x(x + 4)$, the equation becomes:

$$480[2(x + 4)] - 1[x(x + 4)] = 480(2x)$$

$$960x + 3840 - x^2 - 4x = 960x$$

$$x^2 + 4x - 3840 = 0$$

$$(x + 64)(x - 60) = 0$$

$$x = 60$$

60 mph is the original speed, 64 mph is the faster return speed.

Solving for a Variable

To solve an algebraic formula for some variable R, use the following steps:

1. Eliminate any parentheses using the distributive property

2. Multiply every term by the LCD of any fractions to write an equivalent equation without any fractions

3. Move all of the terms containing the variable R to one side of the equation. Move all of the terms without the variable to the opposite side of the equation

4. If there are two or more terms containing the variable R, factor only R out of each of those terms as a common factor

5. Divide both sides of the equation by the number or expression being multiplied times the variable R

6. Reduce the fractions if possible

7. Remember that there are restrictions on values allowed for variables because the denominator cannot equal zero

Examples:

Solve $A = p + prt$ for t.

$$A - p = prt$$
$$\frac{A - p}{pr} = \frac{prt}{pr}$$
$$\frac{A - p}{pr} = t$$

Solve $A = p + prt$ for p.

$$A = p(1 + rt)$$
$$\frac{A}{1 + rt} = \frac{p(1 + rt)}{1 + rt}$$
$$\frac{A}{1 + rt} = p$$

Solve $A = \frac{1}{2} h(b_1 + b_2)$ for b_2.

$$A = \frac{1}{2} hb_1 + \frac{1}{2} hb_2 \quad \leftarrow \text{step a}$$

$$2A = hb_1 + hb_2 \quad \leftarrow \text{step b}$$

$$2A - hb_1 = hb_2 \quad \leftarrow \text{step c}$$

$$\frac{2A - hb_1}{h} = \frac{hb_2}{h} \quad \leftarrow \text{step d}$$

$$\frac{2A - hb_1}{h} = hb_2 \quad \leftarrow \text{will not reduce}$$

SKILL 5.3 Applying the laws of exponents and logarithms

Exponentials and logarithms are complementary. The general relationship for logarithmic and exponential functions is

$y = \log_b x$ if and only if $x = b^y$.

For the exponential base e and the natural logarithm (ln) the relationship is

$y = \ln x$ if and only if $e^y = x$.

When changing common logarithms to exponential form,

$y = \log_b x$ if and only if $x = b^y$.

Natural logarithms can be changed to exponential form by using

$\log_e x = \ln x$, or $\ln x = y$ can be written as $e^y = x$.

Logarithms

Example: Express in exponential form.

$\log_3 81 = 4$

$x = 81$ $b = 3$ $y = 4$ Identify values.

$81 = 3^4$ Rewrite in exponential form.

Example: Solve by writing in exponential form.

$\log_x 125 = 3$

$x^3 = 125$ Write in exponential form.

$x^3 = 5^3$ Write 125 in exponential form.

$x = 5$ Bases must be equal if exponents are equal.

Use a scientific calculator to solve.

Example: Find ln 72.

$\ln 72 = 4.2767$

Use the "ln x" key to find natural logs.

Example: Find ln $x = 4.2767$

Write in exponential form to find x.

$e^{4.2767} = x$ Use the "e^x" key (or "2nd" "ln x").

$x = 72.002439$ The small difference is due to rounding.

The following properties of logarithms are helpful in solving equations.

PROPERTIES OF LOGARITHMS	
Multiplication Property	$\log_b mn = \log_b m + \log_b n$
Quotient Property	$\log_b \frac{m}{n} = \log_b m - \log_b n$
Powers Property	$\log_b n^r = r\log_b n$
Equality Property	$\log_b n = \log_b m$ if and only if $n = m$
Change of Base Formula	$\log_b n = \frac{\log n}{\log b}$
	$\log_b b^x = x$ and $b^{\log_b x} = x$

Exponentials

The following properties can be used to simplify expressions involving exponents.

KEY EXPONENT RULES: FOR 'a' NONZERO AND 'm' AND 'n' REAL NUMBERS		
Product Rule	$a^m \times a^n = a^{(m+n)}$	$(3^4)(3^5) = 3^9$
	$a^m \times b^m = (ab)^m$	$(4^2)(5^2) = 20^2$
	$(a^m)^n = a^{mn}$	$(2^3)^2 = 2^6$
Quotient Rule	$\frac{a^m}{a^n} = a^{(m-n)}$	$2^5 \div 2^3 = 2^2$
Rule of Negative Exponents	$a^{-m} = \frac{1}{a^m}$	$2^{-2} = \frac{1}{2^2}$

Example: Simplify $\frac{3^5(3^{-2} + 3^{-3})}{9}$.

$$\frac{3^5(3^{-2} + 3^{-3})}{9} = \frac{3^5(3^{-2} + 3^{-3})}{3^2} = 3^3(3^{-2} + 3^{-3})$$

$$= 3^3 3^{-2} + 3^3 3^{-3} = 3^{3-2} + 3^{3-3} = 3 + 1 = 4$$

Example: Simplify $\frac{3^2 \times 5^{-2} \times 2^5}{6^2 \times 5}$.

$$\frac{3^2 \times 5^{-2} \times 2^5}{6^2 \times 5} = \frac{3^2 \times 5^{-2} \times 2^5}{3^2 \times 2^2 \times 5} = 5^{-2-1} \times 2^{5-2} = \frac{2^3}{5^3} = \frac{8}{125}$$

Unless the negative sign is inside the parentheses and the exponent is outside the parentheses, the sign is not affected by the exponent.

Example:
$$(-2)^4 = (-2) \times (-2) \times (-2) \times (-2) = 16$$
In this case, -2 is multiplied by itself 4 times.
$$-2^4 = -(2 \times 2 \times 2 \times 2) = -16$$
In this case, 2 is multiplied by itself 4 times and the answer is negated.

A radical may also be expressed using a rational exponent.
$$\sqrt[n]{a} = a^{\frac{1}{n}}$$

Example:
$$\sqrt{5} = 5^{\frac{1}{2}}; \quad \sqrt[5]{7} = 7^{\frac{1}{5}}$$

All the exponent laws discussed above also apply to rational exponents.

Example:
$$(\sqrt[5]{6})^3 = (6^{\frac{1}{5}})^3 = 6^{(\frac{1}{5}) \times 3} = 6^{\frac{3}{5}}$$

Example: Simplify $(-32)^{\frac{3}{5}} + 16^{\frac{3}{4}}$.
$$(-32)^{\frac{3}{5}} + 16^{\frac{3}{4}} = (\sqrt[5]{-32})^3 + (\sqrt[4]{16})^3 = (-2)^3 + 2^3 = -8 + 8 = 0$$

Solving equations involving exponentials or logarithms typically involves isolating the terms with the exponential or logarithmic function and using the inverse operation to "extract" the argument. For instance, given the following equation
$$\ln f(x) = c,$$

the function $f(x)$ can be determined by raising e to each side of the equation.
$$e^{\ln f(x)} = f(x) = e^c$$

Alternatively, if the function is in terms of an exponent e, $e^{f(x)} = c,$

solve by taking the natural logarithm of both sides.
$$\ln e^{f(x)} = f(x) = \ln c$$

Although these examples are in terms of e and the natural logarithm, the same logic applies to exponentials and logarithms involving different bases as well.

Example: Solve $\log_6 (x - 5) + \log_6 x = 2$.

$\log_6 x(x - 5) = 2$	Use product property.
$\log_6 x^2 - 5x = 2$	Distribute.
$x^2 - 5x = 6^2$	Write in exponential form.
$x^2 - 5x - 36 = 0$	Solve quadratic equation.
$(x + 4)(x - 9) = 0$	
$x = -4 \quad x = 9$	

***Be sure to check results. Remember, x must be greater than zero in $\log x = y$.

$$\log_6(x - 5) + \log_6 x = 2$$

$\log_6(-4 - 5) + \log_6(-4) = 2$ Substitute the first answer.

$\log_6(-9) + \log_6(-4) = 2$ This is undefined (the argument is less than zero).

$\log_6(9 - 5) + \log_6 9 = 2$ Substitute the second answer.

$$\log_6 4 + \log_6 9 = 2$$

$\log_6(4)(9) = 2$ Multiplication property.

$$\log_6 36 = 2$$

$6^2 = 36$ Write in exponential form.

$$36 = 36$$

SKILL 5.4 Demonstrating knowledge of linear algebra, including vectors and matrix operations on vectors

Vectors

A VECTOR is any quantity that has magnitude (or length) and direction. For instance, unlike temperature (which is just a scalar), velocity is a vector because it has magnitude (speed) and direction (the direction of travel). Because vectors do not have specified locations, they can be translated as long as their direction and magnitude remain the same. A vector is often written in the same form as a point; for instance, a vector can be written as (x_1, y_1, z_1). In this case, the direction and magnitude of the vector are defined by a ray that starts at the origin and terminates at the point (x_1, y_1, z_1).

> **VECTOR:** any quantity that has a magnitude (or length) and direction

> *Because vectors do not have specified locations, they can be translated as long as their direction and magnitude remain the same.*

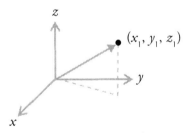

As noted before, however, the vector is not confined to the location shown above. The magnitude of a vector is simply the distance from the origin to the point (x_1, y_1, z_1). If $\vec{A} = (x_1, y_1, z_1)$, then the magnitude is written as $|\vec{A}|$.

$$|\vec{A}| = \sqrt{x_1^2 + y_1^2 + z_1^2}$$

Note that the direction of a vector can be written as a unit vector $\vec{u}$ of length 1, such that

$$\vec{A} = \vec{u}|\vec{A}|$$

Vectors obey the laws of associativity, commutativity, identity, and additive inverses:

$$\overrightarrow{A} + (\overrightarrow{B} + \overrightarrow{C}) = (\overrightarrow{A} + \overrightarrow{B}) + \overrightarrow{C}$$
$$\overrightarrow{A} + \overrightarrow{B} = \overrightarrow{B} + \overrightarrow{A}$$
$$\overrightarrow{A} + 0 = \overrightarrow{A}$$
$$\overrightarrow{A} + (-\overrightarrow{A}) = 0$$

As such, vectors have some of the same properties as real numbers.

Matrices

Matrices are slightly more complicated than vectors, and operations involving matrices likewise require more subtle analysis. In fact, vectors can simply be viewed as a type of matrix. Like vectors, matrices obey some of the same rules and principles as do real numbers; in other cases, however, such as commutativity, matrices and real numbers differ.

A **MATRIX** is an ordered set of numbers written in rectangular form. An example matrix is shown below.

$$\begin{pmatrix} 0 & 3 & 1 \\ 4 & 2 & 3 \\ 1 & 0 & 2 \end{pmatrix}$$

> **MATRIX:** an ordered set of numbers written in rectangular form

Since this matrix has 3 rows and 3 columns, it is called a 3×3 matrix. The element in the second row of the third column would be denoted as $3_{2,3}$. In general, a matrix with r rows and c columns is an $r \times c$ matrix.

> In general, a matrix with r rows and c columns is an $r \times c$ matrix.

Matrix addition and subtraction obey the rules of associativity, commutativity, identity, and additive inverse.

$$\overline{A} + (\overline{B} + \overline{C}) = (\overline{A} + \overline{B}) + \overline{C}$$
$$\overline{A} + \overline{B} = \overline{B} + \overline{A}$$
$$\overline{A} + 0 = \overline{A}$$
$$\overline{A} + (-\overline{A}) = 0$$

Addition, Subtraction, and Scalar Multiplication of Vectors

Addition and subtraction of two vectors $\overrightarrow{A} = (x_1, y_1, z_1)$ and $\overrightarrow{B} = (x_2, y_2, z_2)$ can be performed by adding or subtracting corresponding components of the vectors.

$$\overrightarrow{A} + \overrightarrow{B} = (x_1 + x_2, y_1 + y_2, z_1 + z_2)$$
$$\overrightarrow{A} - \overrightarrow{B} = (x_1 - x_2, y_1 - y_2, z_1 - z_2)$$

Geometrically, addition involves placing the tail of $\vec{B}$ on the head of $\vec{A}$, as shown below. The result is a vector that starts from the tail of $\vec{A}$ and ends at the head of $\vec{B}$.

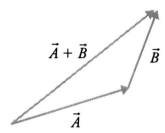

Subtraction of two vectors involves the same process, except that the direction of $\vec{B}$ must be reversed.

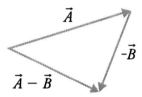

Multiplication of a vector by a scalar simply involves multiplying each component by the scalar.

$$c\vec{A} = (cx_1, cy_1, cz_1)$$

Geometrically, this operation extends the length of the vector by a factor c.

Vector Multiplication

Vector multiplication takes two forms: the dot product (or scalar product) and the cross product (or vector product). The DOT PRODUCT is calculated by multiplying corresponding components of two vectors. The operator for this product is typically a small dot (·).

$$\vec{A} \cdot \vec{B} = x_1 x_2 + y_1 y_2 + z_1 z_2$$

Notice that the dot product yields a single scalar value. Also note that the magnitude of a vector can be written in terms of the dot product.

$$|\vec{A}| = \sqrt{\vec{A} \cdot \vec{A}}$$

DOT PRODUCT: the product of two vectors is found by multiplying corresponding components of the vectors; the result is a scalar

Geometrically, the dot product is a projection of one vector onto another.

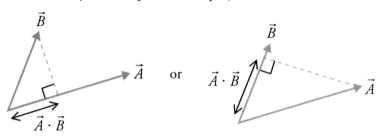

It can be shown that the dot product of two vectors is equivalent to the following:
$$\vec{A} \cdot \vec{B} = |\vec{A}| \, |\vec{B}| \cos \theta$$

> *If two vectors are perpendicular, then their dot product is zero.*

It is clear, both from the geometric and the algebraic definitions of the dot product, that if two vectors are perpendicular, then their dot product is zero.

The cross product of two vectors, typically symbolized by a "×" operator, yields a third vector. The cross product is defined as follows.
$$\vec{A} \times \vec{B} = (y_1 z_2 - y_2 z_1,\ z_1 x_2 - z_2 x_1,\ x_1 y_2\, x_2 y_1)$$

> **CROSS PRODUCT:** a third vector that is perpendicular to both original vectors (that is to the plane formed by the two original vectors)

Geometrically, the CROSS PRODUCT of $\vec{A}$ and $\vec{B}$ is a third vector that is perpendicular to both $\vec{A}$ and $\vec{B}$ (that is, to the plane formed by $\vec{A}$ and $\vec{B}$), with the direction defined by the so-called right-hand screw rule. If a right-hand screw is turned in the direction from $\vec{A}$ to $\vec{B}$, the direction in which the screw advances is the direction of the cross product.

The magnitude of $\vec{A} \times \vec{B}$ is the area of the parallelogram defined by $\vec{A}$ and $\vec{B}$.

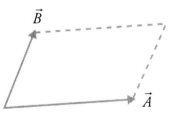

The magnitude of the cross product can also be written as follows.
$$|\vec{A} \times \vec{B}| = |\vec{A}| \, |\vec{B}| \sin \theta$$

> *If two vectors are parallel, their cross product is zero.*

From both the algebraic and geometric definitions of the cross product, it is apparent that if two vectors are parallel, their cross product is zero.

Multiplication of vectors, either by the dot product or cross product, obeys the rule of distibutivity, where $*$ symbolizes either $\cdot$ or $\times$.

$$\vec{A} * (\vec{B} + \vec{C}) = \vec{A} * \vec{B} + \vec{A} * \vec{C}$$

Only the dot product obeys commutativity, however. There is a similar rule for cross products, though.

$$\vec{A} \cdot \vec{B} = \vec{B} \cdot \vec{A}$$
$$\vec{A} \times \vec{B} = -\vec{B} \times \vec{A}$$

Example: Find the cross product $\vec{a} \times \vec{b}$, *where* $\vec{a} = (\text{-}1, 4, 2)$ *and* $\vec{b} = (3, \text{-}1, 4)$.

Use the expression given to calculate the cross product.

$$\vec{a} \times \vec{b} = (4 \cdot 4 - (\text{-}1) \cdot 2, \; 2 \cdot 3 - 4 \cdot (\text{-}1), \; (\text{-}1) \cdot (\text{-}1) - 3 \cdot 4)$$
$$\vec{a} \times \vec{b} = (16 + 2, \; 6 + 4, \; 1 - 12) = (18, 10, \text{-}11)$$

Example: Find the following for $\vec{a} = (1, 2, 3)$, $\vec{b} = (2, 3, 1)$ *and* $c = 2$: $c(\vec{a} \cdot \vec{b})$.

First, find the dot product; then multiply. Note that the result must be a scalar.

$$c(\vec{a} \cdot \vec{b}) = 2[1(2) + 2(3) + 3(1)] = 2[11] = 22$$

For matrix operations on vectors see *Skill 10.5*

COMPETENCY 6
ANALYZE LINEAR AND NONLINEAR FUNCTIONS AND THEIR APPLICATIONS

SKILL 6.1 Analyzing linear and nonlinear functions *(e.g., slope, intercept, roots, asymptotes)*

A LINEAR FUNCTION is a function defined by the equation $f(x) = mx + b$ where m is the slope of the line representing the function and b is the y-intercept, or the y-coordinate where the line crosses the y-axis. In a linear function, the rate of change is constant.

LINEAR FUNCTION: a function defined by the equation $f(x) = mx + b$ where m is the slope of the line representing the function and b is the y-intercept, or the y-coordinate where the line crosses the y-axis

Many real world situations involve linear relationships. One example is the relationship between the elapsed time and the distance traveled when a car is moving at a constant speed. The relationship between the price and the quantity of a bulk item bought at a store is also linear, assuming that the unit price remains constant. These relationships can be expressed using the equation of a straight line, and the slope is often used to describe a constant or average rate of change expressed in miles per hour or dollars per year, for instance. Where the line intercepts an axis indicates a starting point or a point at which values change from positive to negative or negative to positive.

Example: A man drives a car at a speed of 30 mph along a straight road. Express the distance d traveled as a function of the time t assuming the man's initial position is d_0.

The equation relating d and t in this case is

$$d = 30t + d_0.$$

Notice that this equation is in the familiar slope-intercept form $y = mx + b$. In this case, time t (in hours) is the independent variable, the distance d (in miles) is the dependent variable. The slope is the rate of change of distance in relation to time, i.e., the speed (in mph). The y-intercept, or intercept on the distance axis d_0, represents the initial position of the car at the start time $t = 0$.

The above equation is plotted below with $d_0 = 15$ miles (the point on the graph where the line crosses the y-axis).

$$d = 30t + d_0$$

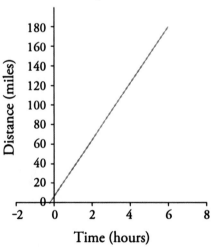

The x-intercept, or intercept on the time axis, represents the time at which the car would have been at $d = 0$ assuming it was traveling with the same speed before $t = 0$. This value can be found by setting d equal to 0 in the equation.

$$0 = 30t + 15$$
$$30t = -15$$
$$t = \frac{-15}{30} = -\frac{1}{2} \text{ hr.}$$

This simply means that if the car was at $d = 15$ miles when we started measuring the time ($t = 0$), it was at $d = 0$ miles half an hour before that.

A model for the distance traveled by a migrating monarch butterfly is $f(t) = 80t$, where t represents time in days. We interpret this to mean that the average speed of the butterfly is 80 miles per day, and distance traveled may be computed by substituting the number of days traveled for t.

Example: The town of Verdant Slopes has been experiencing a boom in population growth. By the year 2000, the population had grown to 45,000, and by 2005, the population had reached 60,000.

Using the formula for slope as a model, find the average rate of change in population growth, expressing your answer in people per year. Then using the average rate of change determined, predict the population of Verdant Slopes in the year 2010.

Let t represent the time and p represent population growth. The two observances are represented by (t_1, p_1) and (t_2, p_2).

1st observance $= (t_1, p_1) = (2000, 45000)$
2nd observance $= (t_2, p_2) = (2005, 60000)$

Use the formula for slope to find the average rate of change.

$$\text{Rate of change} = \frac{p_2 - p_1}{t_2 - t_1}$$
$$= \frac{60000 - 45000}{2005 - 2000}$$
$$= \frac{15000}{5} = 3000 \text{ people/year}$$

The average rate of change in population growth for Verdant Slopes between the years 2000 and 2005 was 3,000 people per year. The population of Verdant Slopes can be predicted using the following:

3,000 people per year $\times$ 5 years $= 15,000$ people,
60,000 people $+$ 15,000 people $= 75,000$ people.

At a continuing average rate of growth of 3000 people per year, the population of Verdant Slopes could be expected to reach 75,000 by the year 2010.

Graphing Quadratic Functions

The general technique for graphing quadratics is the same as that for graphing linear equations. Graphing a quadratic equation, however, results in a parabola instead of a straight line.

The general technique for graphing quadratics is the same as that for graphing linear equations. Graphing a quadratic equation, however, results in a parabola instead of a straight line.

The general form of a quadratic function is $y = ax^2 + bx + c$. Once a function is identified as quadratic, it is helpful to recognize several features that can indicate the form of the graph. The parabola has an axis of symmetry along $x = -\frac{b}{2a}$ which is the x-coordinate of the vertex (turning point) of the graph.

This can be understood more clearly if we consider an alternate form of a quadratic equation, the standard form for a parabola

$$y = a(x - h)^2 + k,$$

where point (h, k) denotes the coordinates of the vertex of the parabola.

By transforming the general form $y = ax^2 + bx + c$ into the above form, we get

$$y = a\left(x^2 + \frac{b}{a}x\right) + c$$
$$y = a\left(x^2 + 2\frac{b}{2a}x + \left(\frac{b}{2a}\right)^2\right) - \frac{b^2}{4a} + c$$
$$y = a\left(x + \frac{b}{2a}\right)^2 - \frac{b^2}{4a} + c$$

The coordinates of the vertex are given as $\left(-\frac{b}{2a}, -\frac{b^2}{4a} + c\right)$.

Example: Graph $y = 3x^2 + x - 2$.

Expressing this function in standard form we get

$$y = 3\left(x + \frac{1}{6}\right)^2 - \frac{25}{12}.$$

The graph is a parabola with an axis of symmetry $x = -\frac{1}{6}$,

and the vertex is located at the point $\left(-\frac{1}{6}, -\frac{25}{12}\right)$.

x	$y = 3x^2 + x - 2$
-2	8
-1	0
0	-2
1	2
2	12

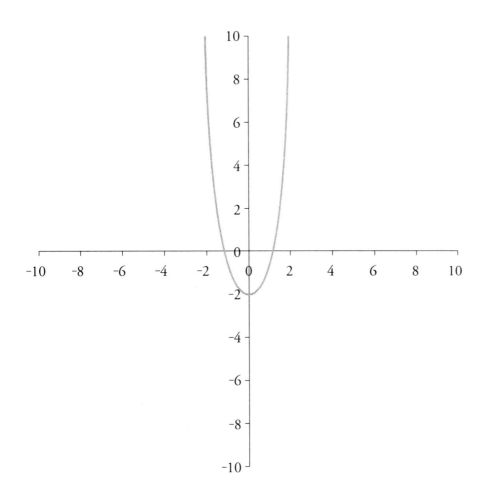

If the quadratic term is positive, the parabola is concave up; if the quadratic term is negative, the parabola is concave down. The function $-x^2 - 2x - 3$ is one such example and is shown below.

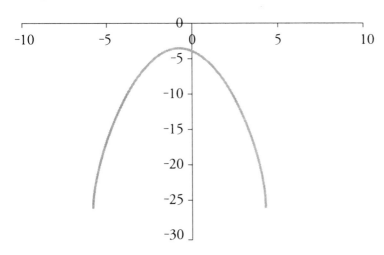

A quadratic function with two real roots (see example problems above) will have two crossings of the x-axis. A quadratic function with one real root will graph as a parabola that is tangent to the x-axis. An example of such a quadratic function is shown in the example below for the function $x^2 + 2x + 1$. The function has a single real root at $x = -1$.

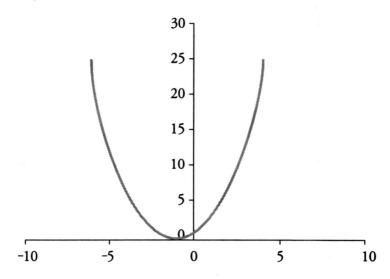

A quadratic function with no real roots will not cross the x-axis at any point. An example is the function $x^2 + 2x + 2$, which is plotted below.

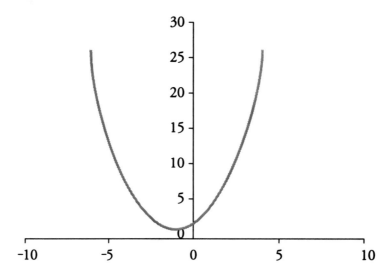

Example: Solve by graphing: $x^2 - 8x + 15 = 0.$

The roots of the polynomial $x^2 - 8x + 15$ are the x values for which the graph intersects the x-axis.

x	$y = x^2 - 8x + 15$
-2	35
-1	24
0	15
1	8
2	3

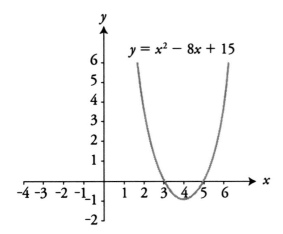

From the above graph, the x-intercepts, or zeros, are 3 and 5. So the solutions of the given quadratic equation are 3 and 5.

To graph a quadratic inequality, graph the quadratic as if it were an equation; however, if the inequality sign is $>$ or $<$, the curved line is dotted; if the inequality sign is $\geq$ or $\leq$, the curved line is solid. Shade above the curve for $>$ or $\geq$. Shade below the curve for $<$ or $\leq$.

Example: Graph the inequality $y < -x^2 + x - 2$.

The quadratic function $-x^2 + x - 2$ is plotted with a dotted line since the inequality sign is $<$ and not $\leq$. Since y is "less than" this function, the shading is done below the curve.

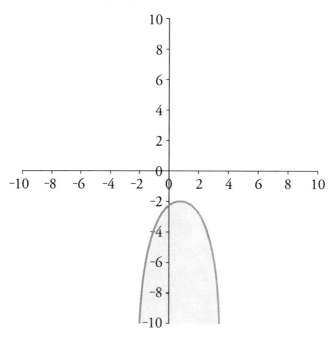

Example: Graph the inequality $y \geq x^2 - 2x - 9$.

The quadratic function $x^2 - 2x - 9$ is plotted with a solid line since the inequality sign is $\geq$. Since y is "greater than or equal to" this function, the shading is done above the curve.

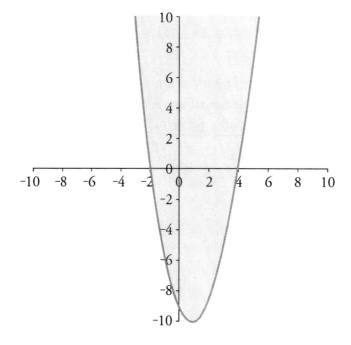

Polynomial Functions

A polynomial is a sum of terms where each term is a constant multiplied by a variable raised to a positive integer power. The general form of a polynomial $P(x)$ is

$$P(x) = a_n x^n + a_{n-1} x^{n-1} + \ldots + a_2 x^2 + a_1 x + a_0$$

Polynomials written in standard form have the terms written in decreasing exponent value, as shown above. The DEGREE OF A POLYNOMIAL FUNCTION IN ONE VARIABLE is the value of the largest exponent to which the variable is raised. The above expression is a polynomial of degree n (assuming that $a_n \neq 0$). Any function that represents a line is a polynomial function of degree one. Quadratic functions are polynomials of degree two. For instance, $5x^2 - 4x - 6$ is a second degree polynomial whereas $2x^3 - 5x^2 + x$ is a polynomial of degree three. If a term has more than one variable (e.g., $2xy$) it is necessary to add the exponents of the variables within the term to get the degree of the polynomial. Since $1 + 1 = 2$, $2xy$ is a polynomial of the second degree.

A polynomial may also be represented in tabular or graphical form as shown in the example below.

Example: Express the polynomial $x^3 - 6x + 4$ in tabular and graphical form.

x	y
-3	-5
-2	8
-1	9
0	4
1	-1
2	0
3	13

Note the change in sign of the y value between $x = -3$ and $x = -2$. This indicates there is a zero between $x = -3$ and $x = -2$. Since there is another change in sign of the y value between $x = 0$ and $x = -1$, there is a second root there. When $x = 2$, $y = 0$ so $x = 2$ is an exact root of this polynomial.

DEGREE OF A POLY-NOMIAL FUNCTION IN ONE VARIABLE: the value of the largest exponent to which the variable is raised

Any function that represents a line is a polynomial function of degree one. Quadratic functions are polynomials of degree two. For instance, $5x^2 - 4x - 6$ is a second degree polynomial whereas $2x^3 - 5x^2 + x$ is a polynomial of degree three.

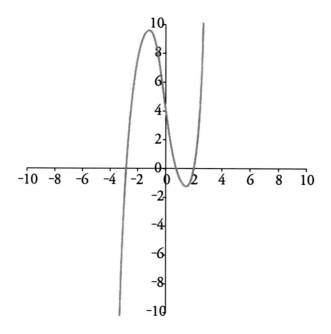

Rational functions

A rational function can be written as the ratio of two polynomial expressions. A rational function is given in the form $f(x) = \frac{p(x)}{q(x)}$. In the equation, $p(x)$ and $q(x)$ both represent polynomial functions ($q(x)$ does not equal zero).

Examples of rational functions are $r(x) = \frac{x^2 + 2x + 4}{x - 3}$ and $r(x) = \frac{x}{x - 3}$, both of which are ratios of two polynomials.

The branches of rational functions approach asymptotes. Setting the denominator equal to zero and solving will give the value(s) of the vertical asymptotes since the function will be undefined at this point. If the value of $f(x)$ approaches b as $|x|$ increases, the equation $y = b$ is a horizontal asymptote. To find the horizontal asymptote, it is necessary to make a table of values for x that are to the right and left of the vertical asymptotes. The pattern for the horizontal asymptotes will become apparent as $|x|$ increases.

If there is more than one vertical asymptote, remember to choose numbers to the right and left of each one in order to find the horizontal asymptotes and have sufficient points to graph the function.

Example: Graph $f(x) = \dfrac{3x + 1}{x - 2}$.

$x - 2 = 0$

$x = 2$

1. Set the denominator equal to 0 to find the vertical asymptote.

x	f(x)
3	10
10	3.875
100	3.07
1000	3.007
1	-4
-10	2.417
-100	2.93
-1000	2.99

2. Make a table choosing numbers to the right and left of the vertical asymptote

3. The pattern shows that as $|x|$ increases, $f(x)$ approaches the value 3, therefore an asymptote exists at $y = 3$

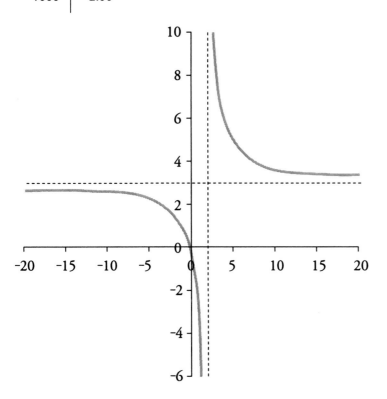

Note that $x = 2$ is excluded from the domain of the function and $y = 3$ is excluded from the range.

In some cases, the restriction on a rational function owing to the denominator being zero will not be a vertical asymptote but simply a hole in the graph. This happens when the value of x that reduces the denominator to zero is also a zero of the numerator.

Example: Plot the function $\frac{x-2}{x^2-4}$.

Factoring the denominator, we see that the denominator goes to zero at $x = -2$ and $x = 2$.

$$\frac{x-2}{x^2-4} = \frac{x-2}{(x+2)(x-2)}$$

There is a vertical asymptote at $x = h - 2$. Since the function can be simplified to the form $\frac{1}{(x+2)}$ by canceling $(x - 2)$ from the numerator and denominator, there is no asymptote at $x = 2$. The point $x = 2$, however, must be excluded from the function. Hence, there is a hole in the graph at $x = 2$.

Studying the function, we see that for large values of x the function goes to zero. Thus there is a horizontal asymptote at $y = 0$.

x	y	
-6	$-\frac{1}{4}$	
-4	$-\frac{1}{2}$	
-3	-1	
-2.5	-2	
-1.5	2	
-1	1	
0	$\frac{1}{2}$	
1	$\frac{1}{3}$	
2	$\frac{1}{4}$	(location of hole)
3	$\frac{1}{5}$	

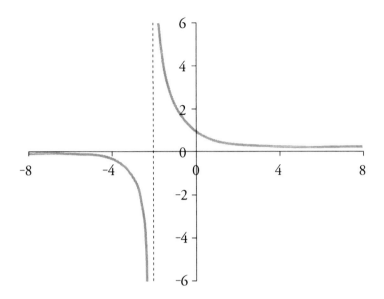

Absolute Value Functions

The absolute value function for a first-degree equation is $y = m|x - h| + k$. Its graph is V-shaped. The point (h, k) is the location of the maximum/minimum point on the graph. The slopes of the two sides of the V are "$\pm m$." The graph opens up if m is positive and down if m is negative.

Following are examples of graphs of absolute value functions.

$$y = |x + 3| + 1$$

$$y = 2|x| - 3$$

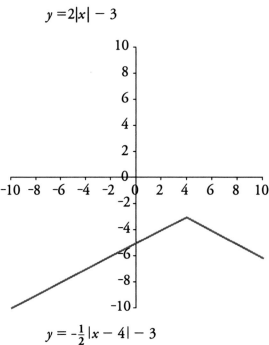

$$y = -\frac{1}{2}|x - 4| - 3$$

Note that on the first graph, the graph opens up since m is $+1$. Its minimum point is (-3, 1). The slopes of the two upward rays are ± 1. The second graph also opens up since m is positive. Its minimum point is (0, -3). The slopes of the two upward rays are ± 2. The third graph opens downward because m is $-\frac{1}{2}$. The maximum point on the graph is (4, -3). The slopes of the two downward rays are $\pm \frac{1}{2}$.

Radical Functions

Radical functions are those that depend on a root of the independent variable x, typically the square root. Some examples are $3\sqrt{x} + 5$, $\sqrt{7 - x}$ and $2\sqrt{x + 3} - 5$.

Plotting a radical function follows a process similar to that of plotting virtually any other function. A set of representative points is needed, and prior knowledge of the domain of the function is helpful (for instance, if only real numbers are considered, the expression under the square root sign must always be positive). Typically, a calculator is needed to find the values of the function for specific variable values.

Plotting a radical function follows a process similar to that of plotting virtually any other function. A set of representative points is needed, and prior knowledge of the domain of the function is helpful (for instance, if only real numbers are considered, the expression under the square root sign must always be positive).

Example: Tabulate and plot the function $3\sqrt{x} + 5$.

x	y
0	5
1	8
4	11
9	14
16	17
25	20

Note that x must always be positive. Hence the domain of the function is $x > 0$.

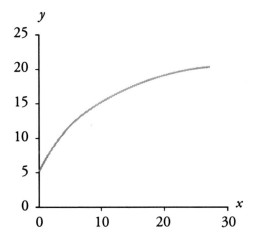

Piecewise Functions

> **PIECEWISE FUNC-TIONS:** functions defined by two or more formulas

Functions defined by two or more formulas are PIECEWISE FUNCTIONS. The formula used to evaluate piecewise functions varies depending on the value of x. The graphs of piecewise functions consist of two or more pieces, or intervals, and are often discontinuous.

Example 1
$$f(x) = x + 1 \quad \text{if } x > 2$$
$$ x - 2 \quad \text{if } x < 2$$

Example 2
$$f(x) = x \quad \text{if } x > 1$$
$$ x^2 \quad \text{if } x < 1$$

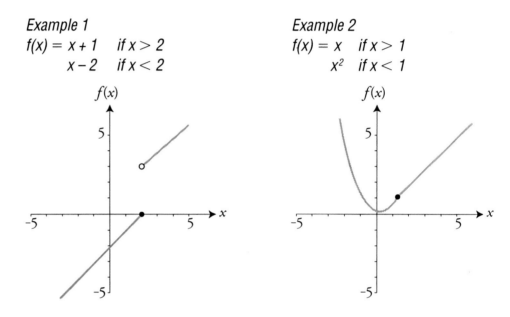

When graphing or interpreting the graph of piecewise functions, it is important to note the points at the beginning and end of each interval because the graph must clearly indicate what happens at the end of each interval. Note that in the graph of Example 1, point (2, 3) is not part of the graph and is represented by an empty circle. On the other hand, point (2, 0) is part of the graph and is represented as a solid circle. Note also that the graph of Example 2 is continuous despite representing a piecewise function.

SKILL 6.2 Identifying the effects of algebraic transformations on the graph of a function

> The basic types of transformation are horizontal and vertical shift, horizontal and vertical scaling, and reflection.

Different types of function transformations affect the graph and characteristics of a function in predictable ways. The basic types of transformation are horizontal and vertical shift, horizontal and vertical scaling, and reflection. As an example of the types of transformations, we will consider transformations of the function $f(x) = x^2$.

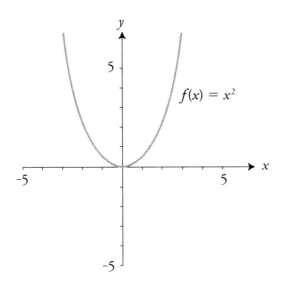

Shifts

Horizontal shifts take the form $g(x) = f(x \pm c)$. For example, we obtain the graph of the function $g(x) = (x + 2)^2$ by shifting the graph of $f(x) = x^2$ two units to the left. The graph of the function $h(x) = (x - 2)^2$ is the graph of $f(x) = x^2$ shifted two units to the right.

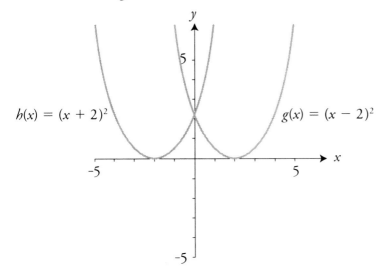

Vertical shifts take the form $g(x) = f(x) \pm c$. For example, we obtain the graph of the function $g(x) = (x^2) - 2$ by shifting the graph of $f(x) = x^2$ two units down. The graph of the function $h(x) = (x^2) + 2$ is the graph of $f(x) = x^2$ shifted two units up.

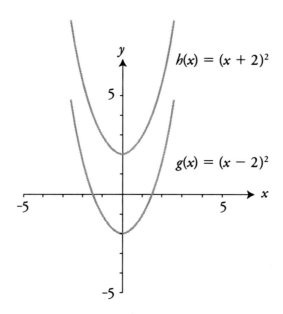

Scaling

Horizontal scaling takes the form $g(x) = f(cx)$. For example, we obtain the graph of the function $g(x) = (2x^2)$ by compressing the graph of $f(x) = x^2$ in the x-direction by a factor of two. If $c > 1$ the graph is compressed in the x-direction, while if $1 > c > 0$ the graph is stretched in the x-direction.

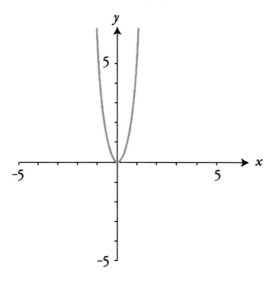

> **SKILL 6.3** Demonstrating knowledge of the use of technology *(e.g., graphing utilities, spreadsheets)* to analyze relationships between different representations *(e.g., equations, graphs)* of functions and inequalities

Using a Graphing Calculator with Polynomial Functions

The following examples are illustrated using the basic functions of a Texas Instruments, or TI-type, graphing calculator. Although the specifics may not apply to all graphing calculators, the general approach should.

Solve $x^2 + 2x - 8$ for its roots by graphing on a calculator.

1. Press "Y=" and enter "X^2+2X−8" for Y1.

2. Press "GRAPH."

3. Identify the *x*-intercepts of the parabola. The *x*-intercepts are -4 and 2.

4. Notice the parabola at $x = -1$. This is the line of the axis of symmetry and the vertex is at the bottom of the line; it is located halfway between the 2 *x*-intercepts.

Using a Graphing Calculator with Rational Functions

Graph the functions *f, g, f+g* for *x* for the interval $[-p, p]$.

1. Press the "GRAPH" key and then choose "*y(x)*=" by pressing the "F1" key.

2. If needed, press the "F4" key until only "y1=" appears on the screen.

3. Type in "X^2," then press the "ENTER" key.

4. Type in "COSX" and press the "ENTER" key.

5. Type in "y1+y2" and press the "ENTER" key. NOTE: Both ys must be lower case.

6. The range settings for the graph above are $[-p, p] \times [-1, 10]$.

7. Note that the graphs of the functions are plotted in the order in which they are entered above. You can plot only one or two of the graphs by using the "SELCT" key on the "y(x)=" screen.

Using a Graphing Calculator with Absolute Value Functions

Solve $2|x - 3|$ using a table on the graphing calculator.

1. Enter the left side of the equation in the "Y=" editor. Press the "MATH" key and use the "NUM" menu for "ABS."

2. Use the defaults for "2nd" "WINDOW" ("TBLSET") and then press "2nd" "GRAPH" "TABLE" to see the values of the equation above when $x = 0, 1, 2, 3, 4...$

3. Note that Y1 = 4 when $x = 1$ and when $x = 5$.

SKILL 6.4 Applying linear and nonlinear functions to model real-world situations and solve problems using a variety of graphic and algebraic methods

Linear Models

For some examples of situations modeled using linear equations, see the beginning of this competency.

Many word problems may be modeled and solved using systems of linear equations and inequalities. Some examples are given below.

Many word problems may be modeled and solved using systems of linear equations and inequalities.

Example: Farmer Greenjeans bought 4 cows and 6 sheep for $1,700. Mr. Ziffel bought 3 cows and 12 sheep for $2,400. If all the cows were the same price and all the sheep were another fixed price, find the price charged for a cow and the price charged for a sheep.

Let x = price of a cow
Let y = price of a sheep

Then Farmer Greenjeans's equation would be: $\qquad 4x + 6y = 1700$
Mr. Ziffel's equation would be: $\qquad 3x + 12y = 2400$

To solve by addition-subtraction:

Multiply the first equation by -2: $\qquad -2(4x + 6y = 1700)$
Keep the other equation the same: $\qquad (3x + 12y = 2400)$

Now the equations can be added to each other to eliminate one variable, and you can solve for the other variable.

$$-8x - 12y = -3400$$
$$\underline{3x + 12y = 2400} \qquad \text{Add these equations.}$$
$$-5x \qquad\quad = -1000$$
$$x = 200 \leftarrow \text{the price of a cow was \$200.}$$

Solving for y, $y = 150 \leftarrow$ the price of a sheep was $150. (This problem can also be solved by substitution or determinants.)

Example: Mrs. Allison bought 1 pound of potato chips, a 2-pound beef roast, and 3 pounds of apples for a total of $8.19. Mr. Bromberg bought a 3-pound beef roast and 2 pounds of apples for $9.05. Kathleen Kaufman bought 2 pounds of potato chips, a 3-pound beef roast, and 5 pounds of apples for $13.25. Find the per pound price of each item.

To solve by substitution:

Let x = price of a pound of potato chips.
Let y = price of a pound of roast beef.
Let z = price of a pound of apples.
Mrs. Allison's equation is $\qquad 1x + 2y + 3z = 8.19.$
Mr. Bromberg's equation is $\qquad 3y + 2z = 9.05.$
K. Kaufman's equation is $\qquad 2x + 3y + 5z = 13.25.$

Solve the first equation for x. (This equation was chosen because x is the easiest variable to isolate in this set of equations.) This equation becomes
$\qquad x = 8.19 - 2y - 3z.$

Substitute this expression into the other equations in place of x.
$\qquad$ Equation 2: $3y + 2z = 9.05$
$\qquad$ Equation 3: $2(8.19 - 2y - 3z) + 3y + 5z = 13.25$

Simplify the equation by combining like terms.
$\qquad$ Equation 2: $3y + 2z = 9.05$
$\qquad$ Equation 3: $-1y - 1z = -3.13$

Solve equation 3 for either y or z.
$\qquad y = 3.13 - z \quad$ (*)

Substitute this into equation 2 for y.
$\qquad$ Equation 2: $3(3.13 - z) + 2z = 9.05$
$\qquad$ Equation 3: $-1y - 1z = -3.13$

Combine like terms in equation 2.
$\qquad 9.39 - 3z + 2z = 9.05$
$\qquad z = \$0.34$ per pound (price of apples)

Substitute .34 for z in the above equation marked with an asterisk (*) and solve for y.
$\qquad y = 3.13 - z$
$\qquad y = 3.13 - .34$
$\qquad y = \$2.79 =$ per pound price of roast beef

Substitute .34 for z and 2.79 for y in one of the original equations and solve for x.

$$1x + 2y + 3z = 8.19$$
$$1x + 2(2.79) + 3(.34) = 8.19$$
$$x + 5.58 + 1.02 = 8.19$$
$$x + 6.60 = 8.19$$
$$x = \$1.59 = \text{per pound of potato chips}$$
$$(x, y, z) = (\$1.59, \$2.79, \$0.37)$$

Example: Aardvark Taxi charges $4.00 initially, plus $1.00 for every mile traveled. Baboon Taxi charges $6.00 initially, plus $.75 for every mile traveled. Determine when it is cheaper to ride with Aardvark Taxi and when it is cheaper to ride with Baboon Taxi.

Aardvark Taxi's equation:	$y = 1x + 4$
Baboon Taxi's equation:	$y = .75x + 6$
Using substitution:	$.75y + 6 = 1x + 4$
Multiplying by 4:	$3y + 24 = 4x + 16$
Solving for x:	$8 = x$

This tells you that at eight miles, the total charge for the two companies is the same. If you compare the charge for one mile, Aardvark charges $5.00 and Baboon charges $6.75. Therefore, Aardvark is cheaper for distances up to eight miles, but Baboon Taxi is cheaper for distances greater than eight miles.

This problem can also be solved by graphing the two equations.

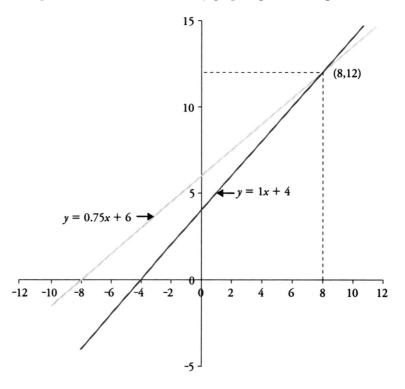

The lines intersect at (8, 12); therefore at eight miles, both companies charge $12.00. At values of less than eight miles, Aardvark Taxi charges less (the graph is below Baboon). At values greater than eight miles, Aardvark charges more (the graph is above Baboon).

LINEAR PROGRAMMING is the optimization of a linear quantity that is subject to constraints expressed as linear equations or inequalities. It is often used in various industries, ecological sciences, and governmental organizations to determine or project production costs, the amount of pollutants dispersed into the air, etc. The key to most linear programming problems is to organize the information in the word problem into a chart or graph of some type.

> **LINEAR PROGRAMMING:** the optimization of a linear quantity that is subject to constraints expressed as linear equations or inequalities

Example: The YMCA wants to sell raffle tickets to raise at least $32,000. If they must pay $7,250 in expenses and prizes out of the money collected from the tickets, how many $25 tickets must they sell?

Since they want to raise *at least* $32,000, that means they would be happy to get 32,000 *or more*. This requires an inequality.

Let x = number of tickets sold.

Then $25x$ = total amount of money collected for x tickets.

The total amount of money minus expenses is greater than $32,000.

$$25x - 7,250 \geq 32,000$$
$$25x \geq 39,250$$
$$x \geq 1,570$$

If they sell 1,570 tickets or more, they will raise at least $32,000.

Example: A printing manufacturer makes two types of printers, a Printmaster and a Speedmaster. The Printmaster requires 10 cubic feet of space and weighs 5,000 pounds; the Speedmaster takes up 5 cubic feet of space and weighs 600 pounds. The total available space for storage before shipping is 2,000 cubic feet and the weight limit for the space is 300,000 pounds. The profit on the Printmaster is $125,000 and the profit on the Speedmaster is $30,000. How many of each machine should be stored to maximize profitability and what is the maximum possible profit?

Let x represent the number of Printmaster units sold and let y represent the number of Speedmaster units sold. The equation for the space required to store the units is

$$10x + 5y \leq 2000$$
$$2x + y \leq 400.$$

Since the number of units for both models cannot be less than 0, also impose the restrictions that $x \geq 0$ and $y \geq 0$. The restriction on the total weight can be expressed as

$$5000x + 600y \leq 300000$$
$$25x + 3y \leq 1500.$$

The expression for the profit P from sales of the printer units is

$$P = \$125{,}000x + \$30{,}000y$$

The solution to this problem is found by maximizing P subject to the constraints given in the preceding inequalities, along with the constraints that $x \geq 0$ and $y \geq 0$. The equations are grouped below for clarity.

$$x \geq 0$$
$$y \geq 0$$
$$2x + y \leq 400$$
$$25x + 3y \leq 1500$$
$$P = \$125{,}000x + \$30{,}000y$$

The two inequalities in two variables are plotted in the graph below. The shaded region represents the set of solutions that obey both inequalities. (Note that the shaded region in fact includes only points where both x and y are whole numbers.)

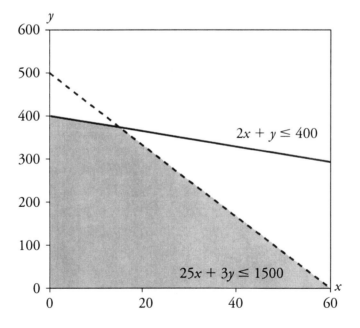

Note that the border of the shaded region that is formed by the two inequalities includes the solutions that constitute the maximum value of y for a given value of x. Note also that x cannot exceed 60 (since it would violate the second inequality). The solution to the problem must lie on the border of the shaded region since the border spans all the possible solutions that maximize the use of space and weight for a given number x.

To visualize the solution, plot the profit as a function of the solutions to the inequalities that lie along the border of the shaded area.

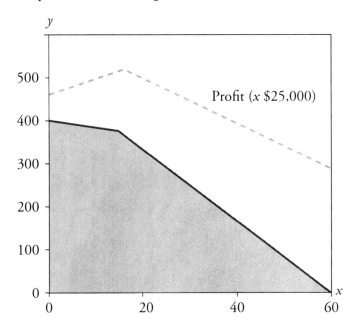

The profit curve shows a maximum at about $x = 16$. Verify this result by using a table to test several values.

x	y	$P(x\$25,000)$
15	370	519
16	366	519.2
17	358	514.6

Also double check to be sure that the result obeys the two inequalities.

$$2(16) + (366) = 398 \leq 400$$
$$25(16) + 3(366) = 1498 \leq 1500$$

The optimum result is storage of 16 Printmaster and 366 Speedmaster printer units.

Example: Sharon's Bike Shoppe can assemble a 3-speed bike in 30 minutes and a 10-speed bike in 60 minutes. The profit on each bike sold is $60 for a 3-speed bike or $75 for a 10-speed bike. How many of each type of bike should be assembled during an 8-hour day (480 minutes) to maximize the possible profit? Total daily profit must be at least $300.

Let x be the number of 3-speed bikes and y be the number of 10-speed bikes. Since there are only 480 minutes to use each day, the first inequality is

$$30x + 60y \leq 480$$
$$x + 2y \leq 16.$$

Since the total daily profit must be at least $300, the second inequality can be written as follows, where P is the profit for the day:

$$P = \$60x + \$75y \geq \$300$$
$$4x + 5y \geq 20.$$

To visualize the problem, plot the two inequalities and show the potential solutions as a shaded region.

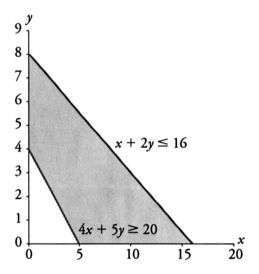

The solution to the problem is the ordered pair of whole numbers in the shaded area that maximizes the daily profit. The profit curve is added as shown below.

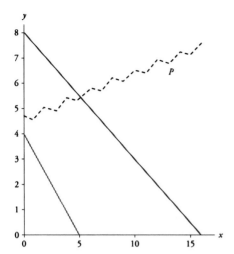

Based on the above plot, it is clear that the profit is maximized for the case where only 3-speed bikes (corresponding to x) are manufactured. Thus, the correct solution can be found by solving the first inequality for x when $y = 0$.

$$x + 2(0) \leq 16$$
$$x \leq 16$$

The manufacture of sixteen 3-speed bikes (and no 10-speed bikes) maximizes profit to $960 per day.

Quadratic Models

Other word problems may be modeled using quadratic equations or inequalities. Examples of this type of problem follow.

Example: A family is planning to add a new room to their house. They would like the room to have a length that is 10 feet more than the width and a total area of 375 square feet. Find the length and width of the room.

Let x be the width of the room. The length of the room is then $x + 10$. The quadratic equation is

$$x(x + 10) = 375$$
$$x^2 + 10x - 375 = 0.$$

Factor the quadratic expression to solve the equation.

$$x^2 + 25x - 15x - 375 = 0 \qquad \text{Break up the middle}$$
$$x(x + 25) - 15(x + 25) = 0 \qquad \text{term using factors of 375}$$
$$(x + 25)(x - 15) = 0$$
$$x = {-25} \text{ or } x = 15$$

Since the dimensions of a room cannot be negative, we choose the positive solution, $x = 15$. The width of the room is 15 feet and the length of the room is 25 feet.

Example: The formula for the maximum height of a projectile fired upward at a velocity of v meters per second from an original height of h meters is y = h + vx − 4.9x². If a rocket is fired from an original height of 250 meters with an original velocity of 4800 meters per second, find the approximate time the rocket would drop to sea level (a height of 0).

Substituting the height and velocity into the equation yields the equation $y = 250 + 4800x - 4.9x^2$. If the height at sea level is 0, then $y = 0$, so $0 = 250 + 4800x - 4.9x^2$. Use the quadratic formula to solve for x.

$$x = \frac{-4800 \pm \sqrt{4800^2 - 4(-4.9)(250)}}{2(-4.9)}$$

$$x \approx 979.53 \text{ or } x \approx -0.05 \text{ seconds}$$

Since the time has to be positive, it will be approximately 980 seconds until the rocket reaches sea level.

Example: A family wants to enclose 3 sides of a rectangular garden, at least 4800 square feet in area, with 200 feet of fence. A wall borders the fourth side of the garden. How long can the garden be?

In order to have a garden with an area of at least 4800 square feet, find the dimensions the garden should have.

Solution:

Let $x = $ distance from the wall

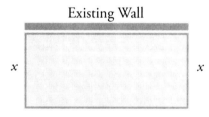

Then amount of fence needed for these 2 sides is $2x$ feet. The side opposite the existing wall would use the remainder of the 200 feet of fence, that is, $200 - 2x$ feet of fence. Therefore the width (w) of the garden is x feet and the length (l) is $(200 - 2x)$ feet.

The area is calculated using the formula $A = lw = x(200 - 2x) = 200x - 2x^2$, and the area needs to be greater than or equal to 4800 square feet. The expression for this inequality is $4800 \leq 200x - 2x^2$. Subtract 4800 from each side and the inequality becomes

$$2(-x^2 + 100x - 2400) \geq 0$$
$$-x^2 + 100x - 2400 \geq 0$$
$$(-x + 60)(x - 40) \geq 0$$
$$-x + 60 \geq 0$$
$$-x \geq -60$$
$$x \leq 60$$
$$x - 40 \geq 0$$
$$x \geq 40.$$

The area will be at least 4800 square feet if the width of the garden is from 40 up to 60 feet. (The length of the rectangle would vary from 120 feet to 80 feet depending on the width of the garden.)

COMPETENCY 7
APPLY KNOWLEDGE OF TRIGONOMETRY AND CALCULUS

SKILL Demonstrating knowledge of the concepts of limits and continuity
7.1

Limits

A LIMIT is the value that a function approaches as a variable of the function approaches a certain value. Thus, the limit L of a function $f(x)$ as x approaches some value c is written

$$\lim_{x \to c} f(x) = L$$

LIMIT: the value that a function approaches as a variable of the function approaches a certain value

This concept can be understood through graphical illustrations, as with the following example. The graph shows a plot of $y = 2x$. A limit in this case might be the limit of y as x approaches 3. Graphically, this involves tracing the plot of the function to the point at $x = 3$.

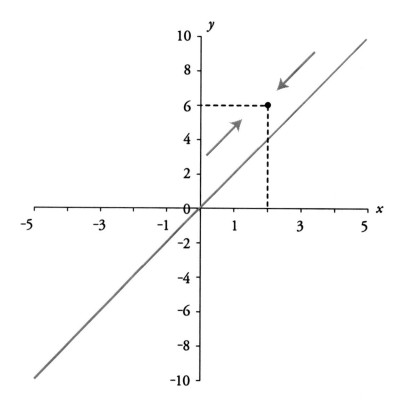

The limit in this case is clearly 6. The limit can be considered either from the right or left (that is, considering x decreasing toward 3 or x increasing toward 3). In the simple example above, the limit is the same from either direction, but, in some cases, the limit may be different from different directions or the function may not even exist on one side of the limit.

When evaluating a limit, especially when dealing with complicated functions, the following two steps should be taken:

1. Factor the expression completely and cancel all common factors in fractions.

2. Substitute the number to which the variable is approaching. In most cases this produces the value of the limit.

For simple functions, evaluating the limit may simply involve calculating $f(c)$ (according to the limit definition given above), but for other functions a more subtle approach may be required. In some instances, such as where the limit of the function differs depending on whether c is approached from the left or right, or where the limit of the function is positive or negative infinity, the limit of $f(x)$ at $x = c$ does not exist.

Evaluation of limits often deals with infinity. If, after simplification, the limit involves positive or negative infinity in the numerator (even if the fraction is simply the numerator divided by unity), then the limit does not exist (sometimes it is stated that "the limit is infinity," but this is not necessarily meaningful). If the denominator includes positive or negative infinity, then the limit is zero (since as the denominator of a fraction gets arbitrarily large, the fraction approaches zero).

Example: Evaluate the limit $\lim\limits_{x \to \infty} \frac{2x^2}{x^5}$.

$\lim\limits_{x \to \infty} \frac{2}{x^3}$ Cancel common factors.

$\frac{2}{\infty^3}$ Substitute.

0 Calculate limit.

As mentioned previously, simplification of the function can, in some cases, eliminate the need to deal with infinity.

Example: Evaluate the limit $\lim\limits_{x \to -3} \frac{x^2 + 5x + 6}{x + 3} + 4x$.

$\lim\limits_{x \to -3} \frac{(x + 3)(x + 2)}{(x + 3)} + 4x$ Factor the numerator.

$\lim\limits_{x \to -3} (x + 2) + 4x$ Cancel common factors.

$(-3 + 2) + 4(-3)$ Substitute -3 for x.

$-1 + -12$ Simplify.

-13

If this example is approached using solely substitution, the denominator becomes infinity and the limit becomes $4(-3) = -12$. Simplification avoids such errors and leads to the correct answer in this case.

The above approach to the evaluation of limits sometimes results in an answer of either $\frac{0}{0}$ or $\frac{\infty}{\infty}$. In such cases, use L'Hopital's rule to find the limit. L'Hopital's rule states that the limit in such cases can be determined by taking the derivative of the numerator of the function and the derivative of the denominator of the function and then calculating the limit of the resulting quotient.

Example: Evaluate the limit $\lim\limits_{x \to \infty} \frac{3x - 1}{x^2 + 2x + 3}$.

$\frac{3\infty - 1}{\infty^2 + 2\infty + 3}$ Substitute ∞ for x.

$\frac{\infty}{\infty}$ The result is not defined.

$\lim\limits_{x \to \infty} \frac{3}{2x + 2}$ Use L'Hopital's rule.

$\frac{3}{2\infty + 2}$ Substitute.

$\frac{3}{\infty}$ Simplify.

0 Evaluate limit.

Example: Evaluate the limit $\lim\limits_{x \to 1} \dfrac{\ln x}{x - 1}$.

$\dfrac{\ln 1}{1 - 1}$ Substitute 1 for *x*.

$\dfrac{0}{0}$ Simplify.

$\lim\limits_{x \to 1} \dfrac{\left(\frac{1}{x}\right)}{1} = \lim\limits_{x \to 1} \dfrac{1}{x}$ Use L'Hopital's rule

$\dfrac{1}{1} = 1$ Evaluate limit.

> *L'Hopital's rule can be used to find the limit in cases where direct substitution yields an undefined result.*

Continuity

Recall that the continuity of a function is easily understood graphically as the absence of missing points or breaks in the plot of the function. A more rigorous definition can be formulated, however. A function $f(x)$ is continuous at a point c if all of the following apply:

1. The function $f(x)$ is defined at $x = c$

2. The limit $\lim\limits_{x \to c} f(x)$ exists

3. The limit can be found by substitution: $\lim\limits_{x \to c} f(x) = f(c)$

A function can then be called continuous on an open interval (a, b) if the above definition applies to the function for every point c in the interval. The function is also continuous at the points $x = a$ and $x = b$ if $\lim\limits_{x \to a^+} f(x) = f(a)$ and $\lim\limits_{x \to b^-} f(x) = f(b)$ both exist. (The $+/-$ notation simply signifies approaching limiting the value from either the right or left, respectively.) If both of these conditions apply, then the function is continuous on the closed interval $[a, b]$.

Example: Determine whether the function ln x is continuous over the closed interval [0, 1].

One approach is to look at a plot of the function.

The limit of the function as x approaches zero from the right does not exist. Algebraically, this can be seen by noting that the equation $\ln x = L$ is the same as the equation $e^L = x$. For $x = 0$, the only possible value of L that satisfies this equation is $-\infty$. In other words,

$$\lim_{x \to 0} \ln x = -\infty$$

The limit does not exist, therefore, and the function is not continuous on the closed interval [0, 1]. The function is continuous on the open interval (0, 1), however. (It is also continuous on the half-open interval (0, 1].) Note that, for all $x > 0$, x is defined, and for $c > 0$, $\lim_{x \to c} \ln x = \ln c$.

Thus, ln x is continuous over (0, ∞).

Example: Determine if the function shown in the graph is continuous at x = 2.

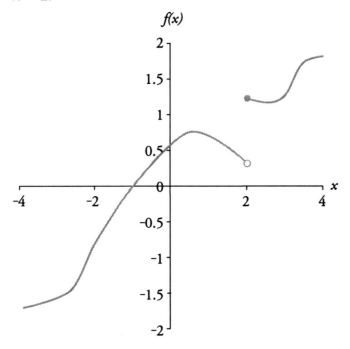

By inspection, it can be seen that the limits of the function as x approaches 2 from the right and left are not equal.

$$\lim_{x \to 2^+} f(x) \neq \lim_{x \to 2^-} f(x)$$

As a result, the function does not meet all of the criteria for continuity at $x = 2$ and is therefore discontinuous.

Example: Determine whether the following function is continuous at

$$x = 1: f(x) = \begin{cases} x^2 & x \neq 1 \\ 0 & x = 1 \end{cases}$$

The plot of this piecewise function is shown below.

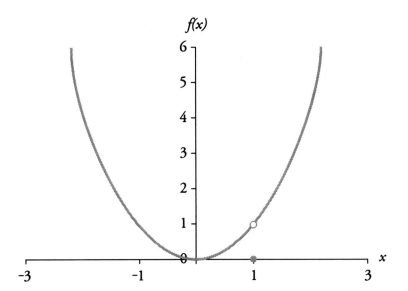

In this case, the function is defined at $x = 1$, and the limits of $f(x)$ as x approaches 1 from both the right and from the left are both equal to 1. Nevertheless, it is not the case that $\lim_{x \to 1} f(x) = f(1)$, since $\lim_{x \to 1} f(x) = 1$ and $f(1) = 0$. Thus, the function is not continuous at $x = 1$.

SKILL 7.2 Applying unit circle trigonometry, identities, and equations to solve problems and model real-world situations

Trigonometric functions can be related to right triangles: each trigonometric function corresponds to a ratio of certain sides of the triangle with respect to a particular angle. Thus, given the generic right triangle diagram below, the following functions can be specified.

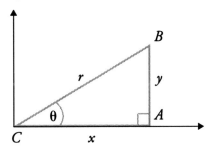

$\sin\theta = \frac{y}{r} \quad \csc\theta = \frac{r}{y}$

$\cos\theta = \frac{x}{r} \quad \sec\theta = \frac{r}{x}$

$\tan\theta = \frac{y}{x} \quad \cot\theta = \frac{x}{y}$

Based on these definitions, the unknown characteristics of a particular right triangle can be calculated based on certain known characteristics. For instance, if the hypotenuse and one of the adjacent angles are both known, the lengths of the other two sides of the triangle can be calculated.

Trigonometry can also be understood in terms of a unit circle on the *x-y* plane. A unit circle has a radius of 1.

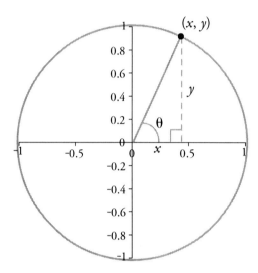

Notice that any given radius forms a right triangle with legs having lengths equal to the position of the point on the circle (*x*, *y*). Since the radius is equal to 1, the values of *x* and *y* are the following:

$$x = \cos\theta$$
$$y = \sin\theta$$

All the properties of trigonometric relationships for right triangles also apply in this case as well.

DEGREE: an angle corresponding to a sector that is $\frac{1}{360}$ of a circle

RADIAN: the angle corresponding to a sector of a circle, where the arc length of the sector is equal to the radius of the circle

PERIODIC FUNCTIONS: functions whose values repeat on regular intervals

The argument of a trigonometric function is an angle that is typically expressed in either degrees or radians. A DEGREE constitutes an angle corresponding to a sector that is $\frac{1}{360}$ of a circle. Therefore, a circle has 360 degrees. A RADIAN, on the other hand, is the angle corresponding to a sector of a circle, where the arc length of the sector is equal to the radius of the circle. In the case of the unit circle (a circle of radius 1), the circumference is 2π. Thus, there are 2π radians in a circle. Conversion between degrees and radians is a simple matter of using the ratio between the total degrees in a circle and the total radians in a circle.

$$(\text{degrees}) = \frac{180}{\pi} \times (\text{radians})$$
$$(\text{radians}) = \frac{\pi}{180} \times (\text{degrees})$$

The trigonometric functions sine, cosine, and tangent (and their reciprocals) are PERIODIC FUNCTIONS. The values of periodic functions repeat on regular intervals.

The period, amplitude, and phase shift are critical properties of periodic functions that can be determined by observation of the graph or by detailed study of the functions themselves.

The PERIOD of a function is the smallest domain containing one complete cycle of the function. For example, the period of a sine or cosine function is the distance between the adjacent peaks or troughs of the graph. The AMPLITUDE of a function is half the distance between the maximum and minimum values of the function.

The PHASE SHIFT of a function is the amount of horizontal displacement of the function from a given reference position.

Below is a generic sinusoidal graph with the period and amplitude labeled.

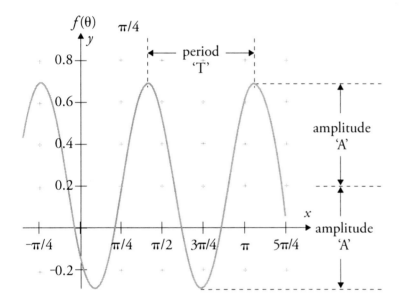

PERIOD: the smallest domain containing one complete cycle of the function

AMPLITUDE: half the distance between the maximum and minimum values of the function

PHASE SHIFT: the amount of horizontal displacement of the function from a given reference position

The period and amplitude for the three basic trigonometric functions are provided in the table below.

PERIOD AND AMPLITUDE OF THE BASIC TRIG FUNCTIONS		
Function	Period (radians)	Amplitude
$\sin \theta$	2π	1
$\cos \theta$	2π	1
$\tan \theta$	π	Undefined

Below are the graphs of the basic trigonometric functions, (a) $y = \sin x$; (b) $y = \cos x$; and (c) $y = \tan x$.

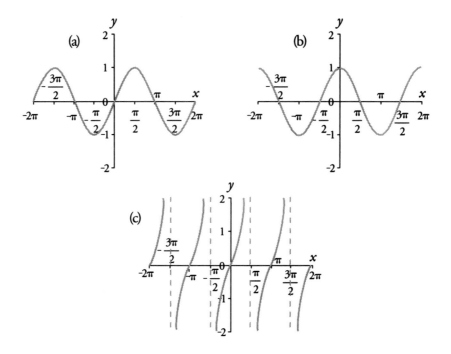

Note that the graph of the tangent function has asymptotes at $x = \frac{2n-1}{2}\pi$, where $n = 0, \pm1, \pm2, \pm3,\ldots$.

The graphs of the reciprocal trigonometric functions are shown below, with (a) $y = \csc x$; (b) $y = \sec x$; and (c) $y = \cot x$.

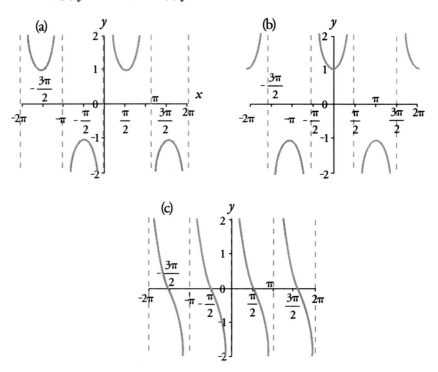

The phase and amplitude for the three reciprocal trigonometric functions are provided in the table below.

PERIOD AND AMPLITUDE OF THE RECIPROCAL TRIG FUNCTIONS		
Function	Period (radians)	Amplitude
csc θ	2π	Undefined
sec θ	2π	Undefined
cot θ	π	Undefined

There are two methods that may be used to prove trigonometric identities. One method is to choose one side of the equation and manipulate it until it equals the other side. The other method is to replace expressions on both sides of the equation with equivalent expressions until both sides are equal.

There are a range of trigonometric identities, including reciprocal and Pythagorean identities, as listed below.

RECIPROCAL IDENTITIES		
$\sin x = \frac{1}{\csc x}$	$\sin x \csc x = 1$	$\csc x = \frac{1}{\sin x}$
$\cos x = \frac{1}{\sec x}$	$\cos x \sec x = 1$	$\sec x = \frac{1}{\cos x}$
$\tan x = \frac{1}{\cot x}$	$\tan x \cot x = 1$	$\cot x = \frac{1}{\tan x}$
$\tan x = \frac{\sin x}{\cos x}$		$\cot x = \frac{\cos x}{\sin x}$

PYTHAGOREAN IDENTITIES		
$\sin^2 x + \cos^2 x = 1$	$1 + \tan^2 x = \sec^2 x$	$1 + \cot^2 x = \csc^2 x$

Example: Prove that $\sin^2 x + \cos^2 x = 1$.

Use the definitions of the sine and cosine functions from right triangle trigonometry.

$$\left(\tfrac{y}{r}\right)^2 + \left(\tfrac{x}{r}\right)^2 = 1$$
$$\frac{x^2 + y^2}{r^2} = 1$$

But the numerator of the above fraction, by the Pythagorean theorem, is simply r^2. Then:

$$\frac{r^2}{r^2} = 1$$

The identity has been proven.

Example: Prove that cot x + tan x = csc x sec x.

Use the reciprocal identities to convert the left side of the equation to sines and cosines. Then combine terms using a common denominator.

$$\frac{\cos x}{\sin x} + \frac{\sin x}{\cos x}$$

$$\frac{\cos^2 x}{\sin x \cos x} + \frac{\sin^2 x}{\sin x \cos x} = \frac{\sin^2 x + \cos^2 x}{\sin x \cos x} = \frac{1}{\sin x \cos x}$$

Finally, convert the expression using the reciprocal identities.

$$\frac{1}{\sin x \cos x} = \csc x \sec x$$

The identity is then proven.

Unlike trigonometric identities, which are true for all values of the defined variable, trigonometric equations and inequalities are true for some, but not all, values of the variable. Most often, trigonometric equations are solved for values between 0 and 360 degrees or between 0 and 2π radians. For inequalities, the solution is often a set of intervals, since trigonometric functions are periodic. Solving trigonometric equations is largely the same as solving algebraic equations. Care must be taken, however, to keep in mind the periodic nature of trigonometric functions. This periodic nature often yields multiple (or an infinite number of) solutions.

Trigonometric identities, including sum and difference formulas, are often indispensable in the problem-solving process. These identities allow many complicated functions to be simplified to forms that are more easily managed algebraically.

> *Some algebraic operations, such as squaring both sides of an equation, will yield extraneous answers. Avoid incorrect solutions by remembering to check all solutions to be sure they satisfy the original equation.*

Some algebraic operations, such as squaring both sides of an equation, will yield extraneous answers. Avoid incorrect solutions by remembering to check all solutions to be sure they satisfy the original equation.

Example: Solve the following equation for x: cos x = 1 − sin x, where 0° ≤ x ≤ 360°.

Start by squaring both sides of the equation.

$$\cos^2 x = (1 - \sin x)^2 = 1 - 2\sin x + \sin^2 x$$

Substitute using the Pythagorean identity to replace the cosine term.

$$1 - \sin^2 x = 1 - 2\sin x + \sin^2 x$$

Simplify the results.

$$2\sin^2 x - 2\sin x = 0$$

$$\sin x (\sin x - 1) = 0$$

There are two possible solutions to the equation:

$$\sin x = 0 \qquad \text{and} \qquad \sin x = 1$$
$$x = 0°, 180° \qquad\qquad x = 90°$$

Thus, the apparent solutions to the problem are $x = 0°$, $90°$, and $180°$. By checking each solution, however, it is found that $x = 180°$ is not a legitimate solution and must be discarded. The actual solutions to the equation are thus $x = 0°$ and $90°$.

Example: Solve the following equation: $\cos^2 x = \sin^2 x$ for $0 \le x \le 2\pi$.
First, use the Pythagorean identity to convert either the cosine or sine term.
$$\cos^2 x = 1 - \cos^2 x$$

Simplify the results.
$$2\cos^2 x = 1$$
$$\cos^2 x = \frac{1}{2}$$
$$\cos x = \pm \frac{1}{\sqrt{2}}$$

Familiarity with the properties of trigonometric functions should lead to the realization that this solution corresponds to odd integer multiples of $\frac{\pi}{4}$. Alternatively, a calculator can be used to calculate the inverse function.
$$x = \arccos(\pm \frac{1}{\sqrt{2}})$$
In either case, the solution is $x = \frac{\pi}{4}, \frac{3\pi}{4}, \frac{5\pi}{4}, \frac{7\pi}{4}$.

Example: Solve for x: $\sin x \ge 0$.
Solving a trigonometric inequality involves the same general process that is used in solving any other inequality. In this case, however, the set of solutions includes an infinite number of intervals, rather than a single interval as is the case for some nonperiodic functions. First, replace the inequality symbol with an equal sign. Solve using the inverse function.
$$\sin x = 0$$
$$\arcsin [\sin x] = \arcsin [0]$$
$$x = \arcsin [0]$$

The solutions for x are the following.
$$x = n\pi \qquad n = 0, \pm 1, \pm 2, \pm 3, \ldots$$

These solutions are the points at which the sine function crosses the x-axis. Thus, some set of intervals bounded by these solutions is the set of solutions for the inequality. It is apparent that the sine function is greater than zero for x between 0 and π, and negative for x between π and 2π. This pattern then repeats. Thus, sin x is greater than zero between $2n\pi$ and $(2n + 1)\pi$ for $n = 0, \pm 1, \pm 2, \pm 3, \ldots$
$$\sin x \ge 0 \text{ for } 2n\pi \le x \le (2n + 1)\pi \text{ where } n = 0, \pm 1, \pm 2, \pm 3, \ldots$$

Note that the endpoints of the intervals are included in the solution set. The validity of this solution can be confirmed by looking at a graph of sin x.

Since trigonometric functions, as seen earlier, can be related to the properties of a circle, they have a cyclical (or periodic) behavior that is suited to modeling periodic phenomena. For instance, the height of a point marked on a wheel, tracked as the wheel rolls, can be modeled using trigonometric functions. The key to modeling such periodic phenomena is identification of the amplitude, period and phase (if necessary) of the phenomenon. This information allows expression of some parameter of the phenomenon as an equation involving a trigonometric function.

Example: Write an equation for the height of sea waves whose crests pass every 5 seconds and whose peaks are 10 feet above their troughs.

In this case, phase information is not needed since there is no fixed position to form a point of comparison (or origin). Thus, either a sine or cosine function can be used. The amplitude of the waves is half the distance between the peaks and troughs, or 5 feet. The period is simply the inverse of the time between peaks: 0.2 sec^{-1}. The equation for the height h of the waves with respect to time t is

$$h = \sin{(0.2t)} \text{ feet}$$

where t is measured in seconds.

Example: Find an equation to model the length of a 6-foot man's shadow with respect to the angle of the sun in the sky measured relative to the plane of the ground at the man's feet. Assume that the sun is directly overhead at midday.

It is helpful to first draw a diagram of the situation. Since it is assumed that the sun is directly overhead at midday, the situation can be drawn in a single plane.

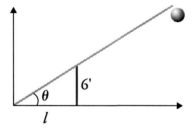

The length l of the shadow can be calculated using the tangent function for the angle θ of the sun in the sky. Use the definition of the tangent to find the function.

$$\tan \theta = \frac{6'}{l}$$

The resulting function can then be written $l(\theta) = \frac{6'}{\tan\theta}$.

To check the result, try some simple cases. For instance, when the sun is overhead, $\theta = 90°$.

$$l(90°) = \frac{6'}{\tan 90°} = \frac{6'}{\infty} = 0'$$

Thus, there is no shadow cast when the sun is overhead. Another example is when the sun approaches the horizon. In this case, the shadow should get very long. Try $\theta = 1°$.

$$l(1°) = \frac{6'}{\tan 1°} = \frac{6'}{0.175} = 342.9'$$

This answer is at least somewhat intuitive. These checks provide confidence in the equation.

SKILL 7.3 Demonstrating knowledge of the definition of the derivative and its relationship to rate of change

The rate of change of a function is equivalent to its slope (change in the vertical direction for a given change in the horizontal direction). For nonlinear functions, the slope is continuously changing over the domain. The rate of change of a function can be found as an average rate of change over some portion of the domain (a difference quotient), or it can be found at a particular domain value (derivative).

Difference Quotient

The DIFFERENCE QUOTIENT is the average rate of change over an interval. For a function f, the difference quotient is represented by the formula

$$\frac{f(x + h) - f(x)}{h}.$$

This formula computes the slope of the secant line through two points on the graph of f. These are the points with x-axis coordinates x and $x + h$.

> **DIFFERENCE QUO-TIENT:** the average rate of change over an interval

Example: Find the difference quotient for the function $f(x) = 2x^2 + 3x - 5$.

Use the difference quotient formula and simplify the results.

$$\frac{f(x + h) - f(x)}{h} = \frac{2(x + h)^2 + 3(x + h) - 5 - (2x^2 + 3x - 5)}{h}$$

$$= \frac{2(x^2 + 2hx + h^2) + 3x + 3h - 5 - 2x^2 - 3x + 5}{h}$$

$$= \frac{2x^2 + 4hx + 2h^2 + 3x + 3h - 5 - 2x^2 - 3x + 5}{h}$$

$$= \frac{4hx + 2h^2 + 3h}{h}$$

$$= 4x + 2h + 3$$

Derivative

DERIVATIVE: the slope of a line tangent to a graph $f(x)$ at x, usually denoted $f'(x)$

The **DERIVATIVE** is the slope of a line tangent to a graph $f(x)$ at x and is usually denoted $f'(x)$. This is also referred to as the instantaneous rate of change. The derivative of $f(x)$ at $x = a$ is found by taking the limit of the average rates of change (computed by the difference quotient) as h approaches zero.

$$f'(a) = \lim_{h \to 0} \frac{f(a + h) - f(a)}{h}$$

Pick a point (for instance, at $x = -3$) on the graph of a function and draw a tangent line at that point. Find the derivative of the function and substitute the value $x = -3$. This result will be the slope of the tangent line.

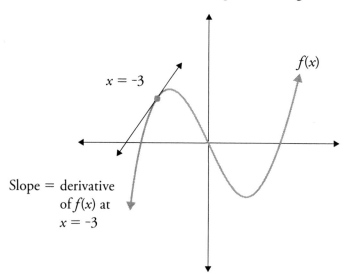

$x = -3$

$f(x)$

Slope = derivative of $f(x)$ at $x = -3$

Example: Suppose a company's annual profit (in millions of dollars) is represented by the above function, $f(x) = 2x^2 + 3x - 5$, and x represents the number of years in the interval. Compute the rate at which the annual profit was changing over a period of 2 years.

$$f'(a) = \lim_{h \to 0} \frac{f(a + h) - f(a)}{h}$$
$$= f'(2) = \lim_{h \to 0} \frac{f(2 + h) - f(2)}{h}$$

Using the difference quotient we computed previously, $4x + 2h + 3$, yields

$$f'(2) = \lim_{h \to 0} (4(2) + 2h + 3)$$
$$= 8 + 3$$
$$= 11.$$

The annual profit for the company has increased at the average rate of $11 million per year over the two-year period.

Rules of Differentiation

The following properties of the derivative allow for differentiation of a wide range of functions (although the process of differentiation may be more or less difficult, depending on the complexity of the function). For illustration, consider two arbitrary functions, $f(x)$ and $g(x)$, and an arbitrary constant, c.

DIFFERENTIATION RULES	
Rule for Multiplicative Constants	$\frac{d}{dx}(cf) = cf'$
Sum and Difference Rules	$\frac{d}{dx}(f + g) = f' + g'$
	$\frac{d}{dx}(f - g) = f' - g'$
Product Rule	$\frac{d}{dx}(fg) = fg' + gf'$
Quotient Rule	$\frac{d}{dx}\left(\frac{f}{g}\right) = \frac{gf' - fg'}{g^2}$
Chain Rule	$\frac{df}{dx} = \frac{df}{du}\frac{du}{dx}$

The chain rule, as expressed above, allows for differentiation of composite functions. The variable u can be an independent variable or it can be a function (of x). Note that the differential elements du in the numerator of the first factor and in the denominator of the second factor can otherwise cancel, making the right side of the equation identical to the left side.

Derivation of Differentiation Rules

As mentioned previously, the formal definition of the derivative can be used to determine the general form of the derivative for certain families of functions. The formal definition of the derivative is expressed in terms of the limit of a difference quotient, as given below.

$$f'(x) = \lim_{\Delta x \to 0} \frac{f(x + \Delta x) - f(x)}{\Delta x}$$

Using this definition, the derivatives of algebraic functions (including, for instance, polynomial, trigonometric, and logarithmic functions) can be derived. In addition, the general differentiation rules above can also be derived by applying in each case the properties of limits to the definition given above.

The use of the formal definition in deriving a general rule of differentiation for a family of functions is best illustrated by way of an example. Consider polynomial functions, as mentioned previously. Note that the sum and difference rules for differentiation, along with the multiplicative constant rule, allow polynomials to be differentiated on a term-by-term basis. Thus, it suffices to simply derive the rule for differentiating the generic term x^n, where n is a constant and x is the variable of the function. Use the formal definition of the derivative given above and substitute this algebraic term for $f(x) =$ (that is, use $f(x) = x^n$).

$$f'(x) = \lim_{\Delta x \to 0} \frac{(x + \Delta x)^n - (x)^n}{\Delta x}$$

Simplify the expression and apply the binomial expansion to the result.

$$f'(x) = \lim_{\Delta x \to 0} \frac{1}{\Delta x}[(x + \Delta x)^n - x^n]$$

$$f'(x) = \lim_{\Delta x \to 0} [\binom{n}{0}x^n + \binom{n}{1}x^{n-1} \Delta x + \binom{n}{2}x^{n-2} (\Delta x)^2 + ... + \binom{n}{n}(\Delta x)^n - x^n]$$

In the above expression, the combinatorial form $\binom{n}{k}$ represents the number of combinations of n objects taken k at a time, or $\frac{n!}{k!(n-k)!}$.

$$f'(x) = \lim_{\Delta x \to 0} \frac{1}{\Delta x}[x^n + nx^{n-1}\Delta x + \binom{n}{2}x^{n-2} (\Delta x)^2 + ... + (\Delta x)^n - x^n]$$

$$f'(x) = \lim_{\Delta x \to 0} \frac{1}{\Delta x}[nx^{n-1}\Delta x + \binom{n}{2}x^{n-2} (\Delta x)^2 + ... + (\Delta x)^n]$$

$$f'(x) = \lim_{\Delta x \to 0} [nx^{n-1} + \binom{n}{2}x^{n-2} \Delta x + ... + (\Delta x)^{n-1}]$$

Note that, with the exception of the first term, all the terms in the brackets have a factor Δx. Thus, when the limit is applied, these terms all become zero, leaving the result of the differentiation.

$$f'(x) = nx^{n-1}$$

This is the well-known rule for differentiating polynomial terms with exponent n.

Example: Find the first derivative of the function $y = 5x^4$.

$$\frac{dy}{dx} = (5)(4)x^{4-1}$$

$$\frac{dy}{dx} = 20x^3$$

Example: Find y' where $y = \frac{1}{4x^3}$.
First, rewrite the function using a negative exponent, then apply the differentiation rule.

$$y' = \frac{1}{4}x^{-3}$$

$$y' = \frac{1}{4}(-3)x^{-3-1}$$

$$y' = -\frac{3}{4}x^{-4} = -\frac{3}{4x^4}$$

Example: Find the first derivative of $y = 3\sqrt{x^5}$.
Rewrite using $\sqrt[z]{x^n} = x^{\frac{n}{z}}$, then take the derivative.

$$y = 3x^{\frac{5}{2}}$$

$$\frac{dy}{dx} = (3)(\frac{5}{2})x^{\frac{5}{2}-1}$$

$$\frac{dy}{dx} = (\frac{15}{2})x^{\frac{3}{2}}$$

$$\frac{dy}{dx} = 7.5\sqrt{x^3} = 7.5x\sqrt{x}$$

The derivatives of other families of functions can be found in a similar manner. Below is a summary of the rules of differentiation for various transcendental (including trigonometric, logarithmic, and exponential) functions.

SUMMARY OF DIFFERENTIATION RULES FOR TRANSCENDENTAL FUNCTIONS	
$\frac{d}{dx}\sin x = \cos x$	$\frac{d}{dx}\csc x = -\csc x \cot x$
$\frac{d}{dx}\cos x = -\sin x$	$\frac{d}{dx}\sec x = \sec x \tan x$
$\frac{d}{dx}\tan x = \sec^2 x$	$\frac{d}{dx}\cot x = -\csc^2 x$
$\frac{d}{dx}\arcsin x = \dfrac{1}{\sqrt{1-x^2}}$	$\frac{d}{dx}\text{arc csc } x = -\dfrac{1}{|x|\sqrt{x^2-1}}$
$\frac{d}{dx}\text{arcccos } x = -\dfrac{1}{\sqrt{1-x^2}}$	$\frac{d}{dx}\text{arc sec } x = \dfrac{1}{|x|\sqrt{x^2-1}}$
$\frac{d}{dx}\arctan x = \dfrac{1}{1+x^2}$	$\frac{d}{dx}\text{arc cot } x = -\dfrac{1}{1+x^2}$
$\frac{d}{dx}\ln x = \frac{1}{x}$	$\frac{d}{dx}e^x = e^x$

Example: Find the derivative of the function $y = 4e^{x2} \sin x$.
Apply the appropriate rules (product and chain rules) to the function.

$$\frac{dy}{dx} = 4(\sin x \frac{d}{dx}e^{x2} + e^{x2}\frac{d}{dx}\sin x)$$
$$\frac{dy}{dx} = 4(\sin x[2xe^{x2}] + e^{x2}\cos x)$$
$$\frac{dy}{dx} = 8xe^{x2}\sin x + 4e^{x2}\cos x$$

Example: Find the derivative of the function $y = \frac{5}{e^{\sin x}}$.
Rewrite the function with a negative exponent and use the chain rule.

$$y = 5e^{-\sin x}$$
$$\frac{dy}{dx} = 5\frac{d}{dx}e^{-\sin x}$$
$$\frac{dy}{dx} = 5e^{-\sin x}[-\cos x]$$
$$\frac{dy}{dx} = 5e^{-\sin x}\cos x = -\frac{5\cos x}{e^{\sin x}}$$

Finding Slope of a Tangent Line at a Point

Using these properties of derivatives, the slopes (and therefore the equations) of tangent lines can be found for a wide range of functions. The procedure simply involves finding the slope of the function at the given point using the derivative then determining the equation of the line using point-slope form.

Example: Find the slope of the tangent line for the given function at the given point: $y = \frac{1}{x-2}$ *at (3, 1).*

Find the derivative of the function.

$$y' = \frac{d}{dx}(x-2)^{-1}$$
$$y' = (-1)(x-2)^{-2}(1) = -\frac{1}{(x-2)^2}$$

Evaluate the derivative at $x = 3$:

$$y' = -\frac{1}{(3-2)^2} = -1$$

Thus, the slope of the function at the point is -1.

Example: Find the points at which the tangent to the curve $f(x) = 2x^2 + 3x$ *is parallel to the line* $y = 11x - 5$.

For the tangent line to be parallel to the given line, the only condition is that the slopes are equal. Thus, find the derivative of f, set the result equal to 11, and solve for x.

$$f'(x) = 4x + 3 = 11$$
$$4x = 8$$
$$x = 2$$

To find the y value of the point, simply substitute 2 into f.

$$f(2) = 2(2)^2 + 3(2) = 8 + 6 = 14$$

Thus, the tangent to f is parallel to $y = 11x - 5$ at the point (2, 14) only.

Example: Find the equation of the tangent line to $f(x) = 2e^{x^2}$ *at* $x = -1$.

To find the tangent line, a point and a slope are needed. The x value of the point is given; the y value can be found by substituting $x = -1$ into f.

$$f(-1) = 2e^{(-1)^2} = 2e$$

Thus, the point is $(-1, 2e)$. The slope is found by substituting -1 into the derivative of f.

$$f'(x) = 2e^{x^2}(2x) = 4xe^{x^2}$$
$$f'(-1) = 4(-1)e^{(-1)^2} = -4e$$

Use the point-slope form of the line to determine the correct equation.

$$y - 2e = -4e(x - [-1])$$
$$y = 2e - 4ex - 4e = -4ex - 2e$$

Thus, the equation of the line tangent to f at $x = -1$ is $y = -4ex - 2e$.

SKILL 7.4 Demonstrating knowledge of the definite integral, area under the curve, and techniques of numerical integration

The formal definition of an integral is based on the Riemann sum. A RIEMANN SUM is the sum of the areas of a set of rectangles that is used to approximate the area under the curve of a function. Given a function f defined over some closed interval $[a, b]$, the interval can be divided into a set of n arbitrary partitions, each of length Δx_i. Within the limits of each partition, some value $x = c_i$ can be chosen such that Δx_i and $f(c_i)$ define the width and height (respectively) of a rectangle. The sum of the aggregate of all the rectangles defined in this manner over the interval $[a, b]$ is the Riemann sum.

> **RIEMANN SUM:** the sum of the areas of a set of rectangles that is used to approximate the area under the curve of a function

Consider, for example, the function $f(x) = x^2 + 1$ over the interval $[0, 1]$. The plot of the function is shown below.

Partition the interval into segments of width 0.2 along the x-axis, and choose the function value $f(c_i)$ at the center of each interval. This function value is the height of the respective rectangle.

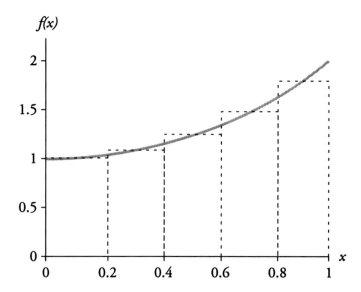

The Riemann sum for this case is expressed below.

$$\sum_{i=1}^{5} 0.2f(0.2i - 0.1) = 1.33$$

This expression is the sum of the areas of all the rectangles shown above. This is an approximation of the area under the curve of the function (and a reasonably accurate one, as well—the actual area is $\frac{4}{3}$).

Generally, the Riemann sum for arbitrary partitioning and selection of the values c_i is the following:

$$\sum_{i=1}^{n} f(c_i)\Delta x_i$$

where c_i is within the closed interval defined by the partition Δx_i.

Definite Integrals

The DEFINITE INTEGRAL is defined as the limit of the Riemann sum as the widths of the partitions Δx_i go to zero (and, consequently, n goes to infinity). Thus, the definite integral can be expressed mathematically as follows:

$$\int_a^b f(x)dx = \lim_{\Delta x_m \to 0} \sum_{i=1}^{n} f(c_i)\Delta x_i$$

where Δx_m is the width of the largest partition. If the partitioning of the interval is such that each partition has the same width, then the definition can be written as follows:

$$\int_a^b f(x)dx = \lim_{\Delta x \to 0} \sum_{i=1}^{n} f(c_i)\Delta x_i$$

Note that $n = \frac{b-a}{\Delta x}$ in this case.

The definite integral, is the area under the curve of f(x) over the interval [a, b].

The definite integral, therefore, is the area under the curve of $f(x)$ over the interval $[a, b]$. By taking the limit of the Riemann sum, the number of rectangles used to find the area under the curve becomes infinite and, therefore, the error in the result goes to zero (since the width of each rectangle becomes infinitesimal).

The Fundamental Theorem of Calculus relates differentiation with definite integration, which is fundamentally defined in terms of the Riemann sum. According to the theorem, definite integration is the inverse of differentiation. The theorem is expressed below for the function $F(x)$, where $f(x) = F'(x)$ and where $f(x)$ is continuous on the interval $[a, b]$.

$$\int_a^b f(x)dx = F(b) - F(a)$$

The function $F(x)$ is also called an antiderivative of $f(x)$, because the derivative of $F(x)$ is $f(x)$. Based on this theorem, it is clear that integrals can be evaluated without the need of finding the limit of a Riemann sum as long as the antiderivative of a function can be determined. Thus, the key to evaluating definite integrals is knowledge of how to find the antiderivative of a function.

The definite integral can thus be interpreted in terms of antiderivatives. Note that the definite integral for the interval $[a, b]$ is the area under the curve $f(x)$ between $x = a$ and $x = b$. The antiderivative, $F(c)$, is the cumulative area under $f(x)$ between $x = 0$ and $x = c$. Thus, the difference between the antiderivative evaluated at b and the antiderivative evaluated at a is the definite integral of $f(x)$ between a and b.

The example graph below shows a function $f(x)$. The antiderivative $F(x)$ evaluated at $x = 1$ is the solid shaded area; the antiderivative evaluated at $x = 2$ is the striped area. The difference $F(2) - F(1)$ is the difference between the two areas (the non-overlapping striped region).

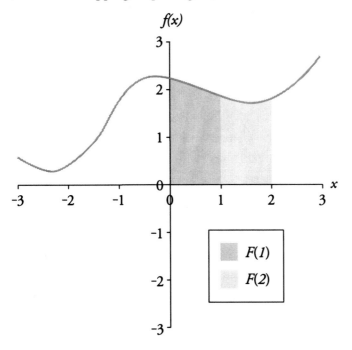

Properties of Integrals

The following summarizes some of the basic rules for integration in terms of some common functions.

BASIC INTEGRATION RULES		
Integration Involving Constants	$\int 0\,dx = C$ $\qquad\qquad$ $\int k\,dx = kx + C$ $\qquad\qquad$ $\int kf(x)\,dx = k\int f(x)\,dx$		
Integration of Sums or Differences of Functions	$\int[f(x) + g(x)]\,dx = \int f(x)\,dx + \int g(x)\,dx$ $\int[f(x) - g(x)]\,dx = \int f(x)\,dx - \int g(x)\,dx$		
Power Rule	$\int x^n\,dx = \frac{x^{n+1}}{n+1} + C$ for $n \neq 1$		
Trigonometric Functions	$\int \sin x\,dx = -\cos x + C$ $\qquad$ $\int \cos x\,dx = \sin x + C$ $\int \tan x\,dx = \ln(\sec x) + C$ $\qquad$ $\int \cot x\,dx = \ln(\sin x) + C$ $\int \csc x\,dx = \ln(\tan \frac{x}{2}) + C$ $\qquad$ $\int \sec x\,dx = \ln(\tan [\frac{x}{2} + \frac{\pi}{4}]) + C$ $\int \sec^2 x\,dx = \tan x + C$ $\qquad$ $\int \sec x \tan x\,dx = \sec x + C$ $\int \csc^2 x\,dx = -\cot x + C$ $\qquad$ $\int \csc x \cot x\,dx = -\csc x + C$		
Logometric Functions	$\int \ln x\,dx = x\ln x - x + C$ $\qquad\qquad$ $\int \frac{1}{x}\,dx = \ln x + C$		
Exponential Functions	$\int e^x\,dx = e^x + C$		

The above rules are helpful for finding the antiderivatives of functions, but they are far from complete, since they do not permit in any obvious manner integration of composite functions or functions with arguments other than simply x. To this end, several helpful strategies can be applied.

Integrating by *u*-Substitution

If a function is expressed in terms of another function (that is, if it is a composite function), then a change of variables permits integration through conversion of the expression into a form similar to a form given in the rules above.

Consider a composite function $f(g(x))$ in the context of the following integral:

$\int f(g(x))\,g'(x)\,dx$

An example of such a composite function might be $f(x) = (x + 1)^2$ or $f(x) = \sin(x^3)$. Assign $g(x)$ a new variable name, u. Then differentiate $g(x)$ in terms of x and rearrange the differentials.

$$u = g(x)$$
$$\frac{dg(x)}{dx} = g'(x) = \frac{du}{dx}$$
$$du = g'(x)dx$$

Use this result in the indefinite integration of the composite function:

$$\int f(g(x))g'(u)dx = \int f(u)du$$

With this simple substitution (sometimes called a u-substitution), the integral can be made to look like one of the general forms. It is sometimes necessary to experiment with different u-substitutions to find one that works (finding a u that allows complete elimination of x from the integral is not always trivial). Follow these steps for integration by substitution:

1. Select an appropriate value for u to perform the substitution.

2. Differentiate u as shown above.

3. Substitute u and du into the integral to eliminate x.

4. Evaluate the integral.

5. Substitute $g(x)$ back into the result to get the antiderivative.

When dealing with definite integrals that require u-substitution, the only difference is that the limits of integration must be modified in accordance with the choice of u. Thus:

$$\int_a^b f(g(x))g'(u)dx = \int_{g(a)}^{g(b)} f(u)du$$

Example: Evaluate the following antiderivative: $\int 2\,x[\sin(x^2) + \cos(x^2)]dx$.
First, split the integral into two parts.

$$\int 2\,x[\sin(x^2) + \cos(x^2)]dx = \int 2\,x \sin(x^2)\,dx + \int 2\,x\cos(x^2)\,dx$$

Next, select an appropriate value for u. In this case, choose $u = x^2$. Then:

$$du = 2x\,dx$$

Rewrite the integral in terms of u.

$$\int \sin(x^2)2x\,dx + \int \cos(x^2)2xdx = \int \sin u\,du + \int \cos u\,du$$

This result is in a form for which the antiderivative can be found easily.

$$\int \sin u\,du + \int \cos u\,du = -\cos u + \sin u + C$$

Substitute the definition of u back into the result to get the antiderivative in terms of x.

$$-\cos u + \sin u + C = -\cos(x^2) + \sin(x^2) + C$$

Example: Evaluate the following antiderivative: $\int e^{\sin x} \cos x\, dx$.

Try choosing $u = \cos x$.

$$du = -\sin x\, dx$$

Substitute into the integral.

$$\int e^{\sin x} \cos x\, dx = -\int \frac{u e^{\sin x}}{\sin x}\, du$$

Note that there is no apparent way to eliminate x from the integral. Thus, this choice of u should be abandoned. Instead, try $u = \sin x$.

$$du = \cos x\, dx$$

Substitute into the integral, as before.

$$\int e^{\sin x} \cos x\, dx = \int e^u du$$

This choice of u was successful. Evaluate the antiderivative and substitute the definition of u back into the result.

$$\int e^u du = e^u = e^{\sin x}$$

Example: Evaluate the definite integral $\int \frac{1}{x \ln x}\, dx$ over the interval $[e, e^e]$.

Substitute using $u = \ln x$. Then, $du = \frac{1}{x}\, dx$.

$$\int \frac{1}{x \ln x}\, dx = \int \frac{1}{xu}x\, du = \int \frac{1}{u}\, du$$

Evaluate the integral and apply the limits of integration, which, using $u = \ln x$, lead to the interval $[\ln e, \ln e^e] = [1, e]$.

$$\int \frac{1}{u}\, du = \ln u \Big|_1^e$$
$$\ln u \Big|_1^e = \ln e - \ln 1 = 1 - 0 = 1$$

Integration by Parts

Another useful technique for evaluating complicated integrals is integration by parts. Since this method is itself complicated, it should only be used as a last resort if simpler methods of integration are not successful. Integration by parts requires two substitutions. To remember the formula for integration by parts, it is helpful to remember that it is based on the product rule of differentiation for two functions, u and v.

$$\frac{d}{dx}(uv) = u\frac{dv}{dx} + v\frac{du}{dx}$$

Naturally, then, integrating this result should return the product uv.

$$\int \frac{d}{dx}(uv)\, dx = \int d(uv) = uv$$

$$\int [u\frac{dv}{dx} + v\frac{du}{dx}]\, dx = \int u\, dv + \int v\, du$$

Rewrite the equation and rearrange to get the formula for integration by parts:

$uv = \int u\,dv + \int v\,du$

$\int u\,dv = uv - \int v\,du$

Thus, by identifying substitution functions for u and v, a method for integration is available. Proper selection of u and v is crucial to making this technique work. Use the following steps to perform integration by parts.

1. Choose dv as the most complicated part of the integral that can be integrated by itself.

2. Choose u as the part of the integral that remains after the dv substitution is made. Preferably, the derivative of u should be simpler than u.

3. Integrate dv to get v.

4. Differentiate u to get du.

5. Rewrite the integral in the form $\int u\,dv = uv - \int v\,du$.

6. Integrate $\int v\,du$.

7. If you cannot integrate $v\,du$, go back to the first step and try a different set of substitutions.

Example: Find the antiderivative of the following function: $\int xe^{3x}dx$.

First, choose $dv = e^{3x}dx$ and $u = x$. Calculate du and v.

$dv = e^{3x}dx \qquad u = x$

$\int dv = \int e^{3x}dx \qquad du = dx$

$v = \frac{e^{3x}}{3}$

Substitute these results into the formula for integration by parts:

$\int u\,dv = \int xe^{3x}dx = uv - \int v\,du = \frac{xe^{3x}}{3} - \int \frac{e^{3x}}{3}dx$

The substitutions fit in this case, and the integration can now be performed easily.

$\int xe^{3x}dx = \frac{xe^{3x}}{3} - \int \frac{e^{3x}}{3}dx = \frac{xe^{3x}}{3} - \frac{e^{3x}}{9} + C$

$\int xe^{3x}dx = \frac{e^{3x}}{3}(x - \frac{1}{3}) + C$

This is the correct solution to the problem.

Example: Evaluate the following indefinite integral: $\int x \cos x\, dx$

Try choosing $u = x$ and $dv = \cos x\, dx$.

$du = dx \qquad\qquad \int dv = \int \cos x\, dx$

$v = \sin x$

Substitute into the formula for integration by parts:

$$\int u \, dv = \int x \cos x dx = uv - \int v \, du = x \sin x - \int \sin x dx$$

The choices of u and dv work, so the integral can be evaluated to find the result.

$$\int x \cos x \, dx = x \sin x + \cos x + C$$

**SKILL Applying the fundamental theorem of calculus to solve
7.5 mathematical and real-world problems**

Applications of Integrals

Area under a curve

Taking the integral of a function and evaluating it over some interval on x provides the total area under the curve (or, more formally, the area bounded by the curve and the x-axis). Thus, the areas of geometric figures can be determined when the figure can be cast as a function or set of functions in the coordinate plane. Remember, though, that regions above the x-axis have "positive" area and regions below the x-axis have "negative" area. It is necessary to account for these positive and negative values when finding the area under curves. The boundaries between positive and negative regions are delineated by the roots of the function. Follow these steps to find the total area under the curve:

1. Determine the interval or intervals on which the area under the curve is to be found. If portions of the function are negative, a given interval may need to be divided appropriately if all areas are to be considered positive.

2. Integrate the function.

3. Evaluate the integral once for each interval.

4. If any of the intervals evaluates to a negative number, reverse the sign (equivalently, take the absolute value of each integral).

5. Add the value of all the integrals to get the area under the curve.

Example: Find the area under the following function on the given interval:
f(x) = sin x; [0, 2π].
First, find the roots of the function on the interval.

$$f(x) = \sin x = 0$$
$$x = 0, \pi$$

The function $\sin x$ is positive over $[0, \pi]$ (since $\sin\frac{\pi}{2} = 1$) and negative over $[\pi, 2\pi]$ (since $\sin\frac{3\pi}{2} = -1$). Use these intervals for the integration to find the area A under the curve.

$$A = \int_0^{2\pi} |\sin x| dx = \left|\int_0^{\pi}\sin x \, dx\right| + \left|\int_{\pi}^{2\pi}\sin x \, dx\right|$$

$$A = \left|-\cos x\big|_0^{\pi}\right| + \left|-\cos x\big|_{\pi}^{2\pi}\right| = |-\cos \pi + \cos 0| + |-\cos 2\pi + \cos \pi|$$

$$A = |1 + 1| + |-1 - 1| = 2 + 2 = 4$$

Thus, the total area under the curve of $f(x) = \sin x$ on the interval $[0, 2\pi]$ is 4 square units.

Area between two curves

Finding the area between two curves is similar to finding the area under one curve. The general process involves integrating the absolute value of the difference between the two functions over the interval of interest. In some instances, it is necessary to find the intervals over which the difference is positive and over which the difference is negative. For the former, the integral can simply be taken with no modifications; for the latter, however, the result of the integral must be negated. To find the points at which the difference between the functions changes from positive to negative (or vice versa), simply set the functions equal to each other and solve. Take the absolute value of each portion of the integral (that is, each integral over a portion of the interval) and add all the parts. This yields the total area between the curves.

Example: Find the area of the regions bounded by the two functions on the indicated interval: f(x) = x + 2 and g(x) = x² on [-2, 3].
The integral of interest is $\int_{-2}^{3}|f(x) - g(x)|dx$.

To eliminate the need to use the absolute-value notation inside the integral, find the values for which $f(x) = g(x)$.

$$f(x) = x + 2 = g(x) = x^2$$
$$x^2 - x - 2 = 0 = (x - 2)(x + 1)$$

The functions are then equal at $x = -1$ and $x = 2$. Perform the integration over the intervals defined by these values.

$$\int_{-2}^{3}|f(x) - g(x)|dx = \left|\int_{-2}^{-1}f(x) - g(x) \, dx\right| + \left|\int_{-1}^{2}f(x) - g(x) \, dx\right| + \left|\int_{2}^{3}f(x) - g(x) \, dx\right|$$

The antiderivative of $f(x) - g(x)$ is the following (ignoring the constant of integration).

$$\int [f(x) - g(x)]dx = \int (x + 2 - x^2)dx = \frac{x^2}{2} + 2x - \frac{x^3}{3}$$

Evaluate over the intervals above.

$$\int_{-2}^{3}|f(x) - g(x)|dx = \left|\left[\tfrac{x^2}{2} + 2x - \tfrac{x^3}{3}\right]_{-2}^{-1}\right| + \left|\left[\tfrac{x^2}{2} + 2x - \tfrac{x^3}{3}\right]_{-1}^{2}\right| + \left|\left[\tfrac{x^2}{2} + 2x - \tfrac{x^3}{3}\right]_{2}^{3}\right|$$

$$\left|\left[\tfrac{x^2}{2} + 2x - \tfrac{x^3}{3}\right]_{-2}^{-1}\right| = \left|(\tfrac{1}{2} - 2 + \tfrac{1}{3}) - (\tfrac{4}{2} - 4 + \tfrac{8}{3})\right| = \left|-\tfrac{7}{6} - \tfrac{2}{3}\right| = \tfrac{11}{6}$$

$$\left|\left[\tfrac{x^2}{2} + 2x - \tfrac{x^3}{3}\right]_{-1}^{2}\right| = \left|(\tfrac{4}{2} + 4 - \tfrac{8}{3}) - (\tfrac{1}{2} - 2 + \tfrac{1}{3})\right| = \left|\tfrac{10}{3} + \tfrac{7}{6}\right| = \tfrac{27}{6}$$

$$\left|\left[\tfrac{x^2}{2} + 2x - \tfrac{x^3}{3}\right]_{2}^{3}\right| = \left|(\tfrac{9}{2} + 6 - \tfrac{27}{3}) - (\tfrac{4}{2} + 4 - \tfrac{8}{3})\right| = \left|\tfrac{3}{2} - \tfrac{10}{3}\right| = \tfrac{11}{6}$$

The sum of these individual parts is $\tfrac{49}{6}$.

Volumes of solids of revolution

SOLID OF REVOLUTION: an area bounded by a curve (or curves) and revolved about a line

An area bounded by a curve (or curves) and revolved about a line is called a SOLID OF REVOLUTION. To find the volume of such a solid, the disc method (called the washer method if the solid has an empty interior of some form) works in most instances. Imagine slicing through the solid perpendicular to the line of revolution. The cross section should resemble either a disc or a washer. The washer method involves finding the sum of the volumes of all "washers" that compose the solid, using the following general formula:

$$V = \pi(r_1^2 - r_2^2)t$$

where V is the volume of the washer, r_1 and r_2 are the interior and exterior radii, and t is the thickness of the washer.

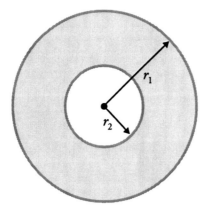

Depending on the situation, the radius is the distance from the line of revolution to the curve; or if there are two curves involved, the radius is the difference between the two functions. The thickness is dx if the line of revolution is parallel to the x-axis and dy if the line of revolution is parallel to the y-axis. The integral is then the following, where dV is the differential volume of a washer.

$$\int dV = \int \pi(r_1^2 - r_2^2)dt$$
$$V = \pi \int (r_1^2 - r_2^2)dt$$

It is assumed here that r_1 is the outer radius and r_2 is the inner radius. For the disc method, where only one radius is needed, $r_2 = 0$.

Example: Find the volume of the solid of revolution made by revolving f(x) = 9 − x² about the x-axis on the interval [0, 4].

This problem can be solved using the disc method. First, note that the radius is $9 - x^2$ and the thickness of the disc is dx. Write the appropriate integral as follows.

$$V = \pi \int_0^4 (9 - x^2)^2 \, dx$$

Next, expand the radius term and evaluate the integral.

$$V = \pi \int_0^4 (81 - 18x^2 + x^4) \, dx$$
$$V = \pi [81x - \frac{18}{3}x^3 + \frac{1}{5}x^5]_0^4$$
$$V = \pi [81(4) - \frac{18}{3}(4)^3 + \frac{1}{5}(4)^5]$$
$$V = \pi [324 - 384 + 204.8] = 144.8\pi \approx 454.9$$

The volume is thus approximately 454.9 cubic units.

Arc length

Finding the arc length of a curve is another useful application of integration. The ARC LENGTH is the distance traversed by a curve over a given interval. Geometrically, the distance d between two points (x_1, y_1) and (x_2, y_2) is given by the following formula.

$$d = \sqrt{(x_2 - x_1)^2 + (y_2 - y_1)^2}$$

If the points are only an infinitesimal distance apart (ds, which is the differential arc length), then the above expression can be written as follows in differential form:

$$ds = \sqrt{dx^2 + dy^2}$$

Factor out the dx term:

$$ds = \sqrt{1 + (\frac{dy}{dx})^2} \, dx$$

But $\frac{dy}{dx}$ is simply the derivative of a function $y(x)$ (which can be expressed as $f(x)$ instead). Thus, the integral of the above expression over the interval $[a, b]$ yields the formula for the arc length.

$$\int ds = = \int_a^b \sqrt{1 + [f'(x)]^2} \, dx$$

> **ARC LENGTH:** the distance traversed by a curve over a given interval

Example: Find the distance traversed by the function f(x) = ln (cos x) on the interval [-$\frac{\pi}{4}$, $\frac{\pi}{4}$].

Use the formula for arc length *s*, applying trigonometric identities as appropriate.

$$s = \int \sqrt{1 + [\tfrac{d}{dx}\ln(\cos x)]^2} = \int \sqrt{1 + [\tfrac{\sin x}{\cos x}]^2}dx$$

$$s = \int \sqrt{1 + [\tan x]^2}dx = \int \sqrt{1 + \tan^2 x}\ dx = \int \sqrt{\sec^2 x}\ dx$$

$$s = \int \sqrt{1 + [\tan x]^2}dx = \int \sqrt{1 + \tan^2 x}\ dx = \int \sec x\ dx$$

Evaluate the integral over the limits of integration.

$$s = \int_{-\pi/4}^{\pi/4} \sec x\ dx = \ln(\sec x + \tan x)\Big|_{-\pi/4}^{\pi/4}$$

$$s = \ln(\sec \tfrac{\pi}{4} + \tan \tfrac{\pi}{4}) - \ln(\sec [-\tfrac{\pi}{4}] + \tan [\tfrac{\pi}{4}])$$

$$s = \ln(\sqrt{2} + 1) - \ln(\sqrt{2} - 1) \approx 1.763$$

The result is approximately 1.763 units.

Linear motion

Integral calculus, in addition to differential calculus, is a powerful tool for analysis of problems involving linear motion. The derivative of the position (or displacement) function is the velocity function, and the derivative of a velocity function is the acceleration function. As a result, the antiderivative of an acceleration function is a velocity function, and the antiderivative of a velocity function is a position (or displacement) function. Solving word problems of this type involve converting the information given into an appropriate integral expression. To find the constant of integration, use the conditions provided in the problem (such as an initial displacement, velocity, or acceleration).

The antiderivative of an acceleration function is a velocity function, and the antiderivative of a velocity function is a position (or displacement) function.

Example: A particle moves along the x-axis with acceleration a(t) = 3t − 1 $\frac{cm}{sec^2}$. At time t = 4 seconds, the particle is moving to the left at 3 cm per second. Find the velocity of the particle at time t = 2 seconds.

Evaluate the antiderivative of the acceleration function *a(t)* to get the velocity function *v(t)* along with the unknown constant of integration *C*.

$$v(t) = \int a(t)dt = \int (3t - 1)dt$$
$$v(t) = \tfrac{3t^2}{2} - t + C$$

Use the condition that at time *t* = 4 seconds, the particle has a velocity of -3 cm/sec.

$$v(4) = \tfrac{3(4)^2}{2} - 4 + C = \text{-}3$$
$$\tfrac{48}{2} - 4 + C = \text{-}3$$
$$C = \text{-}3 + 4 - 24 = \text{-}23\ \tfrac{cm}{sec}$$

Now evaluate $v(t)$ at time $t = 2$ seconds to get the solution to the problem.

$$v(t) = \frac{3t^2}{2} - t - 23 \frac{cm}{sec}$$

$$v(2) = \frac{3(2)^2}{2} - 2 - 23 \frac{cm}{sec} = 6 - 25 \frac{cm}{sec} = -19 \frac{cm}{sec}$$

Example: Find the displacement function of a particle whose acceleration is described by the equation a(t) = 3sin 2t. Assume that the particle is initially motionless at the origin.

Find the antiderivative of the acceleration function $a(t)$ to get the velocity function $v(t)$.

$$v(t) = \int 3 \sin 2t \, dt = -3\frac{1}{2}\cos 2t + C$$

Note that the initial velocity is zero; thus:

$$v(0) = 0 = -\frac{3}{2} \cos 2(0) + C = -\frac{3}{2} + C$$

$$C = \frac{3}{2}$$

$$v(t) = -\frac{3}{2} (1 - \cos 2t)$$

Find the antiderivative of the velocity function to get the displacement function $s(t)$.

$$s(t) = -\int \frac{3}{2} (1 - \cos 2t) dt = -\frac{3}{2} (t - \frac{1}{2}\sin 2t) + C'$$

The initial position is at the origin, so C' can be found.

$$s(0) = 0 = -\frac{3}{2} (0 - \frac{1}{2}\sin 2(0)) + C'$$

$$s(0) = 0 = -\frac{3}{2} (0 - 0) + C'$$

$$C' = 0$$

$$s(t) = -\frac{3}{2} (t - \frac{1}{2}\sin 2t)$$

This last result is the solution to the problem. A necessary (but not sufficient) check of the answer is to differentiate $s(t)$ twice and compare with $a(t)$.

$$s'(t) = \frac{3}{2} (1 - \cos 2t)$$

$$s''(t) = 3 \sin 2t = a(t)$$

DOMAIN III
MEASUREMENT AND GEOMETRY

PERSONALIZED STUDY PLAN

KNOWN MATERIAL/ SKIP IT

PAGE		COMPETENCY AND SKILL	
131	**8:**	**Apply principles of measurement and geometry to solve problems**	☐
	8.1:	Solving problems involving conversions within and between different systems of measurement, including dimensional analysis	☐
	8.2:	Solving mathematical and real-world problems involving measurable attributes of simple or composite figures and shapes	☐
	8.3:	Solving mathematical and real-world problems involving indirect measurement	☐
	8.4:	Solving problems involving the effects of changing the dimensions of a figure or shape on its area and volume	☐
154	**9:**	**Analyze figures and shapes in two and three dimensions**	☐
	9.1:	Applying the properties of polygons and circles to solve mathematical and real-world problems	☐
	9.2:	Applying the properties of two- and three-dimensional shapes to solve mathematical and real-world problems	☐
	9.3:	Analyzing formal and informal arguments and proofs	☐
	9.4:	Evaluating arguments, reasoning, and the validity of conclusions	☐
	9.5:	Analyzing systems of geometry, including Euclidean, non-Euclidean, and projective geometries	☐
177	**10:**	**Analyze figures and shapes using coordinate and transformational geometry**	☐
	10.1:	Analyzing two- and three-dimensional figures and shapes in the coordinate plane	☐
	10.2:	Applying geometric properties and the concepts of distance, midpoint, and slope in coordinate systems to solve mathematical and real-world problems	☐
	10.3:	Applying transformations to figures in the coordinate plane, and analyzing topological properties and transformations	☐
	10.4:	Analyzing the use of the techniques of coordinate geometry in geometric proofs	☐
	10.5:	Applying vectors and polar and parametric equations to solve problems	☐

COMPETENCY 8

APPLY PRINCIPLES OF MEASUREMENT AND GEOMETRY TO SOLVE PROBLEMS

SKILL 8.1 Solving problems involving conversions within and between different systems of measurement, including dimensional analysis

In ancient times, baskets, jars and bowls were used to measure capacity. An inch originated as the length of three barley grains placed end to end. The word "carat," used for measuring precious gems, was derived from carob seeds. Even now, nonstandard units are sometimes used when standard instruments might not be available. For example, students might measure the length of a room by their arm spans. Seeds or stones might be used for measuring weight.

"When you can measure what you are speaking about and express it in numbers, you know something about it; but when you cannot measure it, when you cannot express it in numbers, your knowledge is of a meager and unsatisfactory kind."

—Lord Kelvin

Systems of Units

The Customary (Imperial) System
CUSTOMARY, OR IMPERIAL, UNITS are the familiar everyday units used in the United States.

CUSTOMARY, OR IMPERIAL, UNITS: the familiar everyday units used in the United States

Customary System units
Inch, foot, yard, and mile are commonly used units of length.

1 yard	=	3 feet	=	36 inches
1 mile	=	1,760 yards		

Rod, furlong, and acre (a unit of area) are less familiar units defined in terms of yards:

1 rod	=	$5\frac{1}{2}$ yards		
1 furlong	=	220 yards		
1 acre	=	4,840 sq. yards	=	160 sq. rods

The basic unit of weight is pound (lb).

1 pound	=	16 ounces (oz)		
1 ounce	=	16 drams		
Short ton (U.S.)	=	2,000 lb		
Long ton (British)	=	2,240 lb		

The basic unit of liquid measure or liquid capacity is the gallon.

1 gallon	=	4 quarts	=	8 pints	=	16 cups	=	128 ounces

The basic unit of dry measure or dry capacity is the bushel.

1 bushel	=	4 pecks	=	32 dry quarts	=	64 dry pints	=	2,150.42 cubic inches
1 barrel	=	105 dry quarts						

The metric (SI) system

The metric, or SI system, is commonly used in many countries around the world for making everyday measurements. It is also the standard system used for scientific measurements. The metric system is convenient to use because units at different scales are related by multiples of ten.

The basic metric unit for *length* is the meter (m). The basic metric unit for *weight* or *mass* is the gram (g). The basic metric unit for *volume* is the liter (L).

The following table shows the most commonly used units.

COMMON METRIC UNITS		
1 cm	=	10 mm
1 m	=	1000 mm
1 m	=	100 cm
1 km	=	1000 m
1 L	=	1000 mL

Continued on next page

1 kL	=	1000 L
1 g	=	1000 mg
1 kg	=	1000 g

Appropriate units and equivalents

Different units within the same system of measurement are selected based on the scale at which the measurement is being made. For example, the height of a person is measured in feet whereas the distances between cities are measured in miles. To estimate measurements of familiar objects, it is necessary to first determine the units to be used.

Examples of appropriate units:

LENGTH	
The coastline of Florida	miles or kilometers
The width of a ribbon	inches or millimeters
The thickness of a book	inches or centimeters
The length of a football field	yards or meters
The depth of water in a pool	feet or meters

WEIGHT OR MASS	
A bag of sugar	pounds or grams
A school bus	tons or kilograms
A dime	ounces or grams

CAPACITY	
Bucket of paint for bedroom	gallons or liters
Glass of milk	cups or liters
Bottle of soda	quarts or liters
Medicine for child	ounces or milliliters

To estimate measurements, it is helpful to have a familiar reference with a known measurement. For instance, you can use the knowledge that a dollar bill is about 6 inches long or that a nickel weighs about 5 grams to make estimates of length and weight without actually measuring with a ruler or a balance.

APPROXIMATE MEASUREMENTS OF COMMON ITEMS		
ITEM APPROXIMATELY EQUAL TO	METRIC	IMPERIAL
carton of milk	1 liter	1 quart
yardstick	1 meter	1 yard
distance between highway markers	1 kilometer	1 mile
man's foot	30 centimeters	1 foot
math textbook	1 kilogram	2 pounds
average-sized man	75 kilograms	170 pounds
large paper clip	1 gram	1 ounce
thickness of a dime	2 millimeters	0.1 inch
1 football field	6400 sq. yd.	
boiling point of water	100°C	212°F
freezing point of water	0°C	32°F
1 cup of liquid	240 ml	8 fl. oz.
1 teaspoon	5 ml	

Estimate the measurement of the following items:

The length of an adult cow = _____ meters
The thickness of a compact disc = _____ millimeters
Your height = _____ meters
Length of your nose = _____ centimeters
Weight of your math textbook = _____ kilograms
Weight of an automobile = _____ kilograms
Weight of an aspirin = _____ grams

Conversions: unit analysis

There are many methods for converting measurements to other units within a system or between systems. One method is multiplication of the given measurement by a conversion factor. This conversion factor is the following ratio, which is always equal to unity.

$$\frac{\text{new units}}{\text{old units}} \quad \text{OR} \quad \frac{\text{what you want}}{\text{what you have}}$$

The fundamental feature of *unit analysis* or *dimensional analysis* is that conversion factors may be multiplied together and units cancelled in the same way as numerators and denominators of numerical fractions. The following examples help clarify this point.

Example: Convert 3 miles to yards.

Multiply the initial measurement by the conversion factor, cancel the mile units, and solve:

$$\frac{3 \text{ miles}}{1} \times \frac{1,760 \text{ yards}}{1 \text{ mile}} = 5280 \text{ yards}$$

Example: It takes Cynthia 45 minutes to get ready each morning. How many hours does she spend getting ready each week?

Multiply the initial measurement by the conversion factors from minutes to hours and from days to weeks, cancel the minute and day units and solve:

$$\frac{45 \text{ min}}{\text{day}} \times \frac{1 \text{ hour}}{60 \text{ min.}} \times \frac{7 \text{ days}}{\text{week}} = \frac{5.25 \text{ hours}}{\text{week}}$$

Conversion factors for different types of units are listed below.

Conversion factors

MEASUREMENTS OF LENGTH (ENGLISH SYSTEM)		
12 inches (in)	=	1 foot (ft)
3 feet (ft)	=	1 yard (yd)
1760 yards (yd)	=	1 mile (mi)

MEASUREMENTS OF LENGTH (METRIC SYSTEM)		
Kilometer (km)	=	1000 meters (m)
Hectometer (hm)	=	100 meters (m)

Continued on next page

Decameter (dam)	=	10 meters (m)
Meter (m)	=	1 meter (m)
Decimeter (dm)	=	$\frac{1}{10}$ meter (m)
Centimeter (cm)	=	$\frac{1}{100}$ meter (m)
Millimeter (mm)	=	$\frac{1}{1000}$ meter (m)

CONVERSION OF WEIGHT FROM METRIC TO ENGLISH		
28.35 grams (g)	=	1 ounce (oz)
1 metric ton (t)	=	1.1 ton (t)

MEASUREMENTS OF WEIGHT (METRIC SYSTEM)		
kilogram (kg)	=	1000 grams (g)
gram (g)	=	1 gram (g)
milligram (mg)	=	$\frac{1}{1000}$ gram (g)

CONVERSION OF VOLUME FROM ENGLISH TO METRIC		
1 teaspoon (tsp	≈	5 milliliters
1 fluid ounce	≈	15 milliliters
1 cup	≈	0.24 liters
1 pint	≈	0.47 liters

CONVERSION OF WEIGHT FROM ENGLISH TO METRIC		
28.35 grams	≈	1 ounce
0.454 kilogram	≈	1 pound
1 metric ton	=	1.1 ton

MEASUREMENT OF VOLUME (ENGLISH SYSTEM)		
8 fluid ounces (oz)	=	1 cup (c)
2 cups (c)	=	1 pint (pt)
2 pints (pt)	=	1 quart (qt)
4 quarts (qt)	=	1 gallon (gal)

MEASUREMENT OF VOLUME (METRIC SYSTEM)		
Kiloliter (kl)	=	1000 liters (l)
Liter (l)	=	1 liter (l)
Milliliter (ml)	=	$\frac{1}{1000}$ liter (ml)

CONVERSION OF VOLUME FROM ENGLISH TO METRIC		
1 teaspoon (tsp)	≈	5 milliliters
1 fluid ounce	≈	29.57 milliliters
1 cup	≈	0.24 liters
1 pint	≈	0.47 liters
1 quart	≈	0.95 liters
1 gallon	≈	3.8 liters

Note: (′) represents feet and (″) represents inches.

Example: Convert 8,750 meters to kilometers.

$$\frac{8,750 \text{ meters}}{1} \times \frac{1 \text{ kilometer}}{1000 \text{ meters}} = \underline{\hspace{1.5cm}} \text{km}$$
$$= 8.75 \text{ kilometers}$$

Example: 4 mi. = _____ yd.

1760 yd. = 1 mi.

$$4 \text{ mi.} \times 1760 \frac{\text{yd.}}{\text{mi.}} = 7040 \text{ yd.}$$

Square units can be derived with knowledge of basic units of length by squaring the equivalent measurements.

    1 square foot (sq. ft. or ft^2) = 144 sq. in.

    1 sq. yd. = 9 sq. ft.

    1 sq. yd. = 1296 sq. in.

Example: 14 sq. yd. = _____ sq. ft.

    1 sq. yd. = 9 sq. ft.

    14 sq. yd. $\times$ 9 $\frac{\text{sq. ft.}}{\text{sq. yd.}}$ = 126 sq. ft.

Example: A car skidded 170 yards on an icy road before coming to a stop. How long is the skid distance in kilometers?

Since 1 yard $\approx$ 0.9 meters, multiply 170 yards by 0.9 meters/1 yard.

    170 yd. $\times \frac{0.9 \text{ m}}{1 \text{ yd.}}$ = 153 m

Since 1000 meters = 1 kilometer, multiply 153 meters by 1 kilometer/1000 meters.

    153 m $\times \frac{1 \text{ km}}{1000 \text{ m}}$ = 0.153 km

Example: The distance around a race course is exactly 1 mile, 17 feet, and $9\frac{1}{4}$ inches. Approximate this distance to the nearest tenth of a foot.

Convert the distance to feet.

    1 mile = 1 = 1760 yards = 1760 $\times$ 3 feet = 5280 feet.

    $9\frac{1}{4}$ in. = $\frac{37}{4}$ in. $\times \frac{1 \text{ ft.}}{12 \text{ in.}}$ = $\frac{37}{48}$ ft. = 0.77083 ft.

So 1 mile, 17 ft. and $9\frac{1}{4}$ in. = 5280 ft. + 17 ft. + 0.77083 ft.

    = 5297.$\underline{7}$7083 ft.

Now, we need to round to the nearest tenth digit. The underlined 7 is in the tenths place. The digit in the hundredths place, also a 7, is greater than 5. Therefore, the 7 in the tenths place needs to be rounded up to 8 to get a final answer of 5297.8 feet.

Example: If the temperature is 90° F, what is it expressed in Celsius units?

To convert between Celsius (C) and Fahrenheit (F), use the following formula.

    $\frac{C}{5} = \frac{F - 32}{9}$

If F = 90, then C = $5\frac{(90 - 32)}{9}$ = $\frac{5 \times 58}{9}$ = 32.2.

Example: A map shows a scale of 1 inch = 2 miles. Convert this scale to a numerical ratio so that any unit system (such as metric) can be used to measure distances.

The scale is a ratio—1 inch : 2 miles. If either value is converted so that the two values have the same units, then this scale can be converted to a purely numerical ratio. To avoid fractions, convert miles to inches.

$$2 \text{ mi.} = 2 \text{ mi.} \times \frac{5{,}280 \text{ ft.}}{1 \text{ mi.}} \times \frac{12 \text{ in.}}{1 \text{ ft.}} = 126{,}720 \text{ in.}$$

The ratio is then 1:126,720.

SKILL 8.2 **Solving mathematical and real-world problems involving measurable attributes of simple or composite figures and shapes** *(e.g., length, capacity, angle measure)*

Area Problems

Some problems involve computing the area that remains when sections are cut out of a given figure composed of triangles, squares, rectangles, parallelograms, trapezoids, or circles. The strategy for solving problems of this nature should be to identify the given shapes and choose the correct formulas. Subtract the smaller cut-out shape from the larger shape.

Example: Find the area of one side of the metal in the circular flat washer shown below:

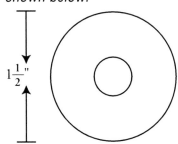

1. The shapes are both circles.

2. Use the formula $A = \pi r^2$ for both. (Inside diameter is $\frac{3}{8}$")

Area of larger circle
$A = \pi r^2$
$A = \pi(.75^2)$
$A = 1.76625 \text{ in}^2$

Area of smaller circle
$A = \pi r^2$
$A = \pi(.1875^2)$
$A = .1103906 \text{ in}^2$

Area of metal washer = larger area − smaller area
$= 1.76625 \text{ in}^2 - .1103906 \text{ in}^2$
$= 1.65585944 \text{ in}^2$

Example: You have decided to fertilize your lawn. The shapes and dimensions of your lot, house, pool, and garden are given in the diagram below. The shaded area will not be fertilized. If each bag of fertilizer costs $7.95 and covers 4,500 square feet, find the total number of bags needed and the total cost of the fertilizer.

Area of Lot	Area of House	Area of Driveway	Area of Garden	Area of Pool
$A = \frac{1}{2} h(b_1 + b_2)$	$A = LW$	$A = LW$	$A = s^2$	$A = \pi r^2$
$A = \frac{1}{2}(100)(180 + 160)$	$A = (80)(50)$	$A = (10)(25)$	$A = (20)^2$	$A = \pi(10)^2$
$A = 17,000$ sq ft	$A = 4,000$ sq ft	$A = 250$ sq ft	$A = 400$ sq ft	$A = 314.159$ sq ft

Total area to fertilize = Lot area − (House + Driveway + Pool + Garden)
$$= 17,000 - (4,000 + 250 + 314.159 + 400)$$
$$= 12,035.841 \text{ sq ft}$$

Number of bags needed = Total area to fertilize/4,500 sq ft. bag
$$= 12,035.841/4,500$$
$$= 2.67 \text{ bags}$$

Since we cannot purchase 2.67 bags we must purchase 3 full bags.

Total cost = Number of bags × $7.95
$$= 3 \times \$7.95$$
$$= \$23.85$$

Examining the change in area or volume of a given figure requires first finding the existing area given the original dimensions and then finding the new area given the increased dimensions.

Example: Given the rectangle below, determine the change in area if the length is increased by 5 and the width is increased by 7.

Draw and label a sketch of the new rectangle.

Find the areas.

Area of original = LW	Area of enlarged shape = LW
$= (7)(4)$	$= (12)(11)$
$= 28 \text{ units}^2$	$= 132 \text{ units}^2$

The change in area is $132 - 28 = 104 \text{ units}^2$.

To find the area of a compound shape, cut the compound shape into smaller, more familiar shapes, and then compute the total area by adding the areas of the smaller parts.

Example: Find the area of the given shape.

1. Using a dotted line, we have cut the shape into smaller parts that are familiar.

2. Use the appropriate formula for each shape and find the sum of all areas.

Area 1 $= LW$ Area 2 $= LW$ Area 3 $= \frac{1}{2}bh$

$\quad\quad = (5)(7)$ $= (12)(8)$ $= \frac{1}{2}(6)(8)$

$\quad\quad = 35 \text{ units}^2$ $= 96 \text{ units}^2$ $= 24 \text{ units}^2$

Total area $=$ Area 1 $+$ Area 2 $+$ Area 3

$\quad\quad\quad\quad = 35 + 96 + 24$

$\quad\quad\quad\quad = 155 \text{ units}^2$

Volume and Surface Area Problems

Use the following formulas to find volume and surface area.

FIGURE	VOLUME	TOTAL SURFACE AREA
Right Cylinder	$\pi r^2 h$	$2\pi rh + 2\pi r^2$
Right Cone	$\dfrac{\pi r^2 h}{3}$	$\pi r\sqrt{r^2 + h^2} + \pi r^2$
Sphere	$\dfrac{4}{3}\pi r^3$	$4\pi r^2$
Rectangular Solid	LWH	$2LW + 2WH + 2LH$

Note: $\sqrt{r^2 + h^2}$ is equal to the slant height of the cone.

Example: Given the figure below, find the volume and the surface area.

$r = 5$ in
$h = 6.2$ in

Volume $= \dfrac{\pi r^2 h}{3}$ First write the formula.

$\quad\quad = \frac{1}{3}\pi(5^2)(6.2)$ Then substitute.

$\quad\quad = 162.23333$ cubic inches   Compute.

Surface area $= \pi r\sqrt{r^2 + h^2} + \pi r^2$ First write the formula.

$\quad\quad = \pi 5\sqrt{5^2 + 6.2^2} + \pi 5^2$ Then substitute.

$\quad\quad = 203.549$ square inches   Compute.

Note: *Volume is always given in cubic units, and area is always given in square units.*

Area and Perimeter Problems

FIGURE	AREA FORMULA	PERIMETER FORMULA
Rectangle	LW	$2(L + W)$
Triangle	$\frac{1}{2}bh$	$a + b + c$
Parallelogram	bh	sum of lengths of sides
Trapezoid	$\frac{1}{2}h(a + b)$	sum of lengths of sides

Example: Find the area and perimeter of a rectangle if its length is 12 inches and its diagonal is 15 inches.

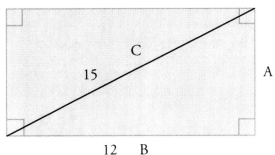

1. Draw and label sketch.
2. Since the height is still needed, use the Pythagorean formula to find missing leg of the triangle.

$A^2 + B^2 = C^2$
$A^2 + 12^2 = 15^2$
$A^2 = 15^2 - 12^2$
$A^2 = 81$
$A = 9$

Now use this information to find the area and perimeter.

$A = LW$	$P = 2(L + W)$	1. Write formula.
$A = (12)(9)$	$P = 2(12 + 9)$	2. Substitute.
$A = 108\ \text{in}^2$	$P = 42$ inches	3. Solve.

Circles

Given a circular figure, the formulas are as follows:

$A = \pi r^2 \quad C = \pi d \text{ or } 2\pi r$

Example:

If the area of a circle is 50 cm², find the circumference.

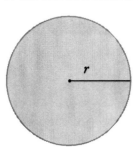

$A = 50$ cm²

1. Draw a sketch.

2. Determine what is still needed.

Use the area formula to find the radius.

$A = \pi r^2$	1. Write the formula.
$50 = \pi r^2$	2. Substitute.
$\frac{50}{\pi} = r^2$	3. Divide by π.
$15.924 = r^2$	4. Substitute.
$\sqrt{15.924} = \sqrt{r^2}$	5. Take the square root of both sides.
$3.99 \approx r$	6. Compute.

Use the approximate answer (due to rounding) to find the circumference.

$A = 2\pi r$	1. Write the formula.
$C = 2\pi(3.99)$	2. Substitute.
$C \approx 25.057$	3. Compute.

When using formulas to solve a geometry problem, it is helpful to use the same strategies used for general problem solving. First, draw and label a sketch if needed. Second, write down the formula and then substitute in the known values. This will assist in identifying what is still needed (the unknown). Finally, solve the resulting equation.

Being consistent in the strategic approach to problem solving is paramount to teaching the concept as well as solving it.

Example: Use the appropriate problem-solving strategies to find the solution.

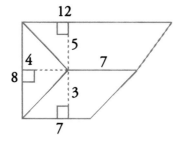

1. Find the area of the given figure.
2. Cut the figure into familiar shapes.
3. Identify what types of figures are given and write the appropriate formulas.

AREA OF FIGURE 1 (TRIANGLE)	AREA OF FIGURE 2 (PARALLELOGRAM)	AREA OF FIGURE 3 (TRAPEZOID)
$A = \frac{1}{2}bh$	$A = bh$	$A = \frac{1}{2}h(a + b)$
$A = \frac{1}{2}(8)(4)$	$A = (7)(3)$	$A = \frac{1}{2}(5)(12 + 7)$
$A = 16$ sq ft	$A = 21$ sq ft	$A = 47.5$ sq ft

Now find the total area by adding the area of all figures:

Total area $= 16 + 21 + 47.5$

$\qquad = 84.5$ sq. ft

Example: Given the figure below, find the area by dividing the polygon into smaller shapes.

1. Divide the figure into two triangles and a rectangle.
2. Find the missing lengths.
3. Find the area of each part.
4. Find the sum of all of the areas.

Find the base of both right triangles using the Pythagorean formula:

$a^2 + b^2 = c^2$	$a^2 + b^2 = c^2$
$a^2 + 12^2 = 15^2$	$a^2 + 12^2 = 20^2$
$a^2 = 225 - 144$	$a^2 = 400 - 144$
$a^2 = 81$	$a^2 = 256$
$a = 9$	$a = 16$

AREA OF TRIANGLE 1	AREA OF TRIANGLE 2	AREA OF RECTANGLE
$A = \frac{1}{2}bh$	$A = \frac{1}{2}bh$	$A = LW$
$A = \frac{1}{2}(9)(12)$	$A = \frac{1}{2}(16)(12)$	$A = (15)(12)$
$A = 54$ sq units	$A = 96$ sq units	$A = 180$ sq units

Find the sum of all three figures:
$54 + 96 + 180 = 330$ square units

Surface Area and Volume of Geometric Solids

To compute the surface area and volume of right prisms, cones, cylinders, spheres, and solids that are combinations of these figures, use the following formulas:

FIGURE	LATERAL AREA	TOTAL AREA	VOLUME
Right Prism	Ph	$2B + Ph$	Bh
Regular Pyramid	$\frac{1}{2}Pl$	$\frac{1}{2}Pl + B$	$\frac{1}{3}Bh$

P = Perimeter; h = height; B = Area of Base; l = slant height

Example: Find the total area of the given figure.

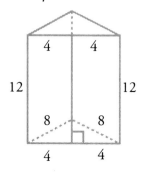

1. Since this is a triangular prism, first find the area of the bases.
2. Find the area of each rectangular lateral face.
3. Add the areas together.

$A = \frac{1}{2}bh$ 　　　　$A = LW$ 　　　 1. Write the formula.

$8^2 = 4^2 + h^2$ 　　　　　　　　　　　 2. Find the height of the base triangle.

　　　　　　　　　　$A = (8)(12)$ 　　 3. Substitute the known values.

$A = 27.713$ sq units 　　$A = 96$ sq units 　　 4. Compute.

Total Area $= 2(27.713) + 3(96)$

　　　　　 $= 343.426$ sq units

FIGURE	VOLUME	TOTAL SURFACE AREA	LATERAL AREA
Right Cylinder	$\pi r^2 h$	$2\pi rh + 2\pi r^2$	$2\pi rh$
Right Cone	$\dfrac{\pi r^2 h}{3}$	$\pi r\sqrt{r^2 + h^2} + \pi r^2$	$\pi r\sqrt{r^2 + h^2}$

Note: $\sqrt{r^2 + h^2}$ is equal to the slant height of the cone.

Example: A water company is trying to decide whether to use traditional cylindrical paper cups or to offer conical paper cups; they both cost the same. The traditional cups are 8 cm wide and 14 cm high. The conical cups are 12 cm wide and 19 cm high. The company will use the cup that holds more water.

Draw and label a sketch of each cup.

$V = \pi r^2 h$	$V = \frac{\pi r^2 h}{3}$	1. Write a formula.
$V = \pi (4)^2 (14)$	$V = \frac{1}{3} \pi (6)^2 (19)$	2. Substitute.
$V = 703.36 \text{ cm}^3$	$V = 715.92 \text{ cm}^3$	3. Solve.

The choice should be the conical cup, since its volume is greater.

FIGURE	VOLUME	TOTAL SURFACE AREA
Sphere	$\frac{4}{3} \pi r^3$	$4 \pi r^2$

Example: How much material is needed to make a basketball that has a diameter of 15 inches? How much air is needed to fill the basketball?

Draw and label a sketch:

$D = 15$ inches

Total surface area

$$\text{TSA} = 4 \pi r^2$$
$$= 4 \pi (7.5)^2$$
$$= 706.5 \text{ in}^2$$

Volume

$$V = \frac{4}{3} \pi r^3$$
$$= \frac{4}{3} \pi (7.5)^3$$
$$= 1766.25 \text{ in}^3$$

1. Write a formula.

2. Substitute.

3. Solve.

SKILL **Solving mathematical and real-world problems involving**
8.3 **indirect measurement** *(e.g., proportional reasoning, Pythagorean theorem, trigonometric ratios, unit circle trigonometry)*

Pythagorean Theorem

RIGHT TRIANGLE: a triangle with one right angle

A RIGHT TRIANGLE is a triangle with one right angle. The side opposite the right angle is called the hypotenuse. The other two sides are the legs.

The Pythagorean Theorem states that, for any right triangle, the square of the length of the hypotenuse is equal to the sum of the squares of the lengths of the legs. Symbolically, this is stated as:

$$c^2 = a^2 + b^2$$

The Pythagorean Theorem states that, for any right triangle, the square of the length of the hypotenuse is equal to the sum of the squares of the lengths of the legs.

Example: Given the right triangle below, find the missing side.

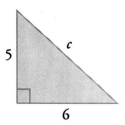

$c^2 = a^2 + b^2$	1. Write formula.
$c^2 = 5^2 + 6^2$	2. Substitute known values.
$c^2 = 61$	3. Take square root.
$c^2 = \sqrt{61}$ or 7.81	4. Solve.

The Converse of the Pythagorean Theorem states that if the square of the longest side of a triangle is equal to the sum of the squares of the other two sides, then the triangle is a right triangle.

The Converse of the Pythagorean Theorem states that if the square of the longest side of a triangle is equal to the sum of the squares of the other two sides, then the triangle is a right triangle.

Example: Given △XYZ, with sides measuring 12, 16, and 20 cm, is this a right triangle?

$$c^2 = a^2 + b^2$$
$$20^2 \overset{?}{\underset{}{=}} 12^2 + 16^2$$
$$400 \overset{?}{\underset{}{=}} 144 + 256$$
$$400 = 400$$

Yes, the triangle is a right triangle.

This theorem can be expanded to determine if triangles are obtuse or acute.

If the square of the longest side of a triangle is greater than the sum of the squares of the other two sides, then the triangle is an obtuse triangle. If the square of the longest side of a triangle is less than the sum of the squares of the other two sides, then the triangle is an acute triangle.

Example: Given △LMN with sides measuring 7, 12, and 14 inches, is the triangle right, acute, or obtuse?

$14^2 \underset{?}{} 7^2 + 12^2$

$196 \underset{?}{} 49 + 144$

$196 > 193$

Therefore, the triangle is obtuse.

When an altitude is drawn to the hypotenuse of a right triangle, then the two triangles formed are similar to the original triangle and to each other.

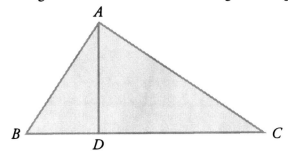

> *When an altitude is drawn to the hypotenuse of a right triangle, then the two triangles formed are similar to the original triangle and to each other.*

Given right triangle *ABC* with right angle at *A*, altitude *AD* drawn to hypotenuse *BC* at *D*, △*ABC* ~ △*ABD* ~ △*ACD*.

If a, b, and c are positive numbers such that $\frac{a}{b} = \frac{b}{c}$, then b is called the GEOMETRIC MEAN of a and c.

> **GEOMETRIC MEAN:** if a, b, and c are positive numbers such that $\frac{a}{b} = \frac{b}{c}$, then b is called the geometric mean of a and c

The geometric mean is significant when the altitude is drawn to the hypotenuse of a right triangle.

The length of the altitude is the geometric mean between each segment of the hypotenuse. Also, each leg is the geometric mean between the hypotenuse and the segment of the hypotenuse that is adjacent to the leg.

Example:

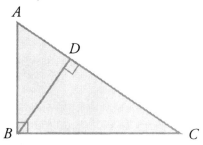

$\triangle ABC$ is a right triangle and $\angle ABC$ is a right angle. $AB = 6$ and $AC = 12$. Find AD, CD, BD, and BC.

$\dfrac{12}{6} = \dfrac{6}{AD}$ $\qquad\qquad$ $\dfrac{3}{BD} = \dfrac{BD}{9}$ $\qquad\qquad$ $\dfrac{12}{BC} = \dfrac{BC}{9}$

$12(AD) = 36$ $\qquad\qquad$ $(BD)^2 = 27$ $\qquad\qquad$ $(BC)^2 = 108$

$AD = 3$

$BD = \sqrt{27} = \sqrt{9 \times 3} = 3\sqrt{3}$

$BC = 6\sqrt{3}$

$CD = 12 - 3 = 9$

Trigonometric Ratios

Trigonometric ratios can be used to solve problems involving distances and angles as in the example below.

Example: Find the length of side x in the triangle below.

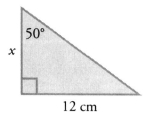

$\tan 50 = \dfrac{\text{opposite}}{\text{adjacent}} = \dfrac{12}{x}$

$1.192 = \dfrac{12}{x}$

$x(1.192) = 12$

$x = 10.07 \text{ cm}$

Trigonometric functions can also be applied to nonright triangles by way of the law of sines and the law of cosines. Consider the arbitrary triangle shown below with angles *A, B,* and *C* and corresponding opposite sides *a, b,* and *c.*

> *Trigonometric functions can be applied to nonright triangles by way of the law of sines and the law of cosines.*

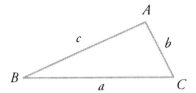

The law of sines is a proportional relationship between the lengths of the sides of the triangle and the opposite angles. The law of sines is given below:

$$\frac{a}{\sin A} = \frac{b}{\sin B} = \frac{c}{\sin C}.$$

The law of cosines permits determination of the length of a side of an arbitrary triangle as long as the lengths of the other two sides, along with the angle opposite the unknown side, are known. The law of cosines is given below:

$$c^2 = a^2 + b^2 - 2ab \cos C.$$

Example: An inlet is 140 feet wide. The lines of sight from each bank to an approaching ship are 79 degrees and 58 degrees. What are the distances from each bank to the ship?

First, draw an appropriate sketch of the situation with the appropriate labels for the parameters.

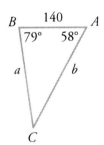

Since the sum of the angles in a triangle is 180°, angle C must be 43°. Use the law of sines to calculate the lengths of sides a and b.

For side b:

$$\frac{b}{\sin 79°} = \frac{140 \text{ feet}}{\sin 43°}$$

$$b = \frac{\sin 79°}{\sin 43°} 140 \text{ feet} \approx 201.5 \text{ feet}$$

And for side a:

$$\frac{a}{\sin 58°} = \frac{140 \text{ feet}}{\sin 43°}$$

$$a = \frac{\sin 58°}{\sin 43°} 140 \text{ feet} \approx 174.1 \text{ feet}$$

Example: Find the length of side b in the triangle below if angle B = 87.5°, a = 12.3, and c = 23.2. (Compute to the nearest tenth.)

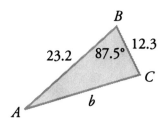

$$b^2 = a^2 + c^2 - (2ac) \cos B$$
$$b^2 = (12.3)^2 + (23.2)^2 - 2(12.3)(23.2)(\cos 87.5)$$
$$b^2 = 664.636$$
$$b = 25.8$$

Proportional Reasoning

The ratio of any two corresponding measurements of similar solids is the scale factor.

Similar solids share the same shape but are not necessarily the same size. The ratio of any two corresponding measurements of similar solids is the scale factor. For example, the scale factor for two square pyramids, one with a side measuring 2 inches and the other with a side measuring 4 inches, is 2:4.

2   4

The base perimeter, the surface area, and the volume of similar solids are directly related to the scale factor. If the scale factor of two similar solids is $a{:}b$, then

- ratio of base perimeters = $a{:}b$

- ratio of areas = $a^2{:}b^2$

- ratio of volumes = $a^3{:}b^3$

Thus, for the above example,

- ratio of base perimeters $= 2:4$

- ratio of areas $= 2^2:4^2 = 4:16$

- ratio of volumes $= 2^3:4^3 = 8:64$

Example: What happens to the volume of a square pyramid when the lengths of the sides of the base are doubled?

scale factor $= a:b = 1:2$

ratio of volume $= 1^3:2^3 = 1:8$

The volume is increased 8 times.

Example: Given the following measurements for two similar cylinders with a scale factor of 2:5 (cylinder A to cylinder B), determine the height, radius, and volume of each cylinder.

cylinder A: $r = 2$

cylinder B: $h = 10$

For cylinder A,

$$\frac{h_a}{10} = \frac{2}{5}$$

$5h_a = 20$ Solve for h_a

$h_a = 4$

Volume of cylinder A $= \pi r^2 h = \pi(2)^2 4 = 16\pi$

For cylinder B,

$$\frac{2}{r_b} = \frac{2}{5}$$

$2r_b = 10$ Solve for r_b

$r_b = 5$

Volume of cylinder B $= \pi r^2 h = \pi(5)^2 10 = 250\pi$

SKILL **Solving problems involving the effects of changing the dimensions**
8.4 **of a figure or shape on its area and volume**

For examples of the effects of changing dimensions, see Skills 8.2 and 8.3.

COMPETENCY 9
ANALYZE FIGURES AND SHAPES IN TWO AND THREE DIMENSIONS

**SKILL Applying the properties of polygons and circles to solve
9.1 mathematical and real-world problems**

POLYGON: a simple closed figure composed of line segments

CONVEX POLYGON: a polygon in which the measure of each internal angle is less than 180 degrees

REGULAR POLYGON: a polygon for which all sides are the same length and all interior angles are the same measure

A **POLYGON** is a simple closed figure composed of line segments. Here we will consider only **CONVEX POLYGONS**, i.e., polygons for which the measure of each internal angle is less than 180°. Of the two polygons shown below, the one on the left is a convex polygon.

A **REGULAR POLYGON** is one for which all sides are the same length and all interior angles are the same measure.

The sum of the measures of the interior angles of a polygon can be determined using the following formula, where n represents the number of angles in the polygon.

Sum of $\angle$s $= 180(n - 2)$

The measure of each angle of a regular polygon can be found by dividing the sum of the measures by the number of angles.

Measure of $\angle = \frac{180(n - 2)}{n}$

Example: Find the measure of each angle of a regular octagon. Since an octagon has eight sides, each angle equals

$$\frac{180(8 - 2)}{8} = \frac{180(6)}{8} = 135°.$$

The sum of the measures of the *exterior angles* of a polygon, taken one angle at each vertex, equals 360°.

The measure of each exterior angle of a regular polygon can be determined using the following formula, where n represents the number of angles in the polygon.

Measure of exterior $\angle$ of regular polygon

$$\angle = 180 - \frac{180(n-2)}{n} = \frac{360}{n}$$

Example: Find the measure of the interior and exterior angles of a regular pentagon.

Since a pentagon has five sides, each exterior angle measures:

$$\frac{360}{5} = 72°$$

Since each exterior angle is supplementary to its interior angle, the interior angle measures $180 - 72$ or $108°$.

Properties of Quadrilaterals

A QUADRILATERAL is a polygon with four sides. The sum of the measures of the angles of a convex quadrilateral is 360°.

A TRAPEZOID is a quadrilateral with exactly one pair of parallel sides.

The two parallel sides of a trapezoid are called the bases, and the two nonparallel sides are called the legs. If the two legs are the same length, then the trapezoid is called an ISOSCELES TRAPEZOID.

The segment connecting the two midpoints of the legs is called the median. The median has the following two properties:

1. The median is parallel to the two bases.

2. The length of the median is equal to one-half the sum of the length of the two bases.

In an isosceles trapezoid, the nonparallel sides are congruent.

An isosceles trapezoid has the following properties:

1. The diagonals of an isosceles trapezoid are congruent.

2. The base angles of an isosceles trapezoid are congruent.

> **QUADRILATERAL:** a polygon with four sides

> **TRAPEZOID:** a quadrilateral with exactly one pair of parallel sides

> **ISOSCELES TRAPEZOID:** a trapezoid with two legs of equal length

Example: An isosceles trapezoid has a diagonal of 10 and a base angle measuring 30°. Find the measures of the other three angles.

Based on the properties of trapezoids, the measure of the other base angle is 30° and the measure of the other diagonal is 10. The other two angles have a measure of:

$$360 = 30(2) + 2x$$
$$x = 150°$$

The other two angles measure 150° each.

> **PARALLELOGRAM:** a quadrilateral with two pairs of parallel sides

A PARALLELOGRAM is a quadrilateral with two pairs of parallel sides. A parallelogram has the following properties:

1. The diagonals bisect each other.

2. Each diagonal divides the parallelogram into two congruent triangles.

3. Both pairs of opposite sides are congruent.

4. Both pairs of opposite angles are congruent.

5. Two adjacent angles are supplementary.

Example: Find the measures of the other three angles of a parallelogram if one angle measures 38°.

Since opposite angles are equal, there are two angles measuring 38°. Since adjacent angles are supplementary, $180 - 38 = 142$. Hence the other two angles measure 142° each.

Example: The measures of two adjacent angles of a parallelogram are 3x + 40 and x + 70. Find the measure of each angle.

$$2(3x + 40) + 2(x + 70) = 360$$
$$6x + 80 + 2x + 140 = 360$$
$$8x + 220 = 360$$
$$8x = 140$$
$$x = 17.5$$
$$3x + 40 = 92.5$$
$$x + 70 = 87.5$$

Thus the angles measure 92.5°, 92.5°, 87.5°, and 87.5°.

> **RECTANGLE:** a parallelogram with a right angle

A RECTANGLE is a parallelogram with a right angle. Since a rectangle is a special type of parallelogram, it exhibits all the properties of a parallelogram. All the angles of a rectangle are right angles because of congruent opposite angles. Additionally, the diagonals of a rectangle are congruent.

A RHOMBUS is a parallelogram with all sides equal in length. A rhombus has all the properties of a parallelogram. Additionally, its diagonals are perpendicular to each other, and they bisect its angles.

RHOMBUS: a parallelogram with all sides equal in length

A SQUARE is a rectangle with all sides equal in length. A square has all the properties of a rectangle and of a rhombus.

SQUARE: a rectangle with all sides equal in length

TRUE OR FALSE?	
All squares are rhombuses	True
All parallelograms are rectangles	False—*Some* parallelograms are rectangles
All rectangles are parallelograms	True
Some rhombuses are squares	True
Some rectangles are trapezoids	False—Trapezoids have only one pair of parallel sides
All quadrilaterals are parallelograms	False—*Some* quadrilaterals are parallelograms
Some squares are rectangles	False—*All* squares are rectangles
Some parallelograms are rhombuses	True

Example: In rhombus ABCD, side AB = 3x − 7 and side CD = x + 15. Find the length of each side.

Since all the sides are the same length,

$$3x − 7 = x + 15$$
$$2x = 22$$
$$x = 11$$

Since $3(11) − 7 = 25$ and $11 + 15 = 25$, each side measures 25 units.

CIRCUMFERENCE: the distance around a circle

The distance around a circle is called the CIRCUMFERENCE. The ratio of the circumference to the diameter is represented by the Greek letter pi, where $\pi \approx$ 3.14. The circumference of a circle is given by the formula $C = 2\pi r$ or $C = \pi d$, where r is the radius of the circle and d is the diameter. The area of a circle is given by the formula $A = \pi r^2$.

We can extend the area formula of a regular polygon to obtain the area of a circle by considering the fact that a circle is essentially a regular polygon with an infinite number of sides. The radius of a circle is equivalent to the apothem of a regular polygon. Thus, applying the area formula for a regular polygon to a circle, we get

$$\tfrac{1}{2} \times \text{perimeter} \times \text{apothem} = \tfrac{1}{2} \times 2\pi r \times r = \pi r^2$$

If two circles have radii that are in a ratio of $a{:}b$, then the following ratios also apply to the circles:

1. The diameters are in the ratio $a{:}b$.

2. The circumferences are in the ratio $a{:}b$.

3. The areas are in the ratio $a^2 : b^2$, or the ratio of the areas is the square of the ratio of the radii.

CENTRAL ANGLE: the angle formed by two radii that intersect in the center of a circle

If you draw two radii in a circle, the angle they form with the center as the vertex is a CENTRAL ANGLE. The piece of the circle "inside" the angle is an arc. Just like a central angle, an arc can have any degree measure from 0 to 360. The measure of an arc is equal to the measure of the central angle that forms the arc. Since a diameter forms a semicircle and the measure of a straight angle like a diameter is 180°, the measure of a semicircle is also 180°.

MINOR ARC: an arc with measure less than 180°

MAJOR ARC: an arc with measure greater than 180°

Given two points on a circle, the two points form two different arcs. Except in the case of semicircles, one of the two arcs will always be greater than 180°, and the other will be less than 180°. The arc less than 180° is a MINOR ARC and the arc greater than 180° is a MAJOR ARC.

Examples:

1.

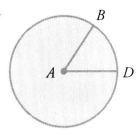

$m\angle BAD = 45°$

What is the measure of the major arc *BD*?

minor arc $BD = m\angle BAD = 45°$

$360 - 45 =$ major arc *BD*

Thus, major arc $BD = 315°$.

A major and minor arc always add up to 360°.

2.

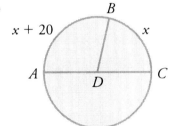

$\overline{AC}$ is a diameter of circle *D*.

What is the measure of $\angle BDC$?

$m\angle ADB + m\angle BDC = 180°$
$x + 20 + x = 180$
$2x + 20 = 180$
$2x = 160$
$x = 80$

A diameter forms a semicircle that has a measure of 180°.

minor arc $BC = 80°$
$m\angle BDC = 80°$

A central angle has the same measure as the arc it forms.

Although an arc has a measure associated to the degree measure of a central angle, it also has a length that is a fraction of the circumference of the circle. For each central angle and its associated arc, there is a sector of the circle that resembles a pie piece. The area of such a sector is a fraction of the area of the circle. The fractions used for the area of a sector and length of its associated arc are both equal to the ratio of the central angle to 360°.

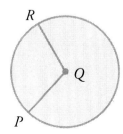

$$\frac{\angle PQR}{360°} = \frac{\text{length of arc } RP}{\text{circumference of circle}} = \frac{\text{area of sector } PQR}{\text{area of circle}}$$

Examples:

1.

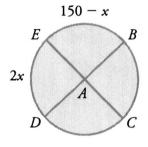

$150 - x$

$2x$

$2x + 150 - x = 180$
$x + 150 = 180$
$x = 30$

Arc $ED = 2(30) = 60°$

Circle A as a radius of 4 cm. What is the length of arc ED?

Arc BE and arc ED make a semicircle.

The ratio 60° to 360° is equal to the ratio of arc length ED to the circumference of circle A.

$\frac{60}{360} = \frac{\text{arc length } ED}{2\pi4}$
$\frac{1}{6} = \frac{\text{arc length}}{8\pi}$
arc length $= \frac{8\pi}{6} = \frac{4\pi}{3}$

Cross multiply and solve for the arc length.

2.

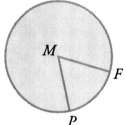

Circumference of circle $M =$
$2\pi(3) = 6\pi$

Area of circle $M = \pi \times 3^2 = 9\pi$

$\frac{\text{area of } MPF}{9\pi} = \frac{2\pi}{6\pi}$

$\frac{\text{area of } MPF}{9\pi} = \frac{1}{3}$
area of $MPF = \frac{9\pi}{3}$
area of $MPF = 3\pi$

The radius of circle M is 3 cm. The length of arc PF is 2π cm. What is the area of sector MPF?

Find the circumference and area of the circle.

The ratio of the sector area to the circle area is the same as the arc length to the circumference.

Solve for the area of the sector.

A TANGENT LINE to a circle intersects or touches the circle in exactly one point. If a radius is drawn to that point, the radius will be perpendicular to the tangent.

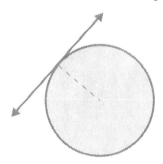

TANGENT LINE: a line that intersects or touches a circle in exactly one point

A SECANT LINE intersects a circle in two points and includes a CHORD, which is a line segment with endpoints on the circle. If a radius or diameter is perpendicular to a chord, the radius will cut the chord into two equal parts and vice versa.

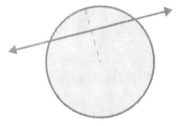

SECANT LINE: a line that intersects a circle in two points

CHORD: a line segment with endpoints on a circle

If two chords in the same circle have the same length, the two chords will have arcs that are the same length, and the two chords will be equidistant from the center of the circle. Distance from the center to a chord is measured by finding the length of a segment from the center perpendicular to the chord.

Examples:

1.

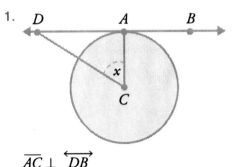

$\overleftrightarrow{DB}$ is tangent to circle C at A.
$m\angle ADC = 40°$. Find x.

$\overline{AC} \perp \overleftrightarrow{DB}$	A radius is $\perp$ to a tangent at the point of tangency.
$m\angle DAC = 90°$	Two segments that are $\perp$ form a 90° angle.
$40 + 90 + x = 180$	The sum of the angles of a triangle is 180°.
$x = 50°$	Solve for x.

2.

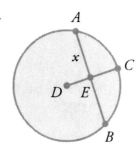

$\overline{CD}$ is a radius and $\overline{CD} \perp$ chord $\overline{AB}$.

$\overline{AB} = 10$. Find x.

$x = \frac{1}{2}(10)$

$x = 5$

If a radius is $\perp$ to a chord, the radius bisects the chord.

INSCRIBED ANGLE: an angle whose vertex is on the circumference of a circle

An INSCRIBED ANGLE is an angle whose vertex is on the circumference of a circle. Such an angle could be formed by two chords, two diameters, two secants, or a secant and a tangent. An inscribed angle has one arc of the circle in its interior. The measure of the inscribed angle is one-half the measure of its intercepted arc. If two inscribed angles intercept the same arc, the two angles are congruent (i.e., their measures are equal). If an inscribed angle intercepts an entire semicircle, the angle is a right angle.

When two chords intersect inside a circle, two sets of vertical angles are formed in the interior of the circle. Each set of vertical angles intercepts two arcs that are across from each other. The measure of an angle formed by two chords in a circle is equal to one-half the sum of the arc intercepted by the angle and the arc intercepted by its vertical angle.

If an angle has its vertex outside of the circle and each side of the angle intersects the circle, then the angle contains two different arcs. The measure of the angle is equal to one-half the difference of the two arcs.

Examples:

1.

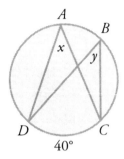

Find *x* and *y*.

$m\angle DAC = \frac{1}{2}(40) = 20°$

$\angle DAC$ and $\angle DBC$ are both inscribed angles, so each one has a measure equal to one-half the measure of arc *DC*.

$m\angle DBC = \frac{1}{2}(40) = 20°$

$x = 20°$ and $y = 20°$

2.

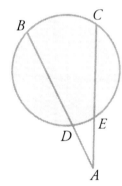

Find the measure of arc *BC* if the measure of arc *DE* is 30° and angle *BAC* = 20°.

$m\angle BAC = \frac{1}{2}(mBC - mDE)$

$\rightarrow 2 \times m\angle BAC = mBC - mDE$

$\rightarrow mBC = 2 \times m\angle BAC + mDE = 2 \times 20° + 30° = 70°$

If *two chords intersect inside a circle*, each chord is divided into two smaller segments. The product of the lengths of the two segments formed from one chord equals the product of the lengths of the two segments formed from the other chord.

If *two tangent segments intersect outside of a circle*, the two segments have the same length.

If *two secant segments intersect outside a circle*, a portion of each segment will lie inside the circle and a portion (called the exterior segment) will lie outside the circle. The product of the length of one secant segment and the length of its exterior segment equals the product of the length of the other secant segment and the length of its exterior segment.

If *a tangent segment and a secant segment intersect outside a circle*, the square of the length of the tangent segment equals the product of the length of the secant segment and its exterior segment.

Examples:

1.

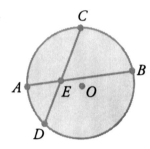

$\overline{AB}$ and $\overline{CD}$ are chords.

$CE = 10$, $ED = x$, $AE = 5$, $EB = 4$

$(AE)(EB) = (CE)(ED)$

Since the chords intersect in the circle, the products of the segment pieces are equal.

$5(4) = 10x$
$20 = 10x$
$x = 2$

Solve for x.

2.

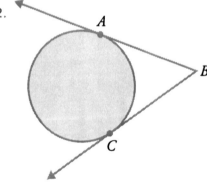

$\overline{AB} = x^2 + x - 2$

$\overline{CB} = 5 - 3x + x^2$

Find the length of $\overline{AB}$ and $\overline{BC}$

$\overline{AB} = x^2 + x - 2$
$\overline{BC} = x^2 - 3x + 5$

Given

$\overline{AB} = \overline{BC}$

Intersecting tangents are equal.

$x^2 + x - 2 = x^2 - 3x + 5$

Set the expressions equal to each other and solve.

$4x = 7$
$x = 1.75$
$(1.75)^2 + 1.75 - 2 = \overline{AB}$
$\overline{AB} = \overline{BC} = 2.81$

Substitute and solve.

Congruence

CONGRUENT figures have the same size and shape; i.e., if one of the figures is superimposed on the other, the boundaries coincide exactly. Congruent line segments have the same length; congruent angles have equal measures. The symbol $\cong$ is used to indicate that two figures, line segments, or angles are congruent.

> **CONGRUENT:** having the same size and shape

The reflexive, symmetric, and transitive properties described for algebraic equality relationships may also be applied to congruence. For instance, if $\angle A \cong \angle B$ and $\angle A \cong \angle D$, then $\angle B \cong \angle D$ (transitive property).

The polygons (pentagons) $ABCDE$ and $VWXYZ$ shown below are congruent since they are exactly the same size and shape.

 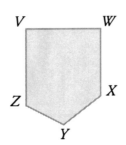

$$ABCDE \cong VWXYZ$$

Corresponding parts are congruent angles and congruent sides. For the polygons shown above:

corresponding angles	corresponding sides
$\angle A \leftrightarrow \angle V$	$AB \leftrightarrow VW$
$\angle B \leftrightarrow \angle W$	$BC \leftrightarrow WX$
$\angle C \leftrightarrow \angle X$	$CD \leftrightarrow XY$
$\angle D \leftrightarrow \angle Y$	$DE \leftrightarrow YZ$
$\angle E \leftrightarrow \angle Z$	$AE \leftrightarrow VZ$

Two triangles are congruent if each of the three angles and three sides of one triangle match up in a one-to-one fashion with congruent angles and sides of the second triangle. To see how the sides and angles match up, it is sometimes necessary to imagine rotating or reflecting one of the triangles so the two figures are oriented in the same position.

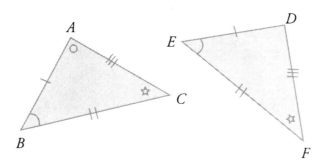

In the example above, the two triangles *ABC* and *DEF* are congruent if these 6 conditions are met:

1. $\angle A \cong \angle D$
2. $\angle B \cong \angle E$
3. $\angle C \cong \angle F$
4. $\overline{AB} \cong \overline{DE}$
5. $\overline{BC} \cong \overline{EF}$
6. $\overline{AC} \cong \overline{DF}$

The congruent angles and segments "correspond" to each other.

It is not always necessary to demonstrate all of the above six conditions to prove that two triangles are congruent. There are several "shortcut" methods described below.

> **SAS POSTULATE:** (side-angle-side) if two sides and the included angle of one triangle are congruent to two sides and the included angle of another triangle, then the two triangles are congruent

The **SAS POSTULATE** (side-angle-side) states that if two sides and the included angle of one triangle are congruent to two sides and the included angle of another triangle, then the two triangles are congruent.

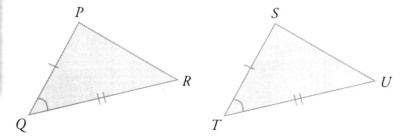

To see why this is true, imagine moving the triangle *PQR* (shown above) in such a way that the point *P* coincides with the point *S*, and line segment *PQ* coincides with line segment ST. Point *Q* will then coincide with *T*, since $PQ \cong ST$. Also, segment *QR* will coincide with *TU*, because $\angle Q \cong \angle T$. Point *R* will coincide with *U*, because $QR \cong TU$. Since *P* and *S* coincide and *R* and *U* coincide, line *PR* will coincide with *SU* because two lines cannot enclose a space. Thus the two triangles match perfectly point for point and are congruent.

Example: Are the following triangles congruent?

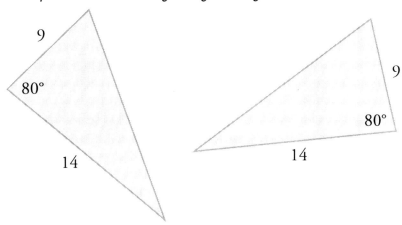

Each of the two triangles has a side that is 14 units and another that is 9 units. The angle included in the sides is 80° in both triangles. Therefore, the triangles are congruent by SAS.

The SSS POSTULATE (side-side-side) states that if three sides of one triangle are congruent to three sides of another triangle, then the two triangles are congruent.

> **SSS POSTULATE:** (side-side-side) if three sides of one triangle are congruent to three sides of another triangle, then the two triangles are congruent

Since $AB \cong XY$, $BC \cong YZ$ and $AC \cong XZ$, then $\triangle ABC \cong \triangle XYZ$.

Example: Given isosceles triangle ABC with D being the midpoint of base AC, prove that the two triangles ABD and ADC are congruent.

Proof:

1. Isosceles triangle *ABC*,
   D midpoint of base *AC*   Given

2. $AB \cong AC$ An isosceles triangle has two congruent sides

3. $BD \cong DC$ Midpoint divides a line into two equal parts

4. $AD \cong AD$ Reflexive property

5. $\triangle ABD \cong \triangle BCD$ SSS

> **ASA POSTULATE:** (angle-side-angle) if two angles and the included side of one triangle are congruent to two angles and the included side of another triangle, the triangles are congruent

The ASA POSTULATE (angle-side-angle) states that if two angles and the included side of one triangle are congruent to two angles and the included side of another triangle, the triangles are congruent.

$\angle A \cong \angle X, \angle B \cong \angle Y, AB \cong XY$ then $\triangle ABC \cong \triangle XYZ$ by ASA

Example: Given two right triangles with one leg (AB and KL) of each measuring 6 cm and the adjacent angle 37°, prove the triangles are congruent.

Proof:

1. Right $\triangle ABC$ and $\triangle KLM$ Given
   $AB = KL = 6$ cm
   $\angle A = \angle K = 37°$

2. $AB \cong KL; \angle A \cong \angle K$ Figures with the same measure are congruent

3. $\angle B \cong \angle L$ All right angles are congruent

4. $\triangle ABC \cong \triangle KLM$ ASA

Example: What method could be used to prove that triangles ABC and ADE are congruent?

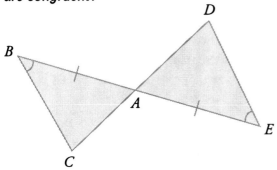

The sides *AB* and *AE* are given as congruent, as are ∠*ABC* and ∠*ADE*. ∠*BAC* and ∠*DAE* are vertical angles and are therefore congruent. Thus triangles *ABC* and *ADE* are congruent by the ASA postulate.

The HL THEOREM (hypotenuse-leg) is a congruence shortcut that can only be used with right triangles. According to this theorem, if the hypotenuse and leg of one right triangle are congruent to the hypotenuse and leg of the other right triangle, then the two triangles are congruent.

HL THEOREM: if the hypotenuse and leg of one right triangle are congruent to the hypotenuse and leg of another right triangle, then the two triangles are congruent

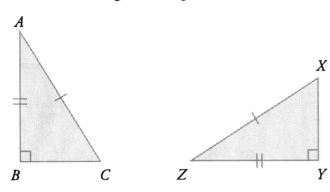

If ∠*B* and ∠*Y* are right angles and *AC* ≅ *XZ* (hypotenuse of each triangle), *AB* ≅ *YZ* (corresponding leg of each triangle), then Δ*ABC* ≅ Δ*XYZ* by HL.

Proof:

1. ∠*B* ≅ ∠*Y*
   AB ≅ *YZ*
   AC ≅ *XZ*   Given

2. $BC = \sqrt{AC^2 - AB^2} =$ Pythagorean theorem

3. $XY = \sqrt{XZ^2 - YZ^2}$ Pythagorean theorem

4. $XY = \sqrt{AC^2 - AB^2} = BC$ Substitution (*XZ* ≅ *AC*, *YZ* ≅ *AB*)

5. Δ*ABC* ≅ Δ*XYZ*   SAS (*AB* ≅ *YZ*, ∠*B* ≅ ∠*Y*, *BC* ≅ *XY*)

SIMILAR: having the same shape but not necessarily the same size

Similarity

Two figures that have the same shape are SIMILAR. To be the same shape, corresponding angles must be equal. Therefore, polygons are similar if and only if there is a one-to-one correspondence between their vertices such that the corresponding angles are congruent. For similar figures, the lengths of corresponding sides are proportional. The symbol ~ is used to indicate that two figures are similar.

For similar figures, the lengths of corresponding sides are proportional.

The polygons *ABCDE* and *VWXYZ* shown below are similar.

 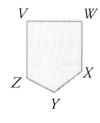

$ABCDE \sim VWXYZ$

Corresponding angles: $\angle A = \angle V, \angle B = \angle W, \angle C = \angle X, \angle D = \angle Y, \angle E = \angle Z$

Corresponding sides: $\frac{AB}{VW} = \frac{BC}{WX} = \frac{CD}{XY} = \frac{DE}{YZ} = \frac{AE}{VZ}$

Example: Given two similar quadrilaterals, find the lengths of sides x, y, and z.

Since corresponding sides are proportional, $\frac{15}{25} = \frac{3}{5}$, so the scale factor is $\frac{3}{5}$.

$$\frac{12}{x} = \frac{3}{5} \qquad \frac{21}{y} = \frac{3}{5} \qquad \frac{z}{30} = \frac{3}{5}$$
$$3x = 60 \qquad 3y = 105 \qquad 5z = 90$$
$$x = 20 \qquad y = 35 \qquad z = 18$$

Just as for congruence, there are shortcut methods that can be used to prove similarity.

AA SIMILARITY POSTULATE: if two angles of one triangle are congruent to two angles of another triangle, then the triangles are similar

According to the AA SIMILARITY POSTULATE, if two angles of one triangle are congruent to two angles of another triangle, then the triangles are similar. It is obvious that if two of the corresponding angles are congruent, the third set of corresponding angles must be congruent as well. Hence, showing AA is sufficient to prove that two triangles are similar.

The SAS SIMILARITY THEOREM states that if an angle of one triangle is congruent to an angle of another triangle, and the sides adjacent to those angles are in proportion, then the triangles are similar.

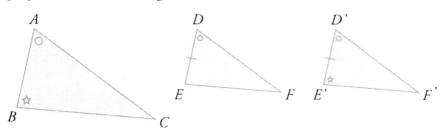

If $\angle A = \angle D$ and $\frac{AB}{DE} = \frac{AC}{DF}$, $\triangle ABC \sim \triangle DEF$.

> **SAS SIMILARITY THEOREM:** if an angle of one triangle is congruent to an angle of another triangle, and the sides adjacent to those angles are in proportion, then the triangles are similar

Example: A graphic artist is designing a logo containing two triangles. The artist wants the triangles to be similar. Determine whether the artist has created similar triangles.

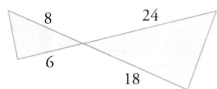

The sides are proportional ($\frac{8}{24} = \frac{6}{18} = \frac{1}{3}$) and vertical angles are congruent. The two triangles are therefore similar by the SAS similarity theorem.

According to the SSS SIMILARITY THEOREM, if the sides of two triangles are in proportion, then the triangles are similar.

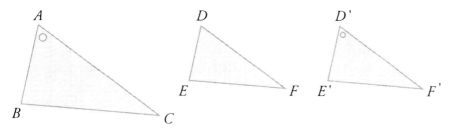

> **SSS SIMILARITY THEOREM:** if the sides of two triangles are in proportion, then the triangles are similar

If $\frac{AB}{DE} = \frac{AC}{DF} = \frac{BC}{EF}$, $\triangle ABC \sim \triangle DEF$

Example: Tommy draws and cuts out 2 triangles for a school project. One of them has sides of 3, 6, and 9 inches. The other triangle has sides of 2, 4, and 6. Is there a relationship between the two triangles?

Determine the proportions of the corresponding sides.

$$\frac{2}{3} \qquad \frac{4}{6} = \frac{2}{3} \qquad \frac{6}{9} = \frac{2}{3}$$

The smaller triangle is $\frac{2}{3}$ the size of the large triangle, therefore they are similar triangles by the SSS similarity theorem.

See Skill 8.3 for a discussion of similar solids

SKILL 9.3 Analyzing formal and informal arguments and proofs

PROOF: an argument that demonstrates the truth (or falsity) of a proposition

Mathematical proofs begin with certain axioms or known propositions and, by some line of reasoning, deduce a particular conclusion.

A **PROOF** is an argument that demonstrates the truth (or falsity) of a proposition. Mathematical proofs begin with certain axioms or known propositions and, by some line of reasoning, deduce a particular conclusion. (For more on deduction and induction, see the next skill section.)

Because not all concepts in mathematics can be proven or otherwise defined (if this were the case, then either circular definitions/proofs would be required—but these are not informative—or an infinite regression of definitions/proofs would be required—but these are impossible), mathematical proofs necessarily start from certain unproven or undefined concepts. In geometry, for instance, the concept of a point is undefined.

Mathematical proofs attempt to reason in a consistent and orderly way from known premises (as long as they are either defined to be true or are proven to be true) to nontrivial conclusions. This process may involve positively demonstrating a proposition through direct proof, which involves showing that the proposition is true, or it may involve indirect proof, which involves showing that the negation (opposite) of the proposition is false. Both approaches are valid, but one or the other may be simpler.

Because some propositions can be shown to be false through a single counter-example, indirect proof is sometimes the simplest method of proof. Indirect proof may also involve using the opposite of the proposition being proved to demonstrate that a contradiction is reached. In such a case, assuming that all other premises are true, then the opposite of the proposition being proved must be false. Consider the following example.

Example: Prove that there are no even prime numbers other than the number 2.

A direct proof of this proposition may be possible, but an indirect proof is much simpler. Assume that the opposite is true: There is an even prime number other than 2. Let this number be called x (an integer). Since x is even, then the following must be true, where y is an integer.

$$\frac{x}{2} = y$$

But if x is evenly divisible by 2, it cannot be a prime number. Thus, a contradiction is reached with the originally assumed proposition that x is prime. This proves that there are no even prime numbers other than 2.

Formal reasoning, which includes deductive reasoning, follows a structured and orderly approach according to various rules of inference. Informal reasoning, which includes inductive reasoning, is less structured and tends not to be as rigorous as formal reasoning. Both of these types of reasoning, however, can be used to justify mathematical ideas.

Formal reasoning is applied for rigorous proofs and deriving conclusions in a way that provides certainty of the results. Informal reasoning is applied to situations where it is necessary to lend evidence to a conjecture or to build a strong (but not necessarily conclusive) case for some conclusion. Because it is less rigorous, informal reasoning tends to provide less certainty, but informal reasoning can be very helpful for finding potential solutions or possible avenues of approach for otherwise intractable problems.

SKILL 9.4 Evaluating arguments, reasoning, and the validity of conclusions

The two forms of reasoning are inductive and deductive. INDUCTIVE REASONING involves making inferences from specific facts to general principles; DEDUCTIVE REASONING involves making inferences from general principles to specific facts. As such, inductive reasoning is generally weaker than deductive reasoning. (Inductive reasoning—or induction—should not be confused with mathematical induction, which is not an example of inductive reasoning, strictly speaking.)

INDUCTIVE REASONING: makes inferences from specific facts to general principles

DEDUCTIVE REASONING: makes inferences from general principles to specific facts

Inductive Reasoning

Inductive reasoning generally involves finding a representative set of examples that support the general application of a broader principle. In a common context, an example of inductive reasoning would be inferring from the fact that only black crows have ever been spotted to the general statement that all crows are black. This inference has a foundation in numerous observations, and it thereby gains significant weight. Nevertheless, it is feasible that somewhere a white (or other-colored) crow does exist but hasn't yet been spotted. Thus, inductive inferences can never acquire 100% certainty, regardless of the amount of information in support of them.

Regardless of the uncertainty associated with induction, inductive inferences can be helpful for building a theory or for making a conjecture about some aspect of life, mathematics, or any other area. The physical sciences are a particular example where induction is commonly used to develop theories about the universe. Although these theories may be founded on a large body of empirical and mathematical evidence, a single counterexample could topple their status. Thus, inductive reasoning can be helpful, but it is much weaker than deductive reasoning.

> *Inductive inferences can be helpful for building a theory or for making a conjecture about some aspect of life, mathematics, or any other area.*

Inductive reasoning, because it is weaker than deduction, is also less rigorous in its application of specific rules for the process of arriving at conclusions. For instance, there is no rule concerning how much evidence constitutes a sufficient reason to inductively accept a particular hypothesis. (Thus, there is no minimum number of sightings of black crows that is required prior to making an inference that all crows are black.) The particular area in which inductive reasoning is applied and the amount of potential evidence that could reasonably be gathered are factors that help determine what constitutes an acceptable inductive inference.

In a mathematical context, induction can serve to make conjectures for which a proof (or a proof of the contrary) can then be sought. For instance, Fermat's Last Theorem states that there are no integer solutions x, y, and z to the expression $x^n + y^n = z^n$ for $n > 2$. Although this theorem was suspected to be true (largely by induction from numerous test cases) for hundreds of years, only recently was a deductive proof discovered. Thus, induction can serve as a less rigorous method of making tentative conclusions pending a formal proof.

Deductive Reasoning

> **INVALID ARGUMENT:** one in which the conclusion does not necessarily follow from the premises

Deductive reasoning is a method of reasoning that is stronger and more rigorous than inductive reasoning. Deductive arguments reason from a set of premises to a conclusion and are classified as invalid, valid, or sound. An INVALID ARGUMENT is one in which the conclusion does not necessarily follow from the premises.

A VALID ARGUMENT is one in which the conclusion necessarily follows from the premises. A SOUND ARGUMENT is a valid argument for which all the premises are true. Thus, the following argument is valid but not sound:

Premise 1:   All dogs are black.
Premise 2:   Rover is a dog.
Conclusion: Rover is black.

Were premises 1 and 2 both true, the conclusion would necessarily be true as well. Premise 1 is false, however, so the argument is valid but not sound. On the other hand, the following argument is both valid *and* sound.

Premise 1:   All integers are real numbers.
Premise 2:   1 is an integer.
Conclusion: 1 is a real number.

Both premises 1 and 2 are true, and the conclusion follows from the premises. Specific examples of deductive logical steps that can be taken in developing or evaluating an argument include *modus ponens* ("if A, then B" and "A is true" necessarily implies "B is true") and *modus tollens* ("if A, then B" and "B is false" necessarily implies "A is false").

Because deductive reasoning is more rigorous and the rules clearer, the process of arriving at an acceptable conclusion from a given set of premises (or the process of evaluating a deductive argument) is likewise clearer. Demonstrating the truth of the premises, however, may still be a complicated process. The premises may even require inductive reasoning to demonstrate their truth (at least tentatively). Thus, whether a deductive argument is sound can still be a matter that rests on the strength of a particular instance of inductive reasoning.

> **VALID ARGUMENT:** one in which the conclusion necessarily follows from the premises

> **SOUND ARGUMENT:** a valid argument for which all the premises are true

SKILL 9.5 Analyzing systems of geometry, including Euclidean, non-Euclidean, and projective geometries

Euclid wrote a set of thirteen books around 330 BCE called the *Elements*. He outlined ten axioms and then deduced 465 theorems. Euclidean geometry is based on the undefined concepts of the point, the line, and the plane.

The fifth of Euclid's axioms (referred to as the parallel postulate) was not as readily accepted as the other nine axioms. Many mathematicians throughout the years have attempted to prove that this axiom is not necessary because it could be proved by the other nine. Among the many who attempted to prove this was Carl Friedrich Gauss; his work led to the development of hyperbolic geometry. Elliptical, spherical, or Riemannian geometry was hypothesized by G.F. Bernhard

Riemann, who based his work on the theory of surfaces and used models as physical interpretations of the undefined terms that satisfy the axioms.

The variants of the Parallel Postulate that lead to non-Euclidean geometries are based on the number of possible unique lines that can be parallel to a line l, where the potential parallel lines must pass through a specific point not on l.

The variants of the Parallel Postulate that lead to non-Euclidean geometries are based on the number of possible unique lines that can be parallel to a line *l*, where the potential parallel lines must pass through a specific point not on *l*.

The chart below lists the fifth axiom (the Parallel Postulate) as it is given in each of the three geometries:

EUCLIDEAN GEOMETRY	SPHERICAL OR RIEMANNIAN GEOMETRY	HYPERBOLIC OR SADDLE GEOMETRY
Through a point not on a line, there is no more than one line parallel to that line.	If *l* is any line and *P* is any point not on *l*, then there are no lines through *P* that are parallel to *l*.	If *l* is any line and *P* is any point not on *l*, then there exists at least two lines through *P* that are parallel to *l*.

EUCLIDEAN GEOMETRY: the study of flat, two-dimensional space

EUCLIDEAN GEOMETRY is the study of flat, two-dimensional space. Non-Euclidean geometries involve curved surfaces, such as that of a sphere. These geometries have a direct connection to our experiences; for instance, the surface of the Earth is (roughly) spherical. Note the results of the Parallel Postulate for spherical geometry. (A line on a sphere is a so-called great circle, which is a circle of the same radius as the sphere.)

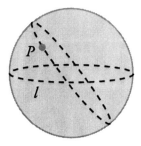

Non-Euclidean geometries have application beyond just abstract mathematical theory. For instance, hyperbolic geometry is a central concept in Einstein's theory of relativity.

The line through point *P* is not parallel to line *l*. Furthermore, it is clear through observation of the figure that, since there is only one great circle through any given point, there are non-collinear parallel lines in spherical geometry. Thus, as is demonstrated by this example, varying the details of the Parallel Postulate leads to various types of non-Euclidean geometries.

COMPETENCY 10
ANALYZE FIGURES AND SHAPES USING COORDINATE AND TRANSFORMATIONAL GEOMETRY

SKILL 10.1 Analyzing two- and three-dimensional figures and shapes in the coordinate plane

Any two-dimensional geometric figure can be represented in the CARTESIAN, or RECTANGULAR, COORDINATE SYSTEM. This system is formed by two perpendicular axes (coordinate axes): the *x*-axis and the *y*-axis. If the dimensions of a two-dimensional, or planar, figure are known, this coordinate system can be used to create a visual representation of the figure.

> **CARTESIAN**, or **RECTANGULAR, COORDINATE SYSTEM**: a system formed by two perpendicular axes: the *x*-axis and the *y*-axis

Example: Represent an isosceles triangle with two sides of length 4.
Draw the two sides along the *x* and *y* axes and connect the points (vertices).

The vertices of the isosceles triangle are found at (0, 0), (4, 0) and (0, 4) with equal sides on the *x* and *y* axes.

If a polygon is shown in the coordinate plane and the coordinates of the vertices must be determined, then the characteristics of the polygon can be used to this end. Consider the following example.

Example: The rectangle shown in the graph below has sides of length 2 parallel to the y-axis and sides of length 4 parallel to the x-axis. Determine the coordinates of the vertices.

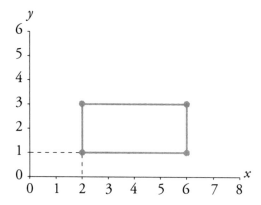

From the graph, it is clear that one of the vertices is located at (2, 1). Using the properties of rectangles (or by inspection of the graph in this case), the other vertices (going in a counter-clockwise direction from the first vertex) are (6, 1), (6, 3) and (2, 3).

Examples that are more difficult may involve polygons with sides that are not parallel to either of the axes. In such cases, knowledge (either given or by inspection) of the location of at least one vertex is necessary, as well as knowldedge of the type of polygon (regular or irregular). Calculation of the slopes of the line segments between vertices may be necessary in some cases to determine the location of unknown vertices. This approach is also helpful in cases where, as with the first example, the polygon must be drawn on the coordinate plane. When possible, it is helpful to draw one or more vertices (or entire sides) of a polygon on the axes. This usually simplifies calculation or representation of the remainder of the polygon.

A three-dimensional geometric figure can be plotted using a basic set of three-dimensional axes, as shown below.

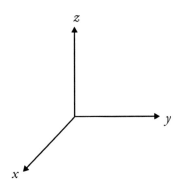

Points can be plotted by traversing the required distance parallel to each axis. Thus, the point (3, 3, 3) is plotted as shown below.

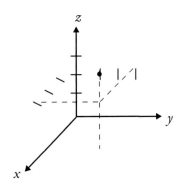

A cube with sides of length 2 can then be represented as shown below.

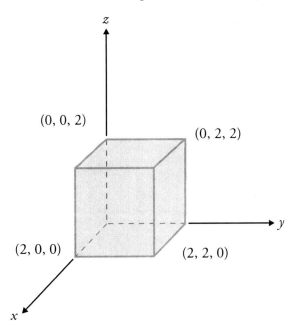

SKILL 10.2 Applying geometric properties and the concepts of distance, midpoint, and slope in coordinate systems to solve mathematical and real-world problems

The Distance Formula

In order to accomplish the task of finding the distance from a given point to another given line, the perpendicular line that intersects the point and the line must be drawn, and the equation of the other line must be written. From this information, the point of intersection can be found. This point and the original point are used in the distance formula given below:

$$D = \sqrt{(x_2 - x_1)^2 + (y_2 - y_1)^2}$$

Example: Given the point (-4, 3) and the line y = 4x + 2, find the distance from the point to the line.

$y = 4x + 2$	Find the slope of the given line by solving for y.
$y = 4x + 2$	The slope is $\frac{4}{1}$; the perpendicular line will have a slope of $-\frac{4}{1}$.
$y = (-\frac{1}{4})x + b$	Use the new slope and the given point to find the equation of the perpendicular line.
$3 = (-\frac{1}{4})(-4) + b$	Substitute (-4, 3) into the equation.
$3 = 1 + b$	Solve.
$2 = b$	Given the value for b, write the equation of the perpendicular line.
$y = (-\frac{1}{4})x + 2$	Write in standard form.
$x + 4y = 8$	Use both equations to solve by elimination to get the point of intersection.
$\begin{aligned} -4x + y &= 2 \\ \underline{x + 4y} &= \underline{8} \end{aligned}$	Multiply the bottom row by 4.
$\begin{aligned} -4x + y &= 2 \\ \underline{4x + 16y} &= \underline{32} \\ 17y &= 34 \\ y &= 2 \end{aligned}$	Solve.
$y = 4x + 2$	Substitute to find the x value.
$2 = 4x + 2$	Solve.
$x = 0$	

(0, 2) is the point of intersection. Use this point on the original line and the original point to calculate the distance between them.

$D = \sqrt{(x_2 - x_1)^2 + (y_2 - y_1)^2}$, where points are (0, 2) and (-4, 3).

$D = \sqrt{(-4 - 0)^2 + (3 - 2)^2}$ Substitute.

$D = \sqrt{(16) + (1)}$ Simplify.

$D = \sqrt{17}$

The distance between two parallel lines, such as line *AB* and line *CD* as shown below, is the line segment *RS*, the perpendicular between the two parallels.

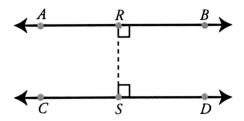

Example: Given the geometric figure below, find the distance between the two parallel sides AB and CD.

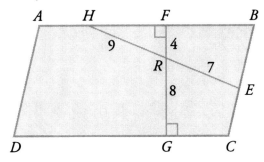

The distance *FG* is 12 units.

The key to applying the distance formula is to understand the problem before beginning.

$D = \sqrt{(x_2 - x_1)^2 + (y_2 - y_1)^2}$,

Example: Find the perimeter of a figure with vertices at (4, 5), (-4, 6), and (-5, -8).

The figure being described is a triangle. Therefore, the distance for all three sides must be found. Carefully identify all three sides before beginning.

Side 1 = (4, 5) to (-4, 6)
Side 2 = (-4, 6) to (-5, -8)
Side 3 = (-5, -8) to (4, 5)

$$D_1 = \sqrt{(-4-4)^2 + (6-5)^2} = \sqrt{65}$$
$$D_2 = \sqrt{((-5-(-4))^2 + (-8-6)^2} = \sqrt{197}$$
$$D_3 = \sqrt{((4-(-5))^2 + (5-(-8))^2} = \sqrt{250} \text{ or } 5\sqrt{10}$$

$$\text{Perimeter} = \sqrt{65} + \sqrt{197} + 5\sqrt{10}$$

The Midpoint Formula

If a line segment has endpoints of (x_1, y_1) and (x_2, y_2), then the midpoint can be found using

$$(\frac{x_1 + x_2}{2}, \frac{y_1 + y_2}{2})$$

Example: Find the center of a circle with a diameter whose endpoints are (3, 7) and (-4, -5).

Midpoint = $(\frac{3 + (-4)}{2}, \frac{7 + (-5)}{2})$
Midpoint = $(-\frac{1}{2}, 1)$

Example: Find the midpoint given the two points (5, $8\sqrt{6}$) and (9, $-4\sqrt{6}$).

Midpoint = $(\frac{5+9}{2}, \frac{8\sqrt{6} + (-4\sqrt{6})}{2})$
Midpoint = $(7, 2\sqrt{6})$

SKILL 10.3 **Applying transformations** *(e.g., rotations, reflections, translations)* **to figures in the coordinate plane, and analyzing topological properties and transformations**

TRANSFORMATIONAL GEOMETRY: the study of the manipulation of objects through movement, rotation, and scaling

Transformational Geometry

TRANSFORMATIONAL GEOMETRY is the study of the manipulation of objects through movement, rotation, and scaling. The transformation of an object is called its image. If the original object is labeled with letters, such as *ABCD*, the image can be labeled with the same letters followed by a prime symbol: *A'B'C'D'*. Transformations can be characterized in different ways.

Types of transformations

An ISOMETRY is a linear transformation that maintains the dimensions of a geometric figure.

SYMMETRY is exact similarity between two parts or halves, as if one were a mirror image of the other.

A TRANSLATION is a transformation that "slides" an object a fixed distance in a given direction. The original object and its translation have the same shape and size, and they face in the same direction.

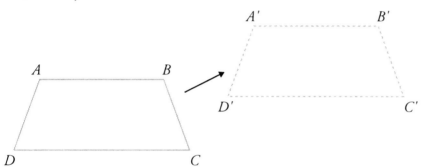

A ROTATION is a transformation that turns a figure about a fixed point, which is called the center of rotation. An object and its rotation are the same shape and size, but the figures may be oriented in different directions. Rotations can occur in either a clockwise or a counterclockwise direction.

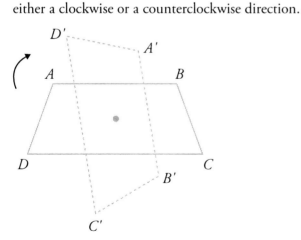

An object and its REFLECTION have the same shape and size, but the figures face in opposite directions. The line (where a hypothetical mirror may be placed) is called the line of reflection. The distance from a point to the line of reflection is the same as the distance from the point's image to the line of reflection.

ISOMETRY: a linear transformation that maintains the dimensions of a geometric figure

SYMMETRY: the exact similarity between two parts or halves, as if one were a mirror image of the other

TRANSLATION: a transformation that "slides" an object a fixed distance in a given direction

ROTATION: a transformation that turns a figure about a fixed point, which is called the center of rotation

REFLECTION: when an object and another figure have the same shape and size, but they face in opposite directions

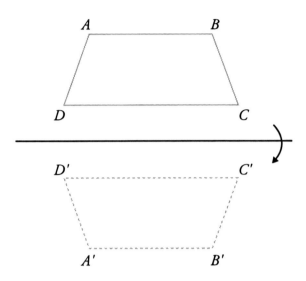

A GLIDE REFLECTION involves a combined translation along and a reflection across a single specified line. The characteristic that defines a glide reflection as opposed to a simple combination of an arbitrary translation and arbitrary reflection is that the direction of translation is parallel with the line of reflection. An example of a glide reflection is shown below.

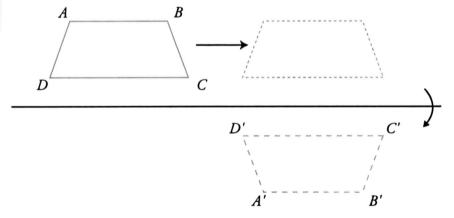

The examples of a translation, a rotation, and a reflection given above are for polygons, but the same principles apply to the simpler geometric elements of points and lines. In fact, a transformation performed on a polygon can be viewed equivalently as the same transformation performed on the set of points (vertices) and lines (sides) that compose the polygon. Thus, to perform complicated transformations on a figure, it is helpful to perform the transformations on all the points (or vertices) of the figure, then reconnect the points with lines as appropriate.

Dilation

DILATIONS involve an expansion of a figure and a translation of that figure while maintaining the figure's angles and relative proportions (the translation may be for a distance zero). These two transformations are obtained by first defining a center of dilation, C, which is some point that acts like an origin for the dilation. The distance from C to each point in a figure is then altered by a scale factor, s. If the magnitude of s is greater than zero, the size of the figure is increased; if the magnitude of s is less than zero, the size is decreased.

> **DILATION:** a simultaneous expansion and translation of a figure while maintaining the figure's angles and relative proportions

The expansion of a geometric figure is a result of the scale factor, s. For instance, if $s = 2$, the expanded figure will be twice the size of the original figure. The translation of a geometric figure is a result of the location of the center of dilation, C. If C is located at the center of the figure, for instance, the figure is dilated without any translation of its center.

Example: Dilate the figure shown by a scale factor of 2 using the origin of the coordinate system as the center of dilation.

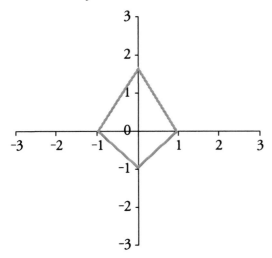

To perform this dilation, the distance between the origin and each point on the figure must be increased by a factor of 2. It is sufficient, however, to simply increase the distance of the vertices of the figure by a factor of 2 and then connect them to form the dilated figure.

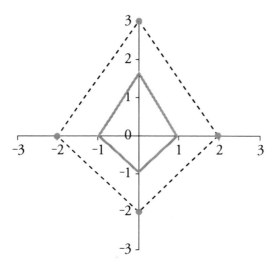

The resulting figure, represented by a dashed line, is the dilation of the original figure.

The points on a figure are dilated by increasing or decreasing their respective distances from a center of dilation, C. As a result, each point P on a figure is essentially translated along the line through P and C. To show that a dilation of this type preserves angles, consider some angle formed by two line segments, with a center of dilation at some arbitrary location. The dilation is for some scale factor s.

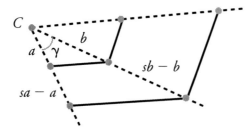

To show that the angles θ and α are equal, it is sufficient to show that the two pairs of overlapping triangles are similar. If they are similar, all the corresponding angles in the figure must be congruent.

The smaller triangle in this case has sides of lengths a and b and an angle γ between them. The larger triangle has sides of lengths sa (or $sa - a + a = sa$) and *sb* and an angle γ between them. Thus, by SAS similarity, these two triangles are similar.

Once this reasoning is applied to the other pair of overlapping triangles, it can be shown that angles θ and α are equal. Furthermore, due to the fact that these triangles have been shown to be similar, it is also true that line segments must scale by the same factor, *s* (this is necessary to maintain the similarity of the triangles above).

As a result of this reasoning, it can be shown that figures that are dilated using an arbitrary scale factor, *s*, and center of dilation, *C*, must maintain all angles through the dilation, and all line segments (or sides) of the figure must also scale by *s*. As a result, figures that are dilated are similar to the original figures.

Since dilations are transformations that maintain similarity of the figures being dilated, they can also be viewed as changes of scale about *C*. For instance, a dilation of a portion of a map would simply result in a change of the scale of the map.

Multiple transformations (or compositions of transformations) can be performed on a geometrical figure. The order of these transformations may or may not be important. For instance, multiple translations can be performed in any order, as can multiple rotations (around a single fixed point) or reflections (across a single fixed line). The order of the transformations becomes important when several types of transformations are performed or when the point of rotation or the line of reflection changes among transformations. For example, consider a translation of a given distance upward and a clockwise rotation by 90° around a fixed point. Changing the order of these transformations changes the result.

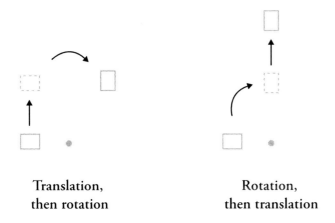

**Translation,
then rotation**

**Rotation,
then translation**

As shown, the final position of the box is different, depending on the order of the transformations. Thus, it is crucial that the proper order of transformations (whether determined by the details of the problem or some other consideration) be followed.

Example: Find the final location of a point at (1, 1) that undergoes the following transformations: rotate 90° counter-clockwise about the origin; translate distance 2 in the negative y direction; reflect about the x-axis.

First, draw a graph of the x and y axes and plot the point at (1, 1).

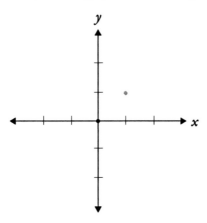

Next, perform the rotation. The center of rotation is the origin and is in the counter-clockwise direction. In this case, the even value of 90° makes the rotation simple to do by inspection. Next, perform a translation of distance 2 in the negative y direction (down). The results of these transformations are shown below.

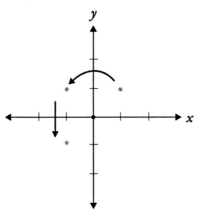

Finally, perform the reflection about the x-axis. The final result, shown below, is a point at (1, −1).

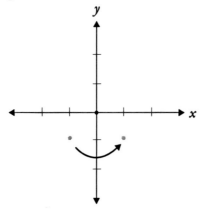

Using this approach, polygons can be transformed on a point-by-point basis.

For some problems, there is no need to work with coordinate axes. For instance, the problem may simply require transformations without respect to any absolute positioning.

Example: Rotate the following regular pentagon by 36° about its center and then reflect it across the horizontal line.

First, perform the rotation. In this case, the direction is not important because the pentagon is symmetric. As it turns out in this case, a rotation of 36° yields the same result as flipping the pentagon vertically (assuming the vertices of the pentagon are indistinguishable).

Finally, perform the reflection. Note that the result here is the same as a downward translation (assuming the vertices of the pentagon are indistinguishable).

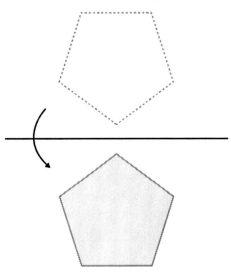

A figure has symmetry when there is an isometry that maps the figure onto itself. A figure has rotational symmetry if there is a rotation of 180 degrees or less that maps the figure onto itself. Point symmetry is where a plane figure can be mapped onto itself by a half-turn or a rotation of 180 degrees around some point. Thus, point symmetry is a specific type of rotational symmetry. An example of a figure with point symmetry is shown below.

> *A figure has symmetry when there is an isometry that maps the figure onto itself. A figure has rotational symmetry if there is a rotation of 180 degrees or less that maps the figure onto itself. Point symmetry is where a plane figure can be mapped onto itself by a half-turn or a rotation of 180 degrees around some point.*

REFLECTIONAL SYMMETRY: an isometry that maps the figure onto itself by reflection across a line

REFLECTIONAL SYMMETRY, or line symmetry, is an isometry that maps the figure onto itself by reflection across a line. An alternative view is that if the figure is folded along a line of symmetry, the two halves will match perfectly. Examples of figures with line symmetry are shown below, with all the potential lines of symmetry marked as broken lines.

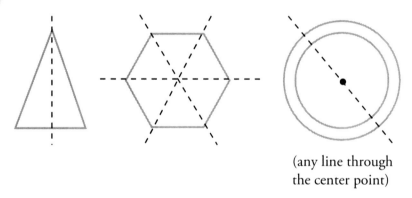

(any line through the center point)

TRANSLATIONAL SYMMETRY: symmetry which allows an image to be translated in a specific direction to produce the same image

TRANSLATIONAL SYMMETRY is where an image can be translated in a specific direction to produce the same image. Necessarily, this requires that the image be infinite in extent and repeating in nature. A TESSELLATION is an image with translational symmetry. A tessellation or tiling, consists of a repeating pattern of figures, which completely cover an area. Below are a couple of examples of art tessellations.

TESSELLATION: an image with translational symmetry

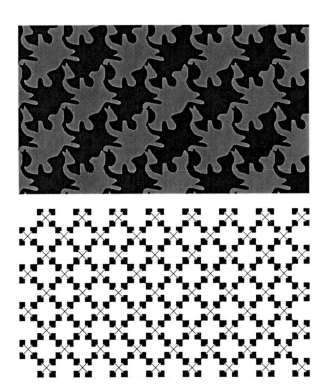

A regular tessellation is made by taking a pattern of polygons that are interlocked and can be extended infinitely. A portion of a tessellation made with hexagons is shown below. This image is made by taking congruent, regular polygons and using them to cover a plane in such a way that there are no holes or overlaps. A semi-regular tessellation is made with polygons arranged exactly the same way at every vertex point. Tessellations occur in frequently in nature. A bee's honeycomb is an example of a tessellation found in nature.

SKILL 10.4 Analyzing the use of the techniques of coordinate geometry in geometric proofs

COORDINATE GEOMETRY involves the application of algebraic methods to geometry. The locations of points in space are expressed in terms of coordinates on a

> **COORDINATE GEOMETRY:** the application of algebraic methods to geometry

Cartesian plane. The relationships between the coordinates of different points are expressed as equations.

Proofs using coordinate geometry techniques employ the following commonly used formulae and relationships:

1. **Midpoint formula:** The midpoint (x, y) of the line joining points (x_1, y_1) and (x_2, y_2) is given by $(x, y) = \left(\frac{x_1 + x_2}{2}, \frac{y_1 + y_2}{2} \right)$.

2. **Distance formula:** The distance between points (x_1, y_1) and (x_2, y_2) is given by $D = \sqrt{(x_2 - x_1)^2 + (y_2 - y_1)^2}$.

3. **Slope formula:** The slope m of a line passing through the points (x_1, y_1) and (x_2, y_2) is given by $m = \frac{y_2 - y_1}{x_2 - x_1}$.

4. **Equation of a line:** The equation of a line is given by $y = mx + b$, where m is the slope of the line and b is the y-intercept, i.e., the y-coordinate at which the line intersects the y-axis.

5. **Parallel and perpendicular lines:** Parallel lines have the same slope. The slope of a line perpendicular to a line with slope m is $\frac{-1}{m}$.

Example: Prove that quadrilateral ABCD with vertices A(-3, 0), B(-1, 0), C(0, 3), and D(2, 3) is in fact a parallelogram using coordinate geometry:

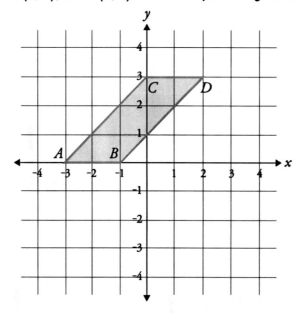

By definition, a parallelogram has diagonals that bisect each other. Using the midpoint formula, $(x, y) = \left(\frac{x_1 + x_2}{2} + \frac{y_1 + y_2}{2}\right)$, find the midpoints of $\overline{AD}$ and $\overline{BC}$.

The midpoint of $\overline{BC} = \left(\frac{-1 + 0}{2}, \frac{0 + 3}{2}\right) = \left(-\frac{1}{2}, \frac{3}{2}\right)$

The midpoint of $\overline{AD} = \left(\frac{-3 + 2}{2}, \frac{0 + 3}{2}\right) = \left(-\frac{1}{2}, \frac{3}{2}\right)$

Since the midpoints of the diagonals are the same, the diagonals bisect each other. Hence the polygon is a parallelogram.

In the above example, the proof involved a specific geometric figure with given coordinates. Coordinate geometry can also be used to prove more general results.

Example: Prove that the diagonals of a rhombus are perpendicular to each other.

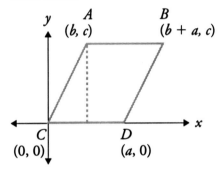

Draw a rhombus $ABCD$ with side of length a such that the vertex C is at the origin and the side CD lies along the x-axis. The coordinates of the corners of the rhombus can then be written as shown above.

The slope m_1 of the diagonal AD is given by $m_1 = \frac{c}{b - a}$.

The slope m_2 of the diagonal BC is given by $m_2 = \frac{c}{b + a}$.

The product of the slopes is $m_1 \times m_2 = \frac{c}{b - a} \times \frac{c}{b + a} = \frac{c^2}{b^2 - a^2}$.

The length of side $AC = \sqrt{b^2 + c^2} = a$ (since each side of the rhombus is equal to a). Therefore,

$b^2 + c^2 = a^2$

$\rightarrow b^2 - a^2 = -c^2$

$\rightarrow \frac{c^2}{b^2 - a^2} = -1$

The product of the slopes of the diagonals $m_1 \times m_2 = -1$.
Hence the two diagonals are perpendicular to each other.

Example: Prove that the line joining the midpoints of two sides of a triangle is parallel to and half the length of the third side.

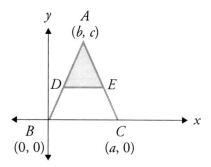

Draw triangle ABC on the coordinate plane in such a way that the vertex B coincides with the origin and the side BC lies along the x-axis. Let point C have coordinates $(a, 0)$ and point A have coordinates (b, c). Point D is the midpoint of side AB and point E is the midpoint of side AC.

We need to prove that segment DE is parallel to and half the length of side BC.

Using the midpoint formula, coordinates of $D = \left(\frac{b}{2}, \frac{c}{2}\right)$; coordinates of $E = \left(\frac{b + a}{2}, \frac{c}{2}\right)$.

The slope of the line segment DE is then given by $\dfrac{\frac{c}{2} - \frac{c}{2}}{\frac{b + a}{2} - \frac{b}{2}} = 0$, which is equal to the slope of the x-axis. Thus DE is parallel to BC.

The length of the line segment $DE = \sqrt{\left(\frac{b + a}{2} - \frac{b}{2}\right)^2 + \left(\frac{c}{2} - \frac{c}{2}\right)^2} = \sqrt{\left(\frac{a}{2}\right)^2} = \frac{a}{2}$.

The length of DE is half that of side BC.

SKILL 10.5 Applying vectors and polar and parametric equations to solve problems

The different types of transformations of geometric figures in the plane, such as translations, rotations, reflections and dilations, can be represented in the coordinate plane or space (especially when the transformations are complicated or when multiple sequential transformations are to be performed) using vectors and matrices.

Points in a geometric figure, such as vertices, can be treated as a vector with two elements—(x_1, y_1), for instance—that specify the location of the point in some coordinate system. Consider the example below.

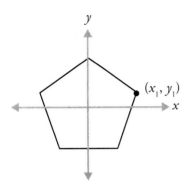

Given that each point on the figure is represented by an ordered pair, a 2 × 2 matrix can be used to perform the transformation. For any given transformation, a particular 2 × 2 matrix $\overline{T}$ can be determined that transforms all the points in the correct manner.

Consider a reflection about the x-axis. This transformation results in the following:

$$(x, y) \rightarrow (x, {}^-y)$$

The result of this transformation is shown below for the pentagon given in the diagram above.

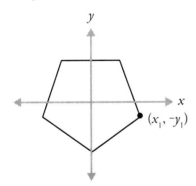

A matrix $\overline{T}$ can be constructed that performs this transformation.

$$\overline{T} \begin{pmatrix} 1 & 0 \\ 0 & -1 \end{pmatrix}$$

Thus:

$$\overline{T} \begin{pmatrix} x \\ y \end{pmatrix} = \begin{pmatrix} 1 & 0 \\ 0 & -1 \end{pmatrix} \begin{pmatrix} x \\ y \end{pmatrix} = \begin{pmatrix} x \\ -y \end{pmatrix}$$

A similar transformation matrix can be constructed for reflections about the y-axis or about an arbitrary line (although this latter case is significantly more difficult).

For a translation, it is sufficient to simply construct a vector that is added to each point (x, y) in the figure. This vector is composed of a length for the translation in the x direction and a length for the translation in the y direction. For instance, to translate a figure a distance a in the positive x direction and a distance b in the negative y direction, use a vector $(a, {}^-b)$. The result is shown below for the pentagon.

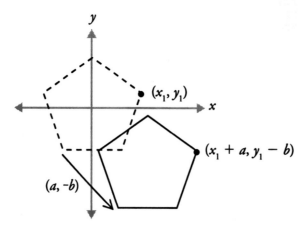

Algebraically, the transformation for the transformed figure in terms of the points (x, y) on the original figure is the following for a general translation (c, d):

$$\begin{pmatrix} x \\ y \end{pmatrix} + \begin{pmatrix} c \\ d \end{pmatrix}$$

Rotations are slightly more complicated transformations. Consider a rotation around the origin of a point specified as (x_1, y_1).

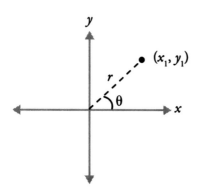

Using polar coordinates, the point can likewise be represented as a distance r from the origin and an angle θ from the x-axis.

$$r = \sqrt{x_1^2 + y_1^2}$$
$$\theta = \arctan\frac{y_1}{x_1}$$

A rotation around the origin simply involves, in this case, changing θ but holding r constant. Consider a rotation α in the counterclockwise direction.

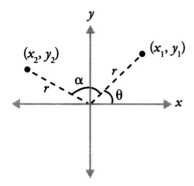

The coordinates of the new point (x_2, y_2) are then the following:

$$x_2 = r \cos (\alpha + \theta)$$
$$y_2 = r \sin (\alpha + \theta)$$

Use the sum formulas for trigonometric functions to expand and then simplify these expressions.

$$x_2 = r (\cos \alpha \cos \theta - \sin \alpha \sin \theta) = (r \cos \theta) \cos \alpha - (r \sin \theta) \sin \alpha$$
$$y_2 = r (\sin \alpha \cos \theta + \cos \alpha \sin \theta) = (r \cos \theta) \sin \alpha + (r \sin \theta) \cos \alpha$$

But $r \cos \theta$ is simply x_1, and $r \sin \theta$ is simply y_1.

$$x_2 = x_1 \cos \alpha - y_1 \sin \alpha$$
$$y_2 = x_1 \sin \alpha + y_1 \cos \alpha$$

Clearly, these two equations can be written in matrix form. Thus, a rotation of point (x_1, y_1) about the origin by angle α can be expressed as follows.

$$\begin{pmatrix} x_2 \\ y_2 \end{pmatrix} = \begin{pmatrix} \cos \alpha & -\sin \alpha \\ \sin \alpha & \cos \alpha \end{pmatrix} \begin{pmatrix} x_1 \\ y_1 \end{pmatrix}$$

$$\begin{pmatrix} x_2 \\ y_2 \end{pmatrix} = \begin{pmatrix} \cos \pi & -\sin \pi \\ \sin \pi & \cos \pi \end{pmatrix} \begin{pmatrix} 1 \\ 0 \end{pmatrix} = \begin{pmatrix} -1 & 0 \\ 0 & -1 \end{pmatrix} \begin{pmatrix} 1 \\ 0 \end{pmatrix} = \begin{pmatrix} -1 \\ 0 \end{pmatrix}$$

This result can be tested using simple cases. For instance, consider a point (1, 0) rotated by π radians.

$$\begin{pmatrix} x_2 \\ y_2 \end{pmatrix} = \begin{pmatrix} \cos \pi & -\sin \pi \\ \sin \pi & \cos \pi \end{pmatrix} \begin{pmatrix} 1 \\ 0 \end{pmatrix} = \begin{pmatrix} -1 & 0 \\ 0 & -1 \end{pmatrix} \begin{pmatrix} 1 \\ 0 \end{pmatrix} = \begin{pmatrix} -1 \\ 0 \end{pmatrix}$$

This result makes intuitive sense. To rotate a figure, simply rotate a set of representative points (such as the vertices); then reconnect them after the rotation. In cases in which a point of rotation is chosen that is not the origin, a change of coordinates to make the origin and the point of rotation coincide may simplify the problem and eliminate the need to handle complicated transformation matrices. Dilations involve a change in the distance r from some point (such as the origin), rather than a change in the angle θ. As with rotations, it is sometimes convenient to perform a change of coordinates so that the center of dilation and the origin of the coordinate system coincide. In such a case, a dilation simply involves multiplying both coordinates of each point in the figure by the dilation factor. Consider the pentagon used above with a dilation factor of 2. For each point (x, y) on the pentagon, the corresponding point (x', y') on the dilated pentagon is simply the following:

$$\begin{pmatrix} x' \\ y' \end{pmatrix} = d \begin{pmatrix} x \\ y \end{pmatrix}$$

where, in this case, the dilation factor d is 2. The result of the dilation is shown below for the pentagon.

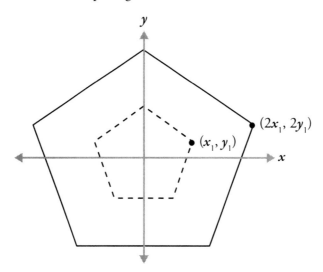

Compound transformations can be made by simply concatenating several transformation operators (whether a multiplicative matrix, a multiplicative constant, or an additive vector).

Example: Find the formula for a transformation involving first a rotation of α counterclockwise around the origin, then a dilation by a factor of 4, then a translation in the positive y direction by 2, and then a clockwise rotation by α.

To solve this problem, consider a point (x, y) on the plane. To rotate counterclockwise by α, use the rotation matrix.

$$\begin{pmatrix} x' \\ y' \end{pmatrix} = \begin{pmatrix} \cos\alpha & -\sin\alpha \\ \sin\alpha & \cos\alpha \end{pmatrix} \begin{pmatrix} x \\ y \end{pmatrix}$$

The dilation simply involves multiplication by a factor of 4.

$$\begin{pmatrix} x'' \\ y'' \end{pmatrix} = 4 \begin{pmatrix} x' \\ y' \end{pmatrix}$$

The translation can be represented as follows.

$$\begin{pmatrix} x''' \\ y''' \end{pmatrix} = \begin{pmatrix} x'' \\ y'' \end{pmatrix} + \begin{pmatrix} 0 \\ 2 \end{pmatrix}$$

The final result requires use of the rotation matrix for -α.

$$\begin{pmatrix} \bar{x} \\ \bar{y} \end{pmatrix} = \begin{pmatrix} \cos\alpha & \sin\alpha \\ -\sin\alpha & \cos\alpha \end{pmatrix} \begin{pmatrix} x''' \\ y''' \end{pmatrix}$$

Rewriting the equation in full yields

$$\begin{pmatrix} \bar{x} \\ \bar{y} \end{pmatrix} = \begin{pmatrix} \cos\alpha & \sin\alpha \\ -\sin\alpha & \cos\alpha \end{pmatrix} \left\{ 4 \begin{pmatrix} \cos\alpha & -\sin\alpha \\ \sin\alpha & \cos\alpha \end{pmatrix} \begin{pmatrix} x \\ y \end{pmatrix} + \begin{pmatrix} 0 \\ 2 \end{pmatrix} \right\}$$

Using this formula, any point or set of points can be transformed in the manner specified by the question.

DOMAIN IV
DATA, PROBABILITY, AND DISCRETE MATH

PERSONALIZED STUDY PLAN

KNOWN MATERIAL/ SKIP IT

PAGE	COMPETENCY AND SKILL	KNOWN MATERIAL/ SKIP IT
203	**11: Apply knowledge of the collection, presentation, and analysis of data**	☐
	11.1: Devising a plan for collecting data using appropriate sampling techniques	☐
	11.2: Selecting an effective format for organizing and describing data distributions	☐
	11.3: Interpreting data presented in a variety of formats	☐
	11.4: Applying descriptive statistics to data	☐
	11.5: Applying inferential statistics and concepts of validity and reliability	☐
218	**12: Understand the principles of probability**	☐
	12.1: Analyzing the relationship between randomness and sampling methods in making statistical claims about populations	☐
	12.2: Determining the probabilities of simple and compound events using counting principles and the concept of sample space	☐
	12.3: Estimating probabilities based on data collection, experiments, and simulations	☐
	12.4: Applying discrete and continuous probability distributions to make inferences about a population	☐
229	**13: Understand the processes and applications of discrete mathematics**	☐
	13.1: Applying systematic counting techniques	☐
	13.2: Applying symbolic logic	☐
	13.3: Performing operations on matrices	☐
	13.4: Applying a variety of models to solve problems	☐

COMPETENCY 11
APPLY KNOWLEDGE OF THE COLLECTION, PRESENTATION, AND ANALYSIS OF DATA

SKILL 11.1 Devising a plan for collecting data using appropriate sampling techniques

Statistical studies typically involve a large number of people or a large pool of data known as the POPULATION. In most cases, it is impractical or impossible to collect data from every member, and therefore a representative sample has to be chosen. The process of selecting a sample must be undertaken with extreme care to ensure that it truly represents a population.

POPULATION: in a statistical study, a large number of people or a large pool of data

In addition to deciding what kind of sample will be selected, one must also select the sample statistic to be used. Different sample statistics can be used to estimate a particular population parameter. In order to estimate a population mean, for instance, one can use the sample median or the sample mean. One way to evaluate whether a sample statistic accurately reflects the value of a population parameter is by studying the characteristics of a sampling distribution. For a study that involves a sample of size n, for example, different samples of the same size and same type will produce slightly different values for the same statistic. A SAMPLE STATISTIC, therefore, is a random variable that follows a probability distribution. Informal inferences about the shape, symmetry, mean, and variance of this sampling distribution can help in selection of the appropriate sampling statistic or estimator.

SAMPLE STATISTIC: a random variable that follows a probability distribution

For an UNBIASED ESTIMATOR, i.e., a sample statistic that accurately reflects a population parameter, the sampling distribution mean is equal to the estimated population parameter and the distribution is centered at the population parameter. The shape of the sample distribution approaches a normal distribution as the sample size increases. Since consistency between samples is desired in the choice of an estimator, a smaller standard deviation indicates a better estimator.

UNBIASED ESTIMATOR: a sample statistic that accurately reflects a population parameter

Surveys and Sampling

In cases where the number of events or individuals is too large to collect data on each one, scientists collect information from only a small percentage. This is known as SAMPLING or SURVEYING. If sampling is done correctly, it should give the investigator nearly the same information he would have obtained by testing

SAMPLING OR SURVEYING: when scientists collect information from only a small percentage of a number of events or individuals because the data pool is too large the entire population. The survey must be carefully designed, considering both the sampling technique and the size of the sample.

There are a variety of sampling techniques, both random and nonrandom. Random sampling is also known as probability sampling, since the methods of probability theory can be used to ascertain the odds that the sample is representative of the whole population. Statistical methods may be used to determine how large a sample is necessary to give an investigator a specified level of certainty (95% is a typical confidence interval). Conversely, if an investigator has a sample of certain size, those same statistical methods can be used to determine how confident one can be that the sample accurately reflects the whole population.

A truly random sample must choose events or individuals without regard to time, place, or result. Simple random sampling is ideal for populations that are relatively homogeneous with respect to the data being collected.

In some cases an accurate representation of distinct sub-populations requires stratified random sampling or quota sampling. For instance, if men and women are likely to respond very differently to a particular survey, the total sample population can be separated into these two subgroups and then a random group of respondents selected from each subgroup. This kind of sampling not only provides balanced representation of different subgroups, it also allows comparison of data between subgroups.

Stratified sampling is sometimes proportional; i.e., the number of samples selected from each subgroup reflects the fraction of the whole population represented by the subgroup.

Sometimes compromises must be made to save time, money, or effort. For instance, when conducting a phone survey, calls are typically made only in a certain geographical area and at a certain time of day. This is an example of cluster random sampling. There are three stages to cluster or area sampling:

1. The target population is divided into many regional clusters (groups).

2. A few clusters are randomly selected for study.

3. A few subjects are randomly chosen from within a cluster.

Systematic random sampling involves the collection of a sample at defined intervals (for instance, every tenth part to come off a manufacturing line). Here, it is assumed that the population is ordered randomly and that there is no hidden pattern that may compromise the randomness of the sampling.

Nonrandom sampling is also known as nonprobability sampling. Convenience sampling is the method of choosing items arbitrarily and in an unstructured manner from the frame. Purposive sampling targets a particular section of the population. Snowball sampling (e.g., having survey participants recommend others) and expert sampling are other types of nonrandom sampling. Obviously, nonrandom samples are far less representative of the whole population than random ones. They may, however, be the only methods available or may meet the needs of a particular study.

**SKILL Selecting an effective format for organizing and describing data
11.2 distributions**

Displaying Statistical Data

The data obtained from sampling may be categorical (e.g., yes or no responses) or numerical. In both cases, results are displayed using a variety of graphical techniques. Geographical data is often displayed superimposed on maps.

Histograms

The most common form of graphical display used for numerical data obtained from random sampling is the histogram. A trend line can be superposed on a histogram to observe the general shape of the distribution. In some cases, the trend line may also be fitted to a probability density function.

If the data set is large, it may be expressed in compact form as a FREQUENCY DISTRIBUTION. The number of occurrences of each data point is the FREQUENCY of that value. The RELATIVE FREQUENCY is defined as the frequency divided by the total number of data points. Since the sum of the frequencies equals the number of data points, the relative frequencies add up to 1. The relative frequency of a data point, therefore, represents the probability of occurrence of that value. Thus, a distribution consisting of relative frequencies is known as a PROBABILITY DISTRIBUTION. The CUMULATIVE FREQUENCY of a data point is the sum of the frequencies from the beginning up to that point.

A histogram is used to display a discrete frequency distribution graphically. It shows the counts of data in different ranges, the center of the data set, the spread of the data, and whether there are any outliers. It also shows whether the data has a single mode or more than one.

FREQUENCY DISTRIBUTION: divides a set of data into classes or intervals

FREQUENCY: the number of occurrences of a certain value in a data set

RELATIVE FREQUENCY: the frequency divided by the total number of data points

The relative frequency of a data point represents the probability of occurrence of that value.

PROBABILITY DISTRIBUTION: a distribution consisting of relative frequencies

CUMULATIVE FREQUENCY: the sum of the frequencies from the beginning up to that point

A histogram is used to display a discrete frequency distribution graphically.

Example: The table below shows the summary of some test results, where people scored points ranging from 0 to 45. The total range of points has been divided into bins 0–5, 6–10, 11–15, and so on. The frequency for the first bin (labeled 5) is the number of people who scored points ranging from 0 to 5; the frequency for the second bin (labeled 10) is the number of people who scored points ranging from 6 to 10; and so on.

Points	Frequency	Cumulative Frequency	Relative Frequency
5	1	1	0.009
10	4	5	0.035
15	12	17	0.105
20	22	39	0.193
25	30	69	0.263
30	25	94	0.219
35	13	107	0.114
40	6	113	0.053
45	1	114	0.009

The histogram of the probability distribution is given below:

The probability distribution can be used to calculate the probability of a particular test score occurring in a certain range. For instance, the probability of a test score lying between 15 and 30 is given by the sum of the areas (assuming width of 1) of the three middle bins in the histogram above:

$$0.193 + 0.263 + 0.219 = 0.675$$

Bar graphs

Bar graphs are used to compare various quantities using bars of different lengths.

Example: A class had the following grades: 4 As, 9 Bs, 8 Cs, 1 D, 3 Fs.
Graph these on a bar graph.

Bar graphs are used to compare various quantities using bars of different lengths.

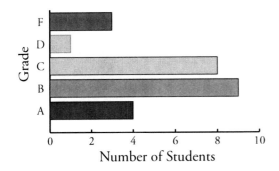

Line graphs

Line graphs are used to show trends, often over a period of time.

Line graphs are used to show trends, often over a period of time.

Example: Graph the following information using a line graph.

THE NUMBER OF NATIONAL MERIT FINALISTS/SCHOOL YEAR						
School	**90-91**	**91-92**	**92-93**	**93-94**	**94-95**	**95-96**
Central	3	5	1	4	6	8
Wilson	4	2	3	2	3	2

Circle graphs (pie charts)

Circle graphs, or pie charts, show the relationships of various parts of a data set to each other and to the whole. Each part is shown as a percentage of the total and occupies a proportional sector of the circular area. To make a circle graph, total all the information that is to be included on the graph. Determine the central angle to be used for each sector of the graph using the following formula:

$$\frac{\text{information}}{\text{total information}} \times 360° = \text{degrees in central } \measuredangle$$

Lay out the central angles according to these sizes, label each section and include its percentage.

Example: Graph this information on a circle graph:

MONTHLY EXPENSES	
Rent	$400
Food	$150
Utilities	$75
Clothes	$75
Savings	$100
Misc.	$200

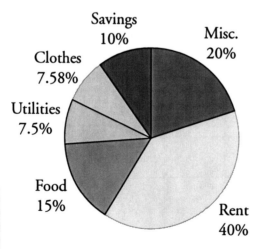

Savings 10% Misc. 20% Clothes 7.58% Utilities 7.5% Food 15% Rent 40%

Scatter plots

Scatter plots compare two characteristics of the same group of things or people and usually consist of a large body of data. They show how much one variable is affected by another. The relationship between the two variables is their

CORRELATION. The closer the data points come to making a straight line when plotted, the closer the correlation.

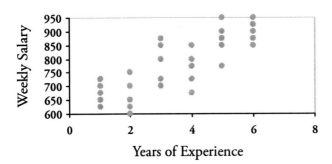

CORRELATION: the relationship between two variables when comparing statistical data

---

SKILL 11.3 Interpreting data presented in a variety of formats

See Skill 11.2

SKILL 11.4 Applying descriptive statistics *(e.g., measures of central tendency, variation)* **to data**

Statistics for Discrete Distributions

Mean, Median, and Mode

The mean, median, and mode are measures of central tendency (i.e., the average, or typical, value) in a data set. They can be defined both for discrete and continuous data sets. For discrete data, the MEAN is the average of the data items, or the value obtained by adding all the data values and dividing by the total number of data items. For a data set of n items with data values $x_1, x_2, x_3, \ldots, x_n$, the mean is given by

$$\bar{x} = \frac{x_1 + x_2 + x_3 + \ldots + x_n}{n}$$

MEAN: for discrete data, the value obtained by adding all the data values and then dividing by the total number of values

The WEIGHTED AVERAGE is the mean of a set of data in which each individual datum has an associated probability or weight. For data values $x_1, x_2, x_3, \ldots, x_n$, with associated probabilities (or weights) $p(x_1), p(x_2), p(x_3), \ldots, p(x_n)$, the mean value is

$$\bar{x} = x_1 p(x_1) + x_2 p(x_2) + x_3 p(x_3) + \ldots + x_n p(x_n) = \sum_i x_i p(x_i)$$

This is the most general definition of the mean.

WEIGHTED AVERAGE: the mean of a set of data in which each individual datum has an associated probability or weight

MEDIAN: found by putting the data in order from smallest to largest and selecting the value in the middle

MODE: the most frequently occurring datum

The MEDIAN is found by putting the data in order from smallest to largest and selecting the value in the middle (or the average of the two values in the middle if the number of data items is even). The MODE is the most frequently occurring datum. There can be more than one mode in a data set.

Example: Find the mean, median, and mode of the test scores listed below:

85	77	65
92	90	54
88	85	70
75	80	69
85	88	60
72	74	95

Mean: sum of all scores ÷ number of scores = 78
Median: Put the numbers in order from smallest to largest. Pick the middle number.

54 60 65 69 70 72 74 75 | 77 80 | 85 85 85 88 88 90 92 95
Two values are in the middle.

Therefore, the median is average of the two numbers in the middle, or 78.5.
The mode is the most frequent number, or 85.

Range, variance, and standard deviation

The RANGE is a measure of variability that is calculated by subtracting the smallest value from the largest value in a set of discrete data.

RANGE: found by subtracting the smallest data value from the largest

VARIANCE: a measure of the "spread" of data about the mean

STANDARD DEVIATION: also a measure of the "spread" of data about the mean; the standard deviation is the square root of the variance

The VARIANCE and STANDARD DEVIATION are measures of the "spread" of data around the mean. It is noteworthy that descriptive statistics involving such parameters as variance and standard deviation can be applied to a set of data that spans the entire population (population parameters, typically represented using Greek symbols) or to a set of data that only constitutes a portion of the population (sample statistics, typically represented by Latin letters).

When making informal inferences about a population based on sample statistics, it is important to ensure that the sample is collected in a manner that adequately represents the population (see the discussion of surveys and sampling below). The confidence in an inference based on sample statistics can increase when, for instance, the size of the sample space approaches that of the population, or when the sampling approach is designed to take into account known aspects of the population. Insofar as the sample represents the population, sample statistics approach (and can be equal to, in some cases) population parameters.

The mean of a set of data, whether for a population (μ) or for a sample ($\bar{x}$), uses the formula discussed above and can be represented as either a set of individual data or as a set of data with associated frequencies. The variance and the standard deviation for the population differ slightly from those of a sample. The population variance (σ^2) and the population standard deviation (σ) are as follows.

$$\sigma^2 = \frac{1}{n} \Sigma \, (x_i - \mu)^2$$

$$\sigma = \sqrt{\sigma^2}$$

For a sample, the data does not include the entire population. As a result, it should be expected that the sample data might not be perfectly representative of the population. To account for this shortcoming in the sample variance (s^2) and standard deviation (s), the sum of the squared differences between the data and the mean is divided by ($n - 1$) instead of just n. This increases the variance and standard deviation slightly, which in turn increases slightly the data spread to account for the possibility that the sample may not accurately represent the population.

$$s^2 = \frac{1}{n-1} \Sigma \, (x_i - \bar{x})^2$$

$$s = \sqrt{s^2}$$

Example: Calculate the range, variance, and standard deviation for the following data set: {3, 3, 5, 7, 8, 8, 8, 10, 12, 21}.

The range is simply the largest data value minus the smallest. In this case, the range is $21 - 3 = 18$.

To calculate the variance and standard deviation, first calculate the mean. If it is not stated whether a data set constitutes a population or sample, assume it is a population. (In this case, if the data were labeled as "ages of the 10 people in a room," this would be a population. If the data were labeled "ages of males at a crowded circus event," the data would be a sample.)

$$\mu = \frac{3 + 3 + 5 + 7 + 8 + 8 + 8 + 10 + 12 + 21}{10} = 8.5$$

Use this mean to calculate the variance.

$$\sigma^2 = \frac{1}{10} \Sigma \, (x_i - 8.5)^2$$

$$\sigma^2 = \frac{1}{10} \{(3 - 8.5)^2 + (3 - 8.5)^2 + (5 - 8.5)^2 + \ldots + (21 - 8.5)^2\}$$

$$\sigma^2 = \frac{246.5}{10} = 24.65$$

The standard deviation is

$$\sigma = \sqrt{\sigma^2} = \sqrt{24.65} \approx 4.96$$

Statistics for Continuous Distributions

The *range* for a continuous data distribution is the same as that for a discrete distribution: the largest value minus the smallest value. Calculation of the mean, variance, and standard deviation are similar, but slightly different. Since a continuous distribution does not permit a simple summation, integrals must be used. The mean μ of a distribution function $f(x)$ is expressed below.

$$\mu \int_{-\infty}^{\infty} xf(x)dx$$

The variance σ^2 also has an integral form and a form similar to that of a discrete distribution.

$$\sigma^2 = \int_{-\infty}^{\infty} (x - \mu)^2 f(x)dx$$

The standard deviation σ is simply

$$\sigma = \sqrt{\sigma^2}$$

Example: Calculate the standard deviation of a data distribution function f(x), where

$$f(x) = \begin{cases} 0 & x < 1 \\ -2x^2 + 2 & -1 \leq x \leq 1 \\ 0 & x > 1 \end{cases}$$

First calculate the mean of the function. Since the function is zero except between 1 and −1, the integral can likewise be evaluated from −1 to 1.

$$\mu = \int_{-1}^{1} (-2x^2 + 2)xdx$$

$$\mu = -2\int_{-1}^{1} (x^3 - x)dx$$

$$\mu = -2 \left[\frac{x^4}{4} - \frac{x^2}{2}\right]_{x=-1}^{x=1}$$

$$\mu = -2 \left\{\left[\frac{(1)^4}{4} - \frac{(1)^2}{2}\right] - \left[\frac{(-1)^4}{4} 2 \frac{(-1)^2}{2}\right]\right\} = 0$$

The mean can also be seen clearly by the fact that the graph of the function $f(x)$ is symmetric about the y-axis, indicating that its center (or mean) is at $x = 0$. Next, calculate the variance of f.

$$\sigma^2 = \int_{-1}^{1} (x - 0)^2 (-2x^2 + 2)dx = -2\int_{-1}^{1} x^2(x^2 - 1)dx$$

$$\sigma^2 = -2\int_{-1}^{1} (x^4 - x^2)dx$$

$$\sigma^2 = -2\left[\frac{x^5}{5} - \frac{x^3}{3}\right]_{x=-1}^{x=1} = -2\left\{\left[\frac{(1)^5}{5} + \frac{(1)^3}{3}\right] - \left[\frac{(-1)^5}{5} - \frac{(-1)^3}{3}\right]\right\}$$

$$\sigma^2 = -2\left\{\frac{1}{5} - \frac{1}{3} - (-\frac{1}{5}) + (-\frac{1}{3})\right\} = -2\left(\frac{2}{5} - \frac{2}{3}\right)$$

$$\sigma^2 = \frac{8}{15} \approx 0.533$$

The standard deviation is

$$\sigma = \sqrt{\sigma^2} = \sqrt{\frac{8}{15}} \approx 0.730$$

Probability density functions

A large data set of continuous data is often represented using a probability distribution expressed as a PROBABILITY DENSITY FUNCTION. The integral of the probability density function over a certain range gives the probability of a data point being in that range of values. The integral of the probability density function over the whole range of values is equal to 1.

The *mean* value for a distribution of a variable x represented by a probability density function $f(x)$ is given by

$$\int_{-\infty}^{+\infty} xf(x)\,dx$$

(Compare this with its discrete counterpart $\bar{x} = \Sigma\, x_i f_i'$.)

The *median* is the upper bound for which the integral of the probability density function is equal to 0.5; i.e., if $\int_{-\infty}^{a} f(x)\,dx = 0.5$, then a is the median of the distribution.

The *mode* is the maximum value or values of the probability density function within the range of the function.

As mentioned before, the mean and median are very close together for symmetric distributions. If a distribution is skewed to the right, the mean is greater than the median. If a distribution is skewed to the left, the mean is smaller than the median.

> PROBABILITY DENSITY FUNCTION: the integral of the probability density function over a certain range gives the probability of a data point being in that range of values

> *If a distribution is skewed to the right, the mean is greater than the median. If a distribution is skewed to the left, the mean is smaller than the median.*

Example: Find the mean, median, and mode for the distribution given by the probability density function

$$f(x) = \begin{cases} 4x(1 - x^2) & 0 \leq x \leq 1 \\ 0 & \text{otherwise} \end{cases}$$

$$\text{Mean} = \int_{0}^{1} 4x^2(1 - x^2)\,dx = \frac{4x^3}{3}\Big|_{0}^{1} - \frac{4x^5}{5}\Big|_{0}^{1} = \frac{4}{3} - \frac{4}{5} = \frac{20 - 12}{15} = \frac{8}{15} = 0.53$$

If $x = a$ is the median, then

$$\int_{0}^{a} 4x(1 - x^2)\,dx = 0.5$$
$$\rightarrow \frac{4x^2}{2}\Big|_{0}^{a} - \frac{4x^4}{4}\Big|_{0}^{a} = 0.5$$
$$\rightarrow 2a^2 - a^4 = 0.5$$
$$\rightarrow 2a^4 - 4a^2 + 1 = 0$$

Solving for a yields

$$a^2 = \frac{4 \pm \sqrt{16 - 8}}{4} = 1 \pm \frac{2\sqrt{2}}{4} = 1 - \frac{\sqrt{2}}{2} \text{ (to keep } x \text{ within the range 0 to 1)}$$
$$a = \sqrt{1 - \frac{1}{\sqrt{2}}} = 0.54$$

The mode is obtained by taking the derivative of the probability density function and setting it to zero as shown below. (Notice that the second derivative is negative at $x = 0.58$, and, hence, this is clearly a maximum.)

$$\frac{d}{dx}(4x - 4x^3) = 4 - 12x^2 = 0$$
$$\rightarrow 12x^2 = 4$$
$$\rightarrow x^2 = \frac{1}{3}$$
$$\rightarrow x = \frac{1}{\sqrt{3}} = 0.58$$

SKILL 11.5 Applying inferential statistics (e.g., confidence intervals, statistical significance) and concepts of validity and reliability

The law of large numbers states that the larger the sample size of a random process (or the more times a random variable is measured), the closer the sample mean will come to the population mean.

The law of large numbers and the central limit theorem are two fundamental concepts in statistics. The law of large numbers states that the larger the sample size of a random process (or the more times a random variable is measured), the closer the sample mean will come to the population mean (in other words, the sample mean will approach the expected value). For example, the average weight of 40 apples out of a population of 100 will more closely approximate the population average weight than will a sample of 5 apples. Thus, the process of statistical inference should take note of the importance of a sufficiently large sample size when making conclusions about a general random variable or process. Although time or monetary considerations can limit sample size, greater confidence is achieved through a larger sample.

The law of large numbers and the central limit theorem show the importance of a large sample size and a large number of samples to the process of statistical inference. As sample size and the number of samples taken increase, the accuracy of conclusions about the population drawn from the sample data increases.

The central limit theorem expands on the law of large numbers by stating that as the number of samples increases, the distribution of sample means (averages) approaches a normal distribution. This holds true regardless of the distribution of the population. Thus, as the number of samples taken increases, the sample mean becomes closer to the population mean. This property of statistics allows for the analysis of the properties of populations with unknown distributions.

STATISTICAL HYPOTHESIS TESTING is a method of determining, to within a certain confidence level, whether a hypothesis can be accepted according to a certain set of data.

The first step of hypothesis testing is to formulate the so-called NULL HYPOTHESIS, which is assumed to be true and is to be accepted unless sufficient evidence warrants its rejection. Thus, the null hypothesis is often a simple or readily accepted statement, and it is typically labeled H_0. The opposite of the null hypothesis is the so-called alternate hypothesis, which is typically labeled H_1 or H_a. If the null hypothesis is rejected, the alternate hypothesis is then accepted.

The next step involves computing some test statistic using the associated sample data. Comparison of this data with a critical value for the test statistic (which is a threshold value for a given confidence) allows determination of whether to accept or reject the null hypothesis.

Common test statistics include the t-test, the z-test, and the χ^2 (chi-square) "goodness of fit" test.

The (Student's) t-test is the method most commonly used to evaluate the difference in means between two groups. The t-test assesses whether the means of two groups are statistically different from each other. The formula for the t-test is a ratio: the numerator of the ratio is the difference between the two means or averages, and the denominator is a measure of the variability or dispersion of the scores.

$$\frac{\text{difference between group means}}{\text{variability of groups}} = \frac{\bar{X}_T - \bar{X}_C}{SE(\bar{X}_T - \bar{X}_C)} = \text{t-value}$$

In this example T refers to a treatment group and C refers to a control group. To compute the numerator of the formula, find the difference between the means. The denominator is called the standard error of the difference. To compute this quantity, take the variance for each group and divide it by the population of that group. Add these two values and then take the square root of the sum.

$$SE\left(\bar{X}_T - \bar{X}_C\right) = \sqrt{\frac{\text{var}_T}{n_T} + \frac{\text{var}_C}{n_C}}$$

The final formula for the t-test is

$$t = \frac{\bar{X}_T - \bar{X}_C}{\sqrt{\frac{\text{var}_T}{n_T} + \frac{\text{var}_C}{n_C}}}$$

Once the t-value is computed, a Student's t distribution table is needed to compare the t-test statistic with the threshold value for a given confidence level. This confidence level is often expressed as a risk, or alpha level, which is usually 0.05.

Another important value is the number of degrees of freedom (df) for the test. In the t-test, df is the sum of the populations in both groups less two. Using the t-value, the alpha level, and df, it is possible to look up the t-value in a standard table to determine whether the t-value is large enough to be significant. If it is, one can conclude (to a confidence defined by the alpha level) that the difference between the means for the two groups is statistically significant.

NULL HYPOTHESIS: a simple or readily accepted statement which is assumed to be true and is to be accepted unless sufficient evidence warrants its rejection

STATISTICAL HYPOTHESIS TESTING: a method of determining, to within a certain confidence level, whether a hypothesis can be accepted according to a certain set of data

Common test statistics include the t-test, the z-test, and the χ^2 (chi-square) "goodness of fit" test.

Example: The national average household income, which is based on a random sample of 500 households, is $43,000 with a standard deviation of $12,000. In a particular region, a 25-household sample indicates that the average household income is $39,000 with a standard deviation of $15,000. Determine if the discrepancy between average incomes is statistically significant.

Define the null and alternate hypotheses as follows:

H_0: There is no significant difference between the average incomes.

H_a: There is a significant difference between the average incomes.

Use the Student's t-test to calculate a test statistic. Assume an alpha level of 0.05. Also, convert standard deviations to variances by squaring.

$$t = \frac{\bar{X}_T - \bar{X}_C}{\sqrt{\frac{var_T}{n_T} + \frac{var_C}{n_C}}} = \frac{\$39{,}000 - \$43{,}000}{\sqrt{\frac{(\$15{,}000)^2}{25} + \frac{(\$12{,}000)^2}{500}}}$$

$$t = \left| \frac{4{,}000}{\sqrt{9{,}000{,}000 + 288{,}000}} \right| \approx 1.31$$

The number of degrees of freedom in this case is $500 + 25 - 2 = 523$. In many cases, the table of values for the Student's t distribution will not list this high a number, so infinity is usually close enough. The critical t-value for an alpha value of 0.05 is 1.65. Since $1.31 < 1.65$, there is not sufficient reason to reject the null hypothesis. Thus, it can be concluded to a confidence level of 95% that there is no statistically significant difference between the regional average income and the national average income.

Chi-square tests are used to determine the acceptability of a null hypothesis. They are useful for testing the "goodness-of-fit" between an observed distribution and an expected distribution or for testing the independence of two variables.

The chi-square value is calculated using the observed and expected frequencies of a distribution. Given that O_i is the observed frequency for the ith value of a data set and E_i is the expected frequency, then the chi-square (χ^2) value is

$$\chi^2 = \sum_{i=1}^{N} \frac{(O_i - E_i)^2}{E_i}.$$

Here, N is the total number of values in the observed data set. Notice that NO_i and NE_i are the total number of observed and expected samples, respectively, of the ith value of the data set. Notice also that χ^2 is a measure of the deviation of the observed values from the expected values. If the observed values are precisely the same as the expected values, then χ^2 is zero. A high χ^2 means that there is large variation.

DEGREES OF FREE-DOM: the total number of possible values or value classes, minus one

Another important parameter in the chi-square test is the degrees of freedom, n. The number of DEGREES OF FREEDOM is the total number of possible values or value classes, minus one. If a problem involves rolling a six-sided die, the number of degrees of freedom is the six possible outcomes minus one, or five.

Problems may involve either finding or using the significance parameter α, which is the probability that χ^2 will exceed a certain amount c.

$$\alpha = P(\chi^2 > c) = 1 - P(\chi^2 \leq c)$$

A common value for α is 0.05, which is intended to ensure that a hypothesis is rejected only if it can reasonably be assumed that the lack of a fit or dependence results from intention rather than chance.

The critical values, c, corresponding to various significance levels, α, and degrees of freedom, n, can be found in χ^2 tables. A sample portion of the χ^2 table is shown below. Note that the probability values, P, correspond to $1 - \alpha$. (The values in the table have limited numerical accuracy, and cases where greater accuracy is needed may require direct calculation of the critical value.)

		$P(\chi^2 \leq C)$						
	0.99	0.95	0.90	0.75	0.50	0.25	0.10	0.05
1	6.63	3.84	2.71	1.32	0.46	0.10	0.02	0.00
2	9.21	5.99	4.61	2.77	1.39	0.58	0.21	0.10
3	11.3	7.81	6.25	4.11	2.37	1.21	0.58	0.35
4	13.3	9.49	7.78	5.39	3.36	1.92	1.06	0.71
5	15.1	11.1	9.24	6.63	4.35	2.67	1.61	1.15

(left column label: $n$)

Example: A coin is flipped 200 times and lands heads up 92 times and tails up 108 times. Determine if the coin is a fair coin.

The "fairness" of the coin can be determined using a chi-square test. First, establish a null hypothesis. In this example, the null hypothesis is that the coin should be equally likely to land heads up or tails up for a given flip. This null hypothesis allows us to state expected frequencies. For 200 tosses we would expect 100 heads and 100 tails.

Next, prepare a table.

	HEADS	TAILS	TOTAL
Observed	92	108	200
Expected	100	100	200
Total	192	208	400

The observed values are the data gathered. The expected values are the frequencies expected, based on the null hypothesis. Calculate χ^2 as follows, noting that there are two sample values: heads up and tails up.

$$\chi^2 = \sum_{i=1}^{2} \frac{(O_i - E_i)^2}{E_i} = \frac{(92 - 100)^2}{100} + \frac{(108 - 100)^2}{100}$$

$$\chi^2 = \frac{64}{100} + \frac{64}{100} = \frac{128}{100} = 1.28$$

Next, determine the degrees of freedom (n) by subtracting one from the number of sample values. In this example, there are two possible sample values (heads and tails), so $n = 1$.

An appropriate significance level (α) must also be chosen. For instance, assume that there should only be a 5% chance that the χ^2 value is greater than the critical value c. Next, consult the table of critical values of the chi-squared distribution.

The chi-squared value corresponding to $n = 1$ is 1.28. In the table above, the corresponding critical value c is 3.84. Since $1.28 < 3.84$, the hypothesis should not be rejected.

Notice, however, that if the number of heads was 114 and the number of tails 86, then the χ^2 value would be 3.92, which exceeds the critical value of $c = 3.84$. In this case, for the chosen significance level, there would be evidence that the coin was loaded, and the null hypothesis (the coin is fair) would be rejected.

COMPETENCY 12
UNDERSTAND THE PRINCIPLES OF PROBABILITY

SKILL 12.1 Analyzing the relationship between randomness and sampling methods in making statistical claims about populations

See Skill 11.1

SKILL 12.2 Determining the probabilities of simple and compound events using counting principles and the concept of sample space

The PROBABILITY of an outcome, given a RANDOM EXPERIMENT (a structured, repeatable experiment for which the outcome cannot be predicted or, alternatively, for which the outcome is dependent on "chance"), is the relative frequency of the outcome. The RELATIVE FREQUENCY of an outcome is the number of times an experiment yields that outcome for a very large (ideally, infinite) number of trials. For instance, if a "fair" coin is tossed a very large number of times, then the relative frequency of a "heads-up" outcome is 0.5, or 50% (that is, one out of every two trials, on average, should be heads up). The probability is this relative frequency.

In probability theory, the SAMPLE SPACE is a list of all possible outcomes of an experiment. For example, the sample space of tossing two coins is the set {HH, HT, TT, TH}, where H is heads and T is tails, and the sample space of rolling a six-sided die is the set {1, 2, 3, 4, 5, 6}. When conducting experiments with a large number of possible outcomes, it is important to determine the size of the sample space. The size of the sample space can be determined by using the fundamental counting principles and the rules of combinations and permutations.

A RANDOM VARIABLE is a function that corresponds to the outcome of some experiment or event, which is in turn dependent on "chance." For instance, the result of a tossed coin is a random variable: the outcome is either heads or tails, and each outcome has an associated probability. A DISCRETE VARIABLE is one that can only take on certain specific values. For instance, the number of students in a class can only be a whole number (e.g., 15 or 16, but not 15.5).

A CONTINUOUS VARIABLE, such as the weight of an object, a variable that can take on a continuous range of values.

The probabilities for the possible values of a random variable constitute the PROBABILITY DISTRIBUTION for that random variable. Probability distributions can be discrete, as with the case of the tossing of a coin (there are only two possible distinct outcomes), or they can be continuous, as with the outside temperature at a given time of day. In the latter case, the probability is represented as a continuous function over a range of possible temperatures, and finite probabilities can only be measured in terms of ranges of temperatures rather than specific temperatures. That is to say, for a continuous distribution, it is not meaningful to say "the probability that the outcome is x"; instead, only "the probability that the outcome is between x and $\triangle x$" is meaningful. (Note that if each potential

---

PROBABILITY: given a random experiment, the relative frequency of an outcome

RANDOM EXPERIMENT: a structured, repeatable experiment for which the outcome cannot be predicted

RELATIVE FREQUENCY: the number of times an experiment yields a certain outcome for a very large number of trials

SAMPLE SPACE: a list of all possible outcomes of an experiment

RANDOM VARIABLE: a function that corresponds to the outcome of some experiment or event

DISCRETE VARIABLE: can take on only certain specific values

CONTINUOUS VARIABLE: can take on a continuous range of values

PROBABILITY DISTRIBUTION: the probabilities for the possible values of a random variable outcome in a continuous distribution has a nonzero probability, then the sum of all the probabilities would be greater than 1, since there are an infinite number of potential outcomes.)

Example: Find the sample space and construct a probability distribution for tossing a six-sided die (with numbers 1 through 6) for which even numbers are twice as likely as odd numbers to come up on a given roll (assume the even numbers are equally likely and the odd numbers are equally likely).

The sample space is simply the set of all possible outcomes that can arise in a given trial. For this die, the sample space is {1, 2, 3, 4, 5, 6}. To construct the associated probability distribution, note first that the sum of the probabilities must equal 1. Let the probability of rolling an odd number (1, 3, or 5) be x; the probability of rolling an even number (2, 4, or 6) is then $2x$.

$$1 = p(1) + p(2) + p(3) + p(4) + p(5) + p(6) = 3x + 6x + 9x$$

$$x = \frac{1}{9}$$

The probability distribution can be shown as a histogram below.

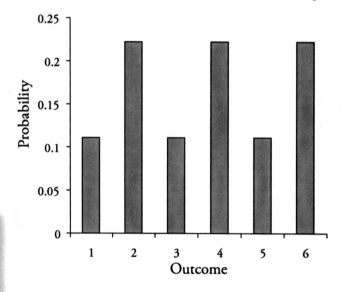

The sum of the probabilities for all the possible outcomes of a discrete distribution (or the integral of the continuous distribution over all possible values) must be equal to unity. The expected value of a probability distribution is the same as the mean value of a probability distribution. The EXPECTED VALUE is thus a measure of the central tendency or average value for a random variable with a given probability distribution.

A BERNOULLI TRIAL is an experiment whose outcome is random and can be either of two possible outcomes, which are called "success" or "failure." Tossing a coin

EXPECTED VALUE: a measure of the central tendency or average value for a random variable with a given probability distribution

BERNOULLI TRIAL: an experiment whose outcome is random and can be either of two possible outcomes, which are called "success" or "failure"

would be an example of a Bernoulli trial. The probability of success is represented by p, with the probability of failure being $q = 1 - p$. Bernoulli trials can be applied to any real-life situation in which there are only two possible outcomes. For example, concerning the birth of a child, the only two possible outcomes for the sex of the child are male or female.

Probability can also be expressed in terms of odds. ODDS are defined as the ratio of the number of favorable outcomes to the number of unfavorable outcomes. The sum of the favorable outcomes and the unfavorable outcomes should always equal the total possible outcomes.

ODDS: the ratio of the number of favorable outcomes to the number of unfavorable outcomes

For example, given a bag of 12 red marbles and 7 green marbles, compute the odds of randomly selecting a red marble.

Odds of red $= \frac{12}{7}$

Odds of not getting red $= \frac{7}{12}$

In the case of flipping a coin, it is equally likely that a head or a tail will be tossed. The odds of tossing a head are 1:1. This is called even odds.

A SIMPLE EVENT is a single event such as a coin toss. A COMPOUND EVENT is a combination of two or more simple events that may or may not be dependent on each other. The counting principles described below are used to calculate probabilities for compound events.

SIMPLE EVENT: a single event such as a coin toss

COMPOUND EVENT: a combination of two or more simple events that may or may not be dependent on each other

The following discussion uses the symbols $\cap$ to mean "and," $\cup$ to mean "or," and $P(x)$ to mean "the probability of x." Also, $N(x)$ means "the number of ways that x can occur."

The Addition Rule

The ADDITION PRINCIPLE OF COUNTING states that if A and B are arbitrary events, then

$$N(A \cup B) = N(A) + N(B) - N(A \cap B).$$

ADDITION PRINCIPLE OF COUNTING: states that if A and B are arbitrary events, then $N(A \cup B) = N(A) + N(B) - N(A \cap B)$

Furthermore, if A and B are MUTUALLY EXCLUSIVE EVENTS, then

$$N(A \cup B) = N(A) + N(B).$$

Correspondingly, the probabilities associated with arbitrary events are

$$P(A \cup B) = P(A) + P(B) - P(A \cap B).$$

MUTUALLY EXCLUSIVE EVENTS: events that cannot occur together or have no outcomes in common

For mutually exclusive events, the probabilities are

$$P(A \cup B) = P(A) + P(B).$$

Example: In how many ways can you select a black card or a jack from an ordinary deck of playing cards?

Let B denote selection of a black card and let J denote selection of a jack. Then, since half the cards (26) are black and four are jacks,

$N(B) = 26$

$N(J) = 4.$

Also, since a card can be both black and a jack (the jack of spades and the jack of clubs),

$N(B \cap J) = 2.$

Thus, the solution is

$N(B \cup J) = N(B) + N(J) - N(B \cap J) = 26 + 4 - 2 = 28.$

Example: A travel agency offers 40 possible trips: 14 to Asia, 16 to Europe, and 10 to South America. In how many ways can you select a trip to Asia or to Europe through this agency?

Let A denote selection of a trip to Asia and let E denote selection of a trip to Europe. Since these are mutually exclusive events, then

$N(A \cup E) = N(A) + N(E) = 14 + 16 = 30$

Therefore, there are 30 ways you can select a trip to Asia or to Europe.

The Multiplication Rule

The MULTIPLICATION PRINCIPLE OF COUNTING FOR DEPENDENT EVENTS states that if A and B are arbitrary events, then the number of ways that A and B can occur in a two-stage experiment is given by

$N(A \cap B) = N(A)N(B \mid A),$

where $N(B \mid A)$ is the number of ways B can occur given that A has already occurred. This expression is also known as the joint probability of events A and B. If A and B are independent events (events for which the probability of one event is not dependent on the outcome of another event), then

$N(A \cap B) = N(A)N(B).$

Also, the probabilities associated with arbitrary events are

$P(A \cap B) = P(A)P(B \mid A).$

For independent events, the probabilities are

$P(A \cap B) = P(A)P(B).$

> **MULTIPLICATION PRINCIPLE OF COUNTING FOR DEPENDENT EVENTS:** if A and B are arbitrary events, then the number of ways that A and B can occur in a two-stage experiment is given by $N(A \cap B) = N(A)N(B \mid A)$ where $N(B \mid A)$ is the number of ways B can occur given that A has already occurred

Example: In how many ways can two jacks from an ordinary deck of 52 cards be drawn in succession if the first card is not replaced into the deck before the second card is drawn (that is, without replacement)?

This is a two-stage experiment. Let A be selection of a jack in the first draw and let B be selection of a jack in the second draw. It is clear that

$$N(A) = 4.$$

If the first card drawn is a jack, however, then there are only three remaining jacks remaining for the second draw. Thus, drawing two cards without replacement means the events A and B are dependent, and

$$N(B|A) = 3.$$

The solution is

$$N(A \cap B) = N(A)N(B|A) = (4)(3) = 12.$$

Example: How many six-letter code "words" can be formed if repetition of letters is not allowed?

Since these are code words, a word does not have to be in the dictionary; for example, *abcdef* could be a code word. Since the experiment requires choosing each letter without replacing the letters from previous selections, the experiment has six stages.

Repetition is not allowed; thus, there are 26 choices for the first letter, 25 for the second, 24 for the third, 23 for the fourth, 22 for the fifth, and 21 for the sixth. Therefore, if A is the selection of a six-letter code word without repetition, then

$$N(A) = (26)(25)(24)(23)(22)(21) = 165,765,600.$$

There are over 165 million ways to choose a six-letter code word with six unique letters.

Finite Probability

Using the fundamental counting principles described above, finite probability problems can be solved. Generally, finding the probability of a particular event or set of events involves dividing the number of ways the particular event can take place by the total number of possible outcomes for the experiment. Thus, by appropriately counting these possible outcomes using the above rules, probabilities can be determined.

Example: Determine the probability of rolling three even numbers on three successive rolls of a six-sided die.

This is a three-stage experiment. First, determine the total number of possible outcomes for three rolls of a die. For each roll,

$N(\text{roll}) = 6.$

There are three possible even rolls for a die: 2, 4, and 6.

$N(\text{even}) = 3$

The probability of rolling an even number on any particular roll is

$P(\text{even}) = \frac{N(\text{even})}{N(\text{roll})} = \frac{3}{6} = \frac{1}{2}.$

For three successive rolls, use the multiplication rule for mutually exclusive events.

$P(3 \text{ even rolls}) = P(\text{even})^3 = (\frac{1}{2})^3 = \frac{1}{8} = 0.125$

Thus, the probability of rolling three successive even numbers using a six-sided die is 0.125.

Dependent and Independent Events

Dependent events occur when the probability of the second event depends on the outcome of the first event. For example, consider these two events: the home team wins the semifinal round (event *A*) and the home team wins the final round (event *B*). The probability of event *B* is contingent on the probability of event *A*. If the home team fails to win the semifinal round, it has a zero probability of winning in the final round. On the other hand, if the home team wins the semifinal round, it may have a finite probability of winning in the final round. Symbolically, the probability of event *B*, given event *A*, is written $P(B|A)$. The conditional probability can be calculated according to the following definition, in which the symbol ∩ means "and," the symbol ∪ means "or," and the notation $P(x)$ means "the probability of *x*."

$P(B|A) = \frac{P(A \cap B)}{P(A)}$

> *Dependent events occur when the probability of the second event depends on the outcome of the first event.*

Consider a pair of dice, one red and one green. First the red die is rolled, followed by the green die. It is apparent that these events do not depend on each other, since the outcome of the roll of the green die is not affected by the outcome of the roll of the red die. The total probability of the two independent events can be found by multiplying the separate probabilities.

$P(A \cap B) = P(A)P(B)$
$P(A \cap B) = (\frac{1}{6})(\frac{1}{6}) = \frac{1}{36}$

In many instances, however, events are not independent. Suppose a jar contains 12 red marbles and 8 blue marbles. If a marble is selected at random and then replaced, the probability of picking a certain color is the same in the second trial as it is in the first trial. If the marble is not replaced, then the probability of picking a certain color is not the same in the second trial, because the total number of marbles is decreased by one. This is an illustration of conditional probability. If R_n signifies selection of a red marble on the nth trial and B_n signifies selection of a blue marble on the nth trial, the probability of selecting a red marble in two trials *with replacement* is

$$P(R_1 \cap R_2) = P(R_1)P(R_2) = \left(\frac{12}{20}\right)\left(\frac{12}{20}\right) = \frac{144}{400} = 0.36$$

The probability of selecting a red marble in two trials *without replacement* is

$$P(R_1 \cap R_2) = P(R_1)P(R \mid R_1) = \left(\frac{12}{20}\right)\left(\frac{11}{19}\right) = \frac{132}{360} \approx 0.367$$

Example: A car has a 75% probability of traveling 20,000 miles without breaking down. It has a 50% probability of traveling 10,000 additional miles without breaking down if it first reaches 20,000 miles without breaking down. What is the probability that the car reaches 30,000 miles without breaking down?

Let event A be that the car reaches 20,000 miles without breaking down.

$$P(A) = 0.75$$

Event B is that the car travels an additional 10,000 miles without breaking down (assuming it didn't break down for the first 20,000 miles). Since event B is contingent on event A, write the probability

$$P(B \mid A) = 0.50$$

Use the conditional probability formula to find the probability that the car travels 30,000 miles $(A \cap B)$ without breaking down.

$$P(B \mid A) = \frac{P(A \cap B)}{P(A)}$$
$$P(B \mid A) = \frac{P(A \cap B)}{0.75}$$
$$P(A \cap B) = (0.50)\,(0.75) = 03.75$$

Thus, the car has a 37.5% probability of traveling 30,000 consecutive miles without breaking down.

SKILL 12.3 **Estimating probabilities based on data collection, experiments, and simulations**

Probability Simulations

Simulations of random events or variables can be helpful in making informal inferences about theoretical probability distributions. Although simulations can involve use of physical situations that bear some similarity to the situation of interest, often simulations involve computer modeling.

Pseudorandom numbers

One of the crucial aspects of modeling probability using a computer program is the need for a random number that can be used to "randomize" the aspect of the program that corresponds to the event or variable. Although there is no function on a computer that can provide a truly random number, most programming languages have some function designed to produce a pseudorandom number. A PSEUDORANDOM NUMBER is not truly random, but it is sufficiently unpredictable that it can be used as a random number in many contexts.

Pseudorandom numbers can serve as the basis for simulation of rolling a die, flipping a coin, selecting an object from a collection of different objects, and a range of other situations. If, for instance, the pseudorandom number generator produces a number between 0 and 1, simply divide up that range in accordance with the probabilities of each particular outcome. (For instance, assign 0 to 0.5 as heads and 0.5 to 1 as tails for the flip of a fair coin.) By performing a number of simulated trials and tallying the results, empirical probability distributions can be created.

Ideally, as the number of trials goes to infinity, the empirical probability distribution should approach the theoretical distribution. As a result, by performing a sufficiently large number of trials (this number must be at least somewhat justified for the particular situation), one should be able to make informal inferences based on the data. Such inferences, however, must take into account the limitations of the computer, such as the inability to perform an infinite number of trials in finite time and the numerical inaccuracies that are an inherent part of computer programming.

> **PSEUDORANDOM NUMBER:** a number that is not truly random but that is sufficiently unpredictable that it can be used as a random number in many contexts

---

SKILL 12.4 **Applying discrete and continuous probability distributions** *(e.g., uniform, binomial, normal)* **to make inferences about a population**

The Normal Distribution

A NORMAL DISTRIBUTION (frequently called a bell curve) is the probability distribution associated with most sets of real-world data. A normal distribution has a continuous random variable X with mean μ and variance σ^2. The normal distribution has the following form.

$$f(x) = \frac{1}{\sigma\sqrt{2\pi}} e^{\frac{1}{2}\left(\frac{x-\mu}{\sigma}\right)^2}$$

> **NORMAL DISTRIBUTION:** the probability distribution associated with most sets of real-world data; also called a bell curve

The total area under the normal curve is 1. Thus,

$$\int_{-\infty}^{\infty} f(x)\,dx = 1.$$

Since the area under the curve of this function is 1, the distribution can be used to determine probabilities through integration. If a continuous random variable x follows the normal distribution, then the probability that x has a value between a and b is

$$P(a < X \le b) = \int_{a}^{b} f(x)\,dx = F(b) - F(a).$$

Since this integral is difficult to evaluate analytically, tables of values are often used. Often, however, the tables use the integral

$$\frac{1}{\sqrt{2\pi}} \int_{a}^{b} e^{-\frac{t^2}{2}}\,dt = F(b) - F(a).$$

To use this form, simply convert x values to t values using

$$t = \frac{x_i - \mu}{\sigma}.$$

where x_i is a particular value for the random variable X. This formula is often called the Z-SCORE.

> **Z-SCORE:** this score gives the number of standard deviations between a data value x and the mean of the x distribution

Example: Albert's Bagel Shop's morning customer load follows a normal distribution, with mean (average) 50 and standard deviation 10. Determine the probability that the number of customers on a particular morning will be less than 42.

First, convert to a form that allows use of normal distribution tables:

$$t = \frac{x - \mu}{\sigma} \quad \frac{42 - 50}{10} = -0.8.$$

Next, use a table to find the probability corresponding to the z-score. The actual integral in this case is

$$P(X < 42) = \frac{1}{\sqrt{2\pi}} \int_{-\infty}^{-0.8} e^{-\frac{t^2}{2}}\,dt.$$

The table gives a value for $x = 0.8$ of 0.7881. To find the value for $x < -0.8$, subtract this result from 1.

$$P(X < 42) = 1 - 0.7881 = 0.2119$$

This means that there is about a 21.2% chance that there will be fewer than 42 customers in a given morning.

Example: The scores on Mr. Rogers' statistics exam follow a normal distribution with mean 85 and standard deviation 5. A student is wondering about the probability that she will score between 90 and 95 on her exam.

To compute $P(90 < x < 95)$, first compute the z-scores for each raw score.

$$z_{90} = \frac{90 - 85}{5} = 1$$

$$z_{95} = \frac{95 - 85}{5} = 2$$

Use the tables to find $P(1 < z < 2)$. To do this, subtract as follows.
$$P(1 < z < 2) = P(z < 2) - P(z < 1)$$

The table yields
$$P(1 < z < 2) = 0.9772 - 0.8413 = 0.1359.$$

It can then be concluded that there is a 13.6% chance that the student will score between a 90 and a 95 on her exam.

The Binomial Distribution

The binomial distribution is a probability distribution for discrete random variables and is expressed as
$$f(x) = \binom{n}{x} p^x q^{n-x},$$

where a sequence of n trials of an experiment are performed and where p is the probability of "success" and q is the probability of "failure." The value x is the number of times the experiment yields a successful outcome. Notice that this probability function is the product of p^x (the probability of successful outcomes in x trials) and q^{n-x} (the probability of unsuccessful outcomes in the remainder of the trials). The factor $\binom{n}{x}$ indicates that the x successful trials can be chosen $\binom{n}{x}$ ways (combinations) from the n total trials. (In other words, the successful trials may occur at different points in the sequence.)

Example: A loaded coin has a probability 0.6 of landing heads up. What is the probability of getting three heads in four successive tosses?
Use the binomial distribution. In this case, p is the probability of the coin landing heads up, and $q = 1 - p$ is the probability of the coin landing tails up. Also, the number of "successful" trials (heads up) is 3. Then,
$$f(3) = \binom{4}{3} (0.6)^3 (1 - 0.6)^{4-3}$$
$$f(3) = \frac{4!}{3!\,(4 - 3)!} (0.6)^3 (0.4)^1$$
$$f(3) = \frac{24}{6(1)} (0.216) (0.4) = 0.3456$$

Thus, there is a 34.56% chance that the loaded coin will land heads up three out of four times.

The Exponential Distribution

The exponential distribution is for continuous random variables and has the following form.
$$f(x) = \lambda e^{-\lambda x}$$

Here, $x \geq 0$. The parameter λ is called the rate parameter. For instance, the exponential distribution is often applied to failure rates. If a certain device has a failure rate of λ failures per hour, then the probability that a device has failed at time T hours is

$$P(T) = \lambda \int_0^T e^{-\lambda t}\, dt = -\lambda \frac{1}{\lambda} e^{-\lambda t} \Big|_0^T = -[e^{-\lambda t} - e^0] = 1 - e^{-\lambda t}.$$

Example: Testing has revealed that a newly designed widget has a failure rate of 1 per 5,000 hours of use. What is the probability that a particular part will be operational after a year of continual use?

Use the formula given above for the exponential distribution.

$$P(1 \text{ year}) = 1 - e^{-\lambda(1 \text{ year})}$$

Write λ in terms of failures per year.

$$\lambda = \frac{1 \text{ failure}}{5,000 \text{ hours}} \left(\frac{24 \text{ hours}}{1 \text{ day}}\right)\left(\frac{365 \text{ days}}{1 \text{ year}}\right) = 1.752 \frac{\text{failures}}{\text{year}}$$

$$P(1 \text{ year}) = 1 - e^{-1.752(1)} = 1 - 0.173 = 0.827$$

Thus, there is an 82.7% probability that the device will be operational after one year of continual use.

COMPETENCY 13
UNDERSTAND THE PROCESSES AND APPLICATIONS OF DISCRETE MATHEMATICS

SKILL 13.1 Applying systematic counting techniques

Example: Suppose you want to order a pizza. You have a choice of three sizes (small, medium, or large), three types of crust (thin, pan, or hand-tossed), four choices of meat (pepperoni, sausage, both, or none), and three choices of cheese (regular, double, or stuffed with cheese). How many different types of pizza could you order?

$3 \times 3 \times 4 \times 3 = 108$ different types of pizza

Another method of basic counting is the tree diagram.

Example: Suppose you want to look at the possible sequence of events for having two children in a family. Since a child will be either a boy or a girl, you would have the following tree diagram to illustrate the possible outcomes:

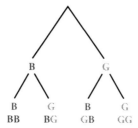

From the diagram, you see that there are four possible outcomes, two of which are the same.

Using Pascal's Triangle to Solve Problems

Pascal's triangle looks like the following:

$$
\begin{array}{ccccccccccc}
& & & & & 1 & & & & & \\
& & & & 1 & & 1 & & & & \\
& & & 1 & & 2 & & 1 & & & \\
& & 1 & & 3 & & 3 & & 1 & & \\
& 1 & & 4 & & 6 & & 4 & & 1 & \\
1 & & 5 & & 10 & & 10 & & 5 & & 1 \\
\end{array}
$$

where the sum of Row 1 = 2^0, Row 2 = 2^1, Row 3 = 2^2, Row 4 = 2^3, Row 5 = 2^4, Row 6 = 2^5. From this, we can see that the sum of row n would be 2^n.

Pascal's Triangle is useful in experiments in which there are only two equally likely possibilities, such as coin tosses.

Example: Find the probability of getting at least 5 heads when tossing 6 coins.

Solution: The fundamental counting property tells us that there are 2^6 possible outcomes when tossing 6 coins. We then construct the row of Pascal's Triangle that begins 1, 6.

$$
\begin{array}{ccccccc}
1 & 6 & 15 & 20 & 15 & 6 & 1 \\
\end{array}
$$

The first five numbers, 1, 6, 15, 20, and 15, represent the number of outcomes for which there are at least 5 heads. Therefore, we find the probability of tossing at least 5 heads with 6 coins as:

$$
\frac{(1 + 6 + 15 + 20 + 15)}{2^6} = \frac{57}{64}.
$$

Permutations and Combinations

A PERMUTATION is the number of possible arrangements of n items, without repetition, where order of selection is important.

A COMBINATION is the number of possible arrangements of n items, without repetition, where order of selection is not important.

Example: If any two numbers are selected from the set {1, 2, 3, 4}, list the possible permutations and combinations.

Combinations	Permutations
12, 13, 14, 23, 24, 34: six ways	12, 21, 13, 31, 14, 41, 23, 32, 24, 42, 34, 43: twelve ways

Note that the list of permutations includes 12 and 21 as separate possibilities since the order of selection is important. In the case of combinations, however, the order of selection is not important and, therefore, 12 is the same combination as 21. Hence, 21 is not listed separately as a possibility.

The number of permutations and combinations may also be found by using the formulae given below.

The number of possible permutations in selecting r objects from a set of n is given by

$$_nP_r = \frac{n!}{(n-r)!}$$ The notation nPr is read "the number of permutations of n objects taken r at a time."

In our example, two objects are being selected from a set of four.

$$_4P_2 = \frac{4!}{(4-2)!}$$ Substitute known values.

$$_4P_2 = 12$$

The number of possible combinations in selecting r objects from a set of n is given by

$$_nC_r = \frac{n!}{(n-r)!r!}$$ The number of combinations when r objects are selected from n objects.

$$_4C_2 = \frac{4!}{(4-2)!2!}$$ Substitute known values.

$$_4C_2 = 6$$

Objects arranged in a row

It can be shown that $_nP_n$, the number of ways n objects can be arranged in a row, is equal to $n!$. We can think of the problem as n positions being filled, one at a time. The first position can be filled in n ways using any one of the n objects. Since one of the objects has already been used, the second position can be filled

PERMUTATION: the number of possible arrangements of n items, without repetition, where order of selection is important

COMBINATION: the number of possible arrangements of n items, without repetition, where order of selection is not important only in $n - 1$ ways. Similarly, the third position can be filled in $n - 2$ ways, and so on. Hence, the total number of possible arrangements of n objects in a row is given by

$$_nP_n = n(n - 1)(n - 2)........1 = n!$$

Example: Five books are placed in a row on a bookshelf. In how many different ways can they be arranged?

The number of possible ways in which 5 books can be arranged in a row is $5! = 1 \times 2 \times 3 \times 4 \times 5 = 120$.

The formula given above for $_nP_r$, the number of possible permutations of r objects selected from n objects, can also be proven in a similar manner. If r positions are filled by selecting from n objects, the first position can be filled in n ways, the second position can be filled in $n - 1$ ways, and so on (as shown before). The rth position can be filled in $n - (r - 1) = n - r + 1$ ways. Hence,

$$_nP_r = n(n - 1)(n - 2).....(n - r + 1) = \frac{n!}{(n - r)!}$$

The formula for the number of possible combinations of r objects selected from n, $_nC_r$, may be derived by using the above two formulae. For the same set of r objects, the number of permutations is $r!$. All of these permutations, however, correspond to the same combination. Hence,

$$_nC_r = \frac{_nP_r}{r!} = \frac{n!}{(n - r)!r!}$$

Objects arranged in a ring

The number of permutations of n objects in a ring is given by $(n - 1)!$. This can be demonstrated by considering the fact that the number of permutations of n objects in a row is $n!$. When the objects are placed in a ring, moving every object one place to its left will result in the same arrangement. Moving each object two places to its left will also result in the same arrangement. We can continue this kind of movement up to n places to get the same arrangement. Thus the count $n!$ is n times too many when the objects are arranged in a ring. Hence, the number of permutations of n objects in a ring is given by $\frac{n!}{n} = (n - 1)!$.

Example: There are 20 people at a meeting. Five of them are selected to lead a discussion. How many different combinations of five people can be selected from the group? If the five people are seated in a row, how many different seating permutations are possible? If the five people are seated around a circular table, how many possible permutations are there?

The number of possible combinations of 5 people selected from the group of 20 is

$$_{20}C_5 = \frac{20!}{15!5!} = \frac{16 \times 17 \times 18 \times 19 \times 20}{1 \times 2 \times 3 \times 4 \times 5} = \frac{1860480}{120} = 15504.$$

The number of possible permutations of the five seated in a row is

$$_{20}P_5 = \frac{20!}{15!} = 16 \times 17 \times 18 \times 19 \times 20 = 1860480.$$

The number of possible permutations of the five seated in a circle is

$$\frac{_{20}P_5}{5} = \frac{20!}{5 \times 15!} = \frac{16 \times 17 \times 18 \times 19 \times 20}{5} = 372096.$$

Sets containing like objects

If the set of n objects contains some objects that are exactly alike, the number of permutations will again be different than $n!$. For instance, if n_1 of the n objects are exactly alike, then switching those objects among themselves will result in the same arrangement. Since we already know that n_1 objects can be arranged in $n_1!$ ways, $n!$ must be reduced by a factor of $n_1!$ to get the correct number of permutations. Thus, the number of permutations of n objects of which n_1 are exactly alike is given by $\frac{n!}{n_1!}$. Generalizing this, we can say that the number of different permutations of n objects of which n_1 are alike, n_2 are alike, ..., n_j are alike, is

$$\frac{n!}{n_1! \, n_2! ... \, n_j!} \text{ where } n_1 + n_2..... + n_j = n.$$

Example: A box contains 3 red, 2 blue, and 5 green marbles. If all the marbles are taken out of the box and arranged in a row, how many different permutations are possible?

The number of possible permutations is

$$\frac{10!}{3!2!5!} = \frac{6 \times 7 \times 8 \times 9 \times 10}{6 \times 2} = 2520.$$

SKILL 13.2 Applying symbolic logic

Logical Connectives and Conditional Statements

A SIMPLE STATEMENT represents a simple idea that can be described either as true or false, but not both. A small letter of the alphabet represents a simple statement.

Example: "Today is Monday."
This is a simple statement, since we can determine that this statement is either true or false. We can write $p = $ "Today is Monday."

Example: "Justin, please be quiet!"
We do not consider this a simple statement in our study of logic, since we cannot assign a truth value to it.

> **SIMPLE STATEMENT:**
> represents a simple idea that can be described either as true or false, but not both

CONNECTIVES: connectives (*and, or, not, if–then,* and *if and only if*)

Simple statements joined by CONNECTIVES (*and, or, not, if–then,* and *if and only if*) result in compound statements. Note that we can also form compound statements using *but, however,* or *nevertheless.* We can assign a truth value to a compound statement.

We frequently write conditional statements in *if–then* form. The *if* clause of the conditional is known as the HYPOTHESIS, and the *then* clause is called the CONCLUSION. In a proof, the hypothesis is the information that is assumed true, while the conclusion is what is to be proven true. We consider a conditional to be of the form "if p, then q," where p is the hypothesis and q is the conclusion.

HYPOTHESIS: known as the *if* clause of the conditional

CONCLUSION: called the *then* clause

$p \rightarrow q$ is read, "if p, then q."

~ (statement) is read, "It is not true that (statement)."

Example: If an angle has a measure of 90 degrees, then it is a right angle.
In this statement, "an angle has a measure of 90 degrees" is the hypothesis, and "it is a right angle" is the conclusion.

Example: If you are in Pittsburgh, then you are in Pennsylvania.
In this statement, "you are in Pittsburgh" is the hypothesis, and "you are in Pennsylvania" is the conclusion.

Logical Quantifiers and Negations

QUANTIFIERS are words that describe a quantity under discussion. These include words such as *all, none* (or *no*), and *some.*

QUANTIFIERS: words that describe a quantity under discussion

NEGATION of a statement: If a statement is true, then its negation must be false (and vice versa).

NEGATION: if a statement is true, then its negation must be false (and vice versa)

NEGATION RULES	
Statement	**Negation**
q	not q
not q	q
π and s	(not π) or (not s)
π or s	(not π) and (not s)
if p, then q	(p) and (not q)

Example: Select the statement that is the negation of "Some winter nights are not cold."

   A. All winter nights are not cold.

   B. Some winter nights are cold.

   C. All winter nights are cold.

   D. None of the winter nights are cold.

The negation of "some are" is "none is." Therefore, the negation statement is "None of the winter nights are cold." Therefore, the answer is D.

Example: Select the statement that is the negation of "If it rains, then the beach party will be called off."

   A. If it does not rain, then the beach party will not be called off.

   B. If the beach party is called off, then it will not rain.

   C. It does not rain, and the beach party will not be called off.

   D. It rains, and the beach party will not be called off.

The negation of "If p, then q" is "p and (not q)." The negation of the given statement is "It rains, and the beach party will not be called off." Select D.

Example: Select the negation of the statement "If they are elected, then all politicians go back on election promises."

   A. If they are elected, then many politicians go back on election promises.

   B. They are elected and some politicians go back on election promises.

   C. If they are not elected, some politicians do not go back on election promises.

   D. None of the above statements is the negation of the given statement.

Identify the key words of "if … then" and "all … go back." The negation of the given statement is "They are elected and none of the politicians goes back on election promises." So select response D, since statements A, B, and C are not the negations.

Example: Select the statement that is the negation of "The sun is shining bright, and I feel great."

A. If the sun is not shining bright, I do not feel great.

B. The sun is not shining bright, and I do not feel great.

C. The sun is not shining bright, or I do not feel great.

D. The sun is shining bright, and I do not feel great.

The negation of "*r* and *s*" is "(not *r*) or (not *s*)." Therefore, the negation of the given statement is "The sun is *not* shining bright, *or* I do not feel great." We select response C.

Inverse, Converse, and Contrapositive

LOGICAL COMPARISONS	
Conditional: If *p*, then *q*	*p* is the hypothesis, and *q* is the conclusion.
Inverse: If ~ *p*, then ~ *q*	Negate both the hypothesis and the conclusion from the original conditional. (If not *p*, then not *q*.)
Converse: If *q*, then *p*	Reverse the two clauses. The original hypothesis becomes the conclusion. The original conclusion then becomes the new hypothesis.
Contrapositive: If ~ *q*, then ~ *p*	Reverse the two clauses. The "If not *q*, then not *p*" original hpothesis becomes the conclusion. The original conclusion then becomes the new hypothesis. Then negate both the new hypothesis and the new conclusion.

Example: Given the conditional:

If an angle has 60°, then it is an acute angle.

Its **inverse**, in the form "If ~ *p*, then ~ *q*," would be

If an angle doesn't have 60°, then it is not an acute angle.

Notice that the inverse is false, even though the conditional statement was true.

Its **converse**, in the form "If *q*, then *p*," would be

If an angle is an acute angle, then it has 60°.

Notice that the converse is false, even though the conditional statement was true.

Its **contrapositive**, in the form "If q, then p," would be

If an angle isn't an acute angle, then it doesn't have 60°.

Notice that the contrapositive is true, assuming the original conditional statement was true.

Example: Find the inverse, converse, and contrapositive of the following conditional statements. Also determine whether each of the four statements is true or false.

Conditional: If $x = 5$ then $x^2 - 25 = 0$.	True
Inverse: If $x \neq 5$, then $x^2 - 25 \neq 0$.	False, x could be -5
Converse: If $x^2 - 25 = 0$, then $x = 5$	False, x could be -5
Contrapositive: If $x^2 - 25 \neq 0$, then $x \neq 5$.	True

Conditional: If $x = 5$, then $6x = 30$.	True
Inverse: If $x \neq 5$, then $6x \neq 30$.	True
Converse: If $6x = 30$, then $x = 5$.	True
Contrapositive: If $6x \neq 30$, then $x \neq 5$	True

Sometimes, as in this example, all four statements can be logically equivalent, but the only statement that will always be logically equivalent to the original conditional is the contrapositive.

Tip: If you are asked to pick a statement that is logically equivalent to a given conditional, look for the contrapositive. The inverse and converse are not always logically equivalent to every conditional. The contrapositive is always logically equivalent.

Venn Diagrams

We can diagram conditional statements using a VENN DIAGRAM. We can draw a diagram with one figure inside another figure. The inner figure represents the hypothesis, and the outer figure represents the conclusion. If we take the hypothesis to be true, then you are located inside the inner figure. If you are located in the inner figure, then you are also inside the outer figure, so that proves that the conclusion is true.

VENN DIAGRAM: a diagram using conditional statements

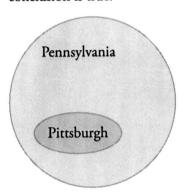

Sometimes that conclusion can then be used as the hypothesis for another conditional, which can result in a second conclusion.

Suppose the following statements were given to you, and you were asked to try to reach a conclusion:

A. All swimmers are athletes.
All athletes are scholars.

In "if-then" form, these would be:
If you are a swimmer, then you are an athlete.
If you are an athlete, then you are a scholar.

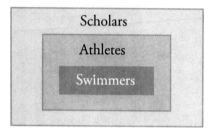

Clearly, if you are a swimmer, then you are also an athlete. This includes you in the group of scholars.

B. All swimmers are athletes.
All wrestlers are athletes.

In "if-then" form, these would be:
If you are a swimmer, then you are an athlete.
If you are a wrestler, then you are an athlete.

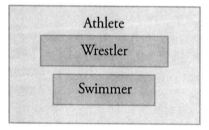

Clearly, if you are a swimmer or a wrestler, then you are also an athlete. This does NOT allow you to come to any other conclusions.

A swimmer may or may NOT also be a wrestler. Therefore, NO CONCLUSION IS POSSIBLE.

C. All rectangles are parallelograms.
Quadrilateral *ABCD* is not a parallelogram.

In "if–then" form, the first statement would be:
If a figure is a rectangle, then it is also a parallelogram.

Note that the second statement is the negation of the conclusion of statement one. Remember also that the contrapositive is logically equivalent to a given conditional—that is, "*If ~ q, then ~ p.*" Since "*ABCD* is not a parallelogram" is like saying "*If ~ q,*" then you can come to the conclusion "*then ~ p.*" Therefore, the conclusion is *ABCD* is not a rectangle.

Looking at the following Venn diagram, if all rectangles are parallelograms, then rectangles are included as part of the parallelograms. Since quadrilateral *ABCD* is not a parallelogram, that it is excluded from anywhere inside the parallelogram box. This allows you to conclude that *ABCD* cannot be a rectangle either.

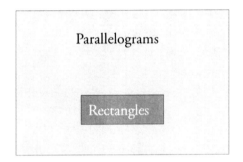

Counterexamples

A COUNTEREXAMPLE is an exception to a proposed rule or conjecture that disproves the conjecture. For example, the existence of a single nonbrown dog disproves the conjecture "All dogs are brown." Thus, any nonbrown dog is a counterexample.

In searching for mathematic counterexamples, one should consider extreme cases near the ends of the domain of an experiment and special cases where an additional property is introduced. Examples of extreme cases are numbers near zero and obtuse triangles that are nearly flat. An example of a special case for a problem involving rectangles is a square because a square is a rectangle with the additional property of symmetry.

Example: Identify a counterexample for the following conjectures.

1. If *n* is an even number, then *n* + 1 is divisible by 3.
   $n = 4$
   $n + 1 = 4 + 1 = 5$
   5 is not divisible by 3.

COUNTEREXAMPLE: an exception to a proposed rule or conjecture that disproves the conjecture

2. If n is divisible by 3, then $n^2 - 1$ is divisible by 4.
$n = 6$
$n^2 - 1 = 6^2 - 1 = 35$
35 is not divisible by 4.

SKILL 13.3 Performing operations on matrices

Addition, Subtraction, and Multiplication of Matrices

Matrices can be added or subtracted only if their dimensions are the same. To add (subtract) compatible matrices, simply add (subtract) the corresponding elements, as with the example below for 2×2 matrices.

$$\begin{pmatrix} a_{11} & a_{12} \\ a_{21} & a_{22} \end{pmatrix} + \begin{pmatrix} b_{11} & b_{12} \\ b_{21} & b_{22} \end{pmatrix} = \begin{pmatrix} a_{11} + b_{11} & a_{12} + b_{12} \\ a_{21} + b_{21} & a_{22} + b_{22} \end{pmatrix}$$

Multiplication of matrices is more complicated, except for the case of multiplication by a scalar. The product of a matrix and a scalar is found by multiplying each element of the matrix by the scalar.

$$c \begin{pmatrix} a_{11} & a_{12} \\ a_{21} & a_{22} \end{pmatrix} = \begin{pmatrix} ca_{11} & ca_{12} \\ ca_{21} & ca_{22} \end{pmatrix}$$

> Multiplication of two matrices is only defined if the number of columns in the first matrix is equal to the number of rows in the second matrix.

Multiplication of two matrices is only defined if the number of columns in the first matrix is equal to the number of rows in the second matrix. Matrix multiplication is not necessarily commutative. Given an $n \times m$ matrix ($\overline{A}$) multiplied by an $m \times p$ matrix ($\overline{B}$) (multiplied in that order), the product is an $n \times p$ matrix. Each element C_{ij} in the product matrix is equal to the sum of each element in the ith row of the $n \times m$ matrix multiplied by each corresponding element in the jth column of the $m \times p$ matrix. Thus, each element C_{ij} of the product matrix $\overline{AB}$ is equal to the following, where $\overline{AB} = \overline{C}$:

$$C_{ij} = \sum_{k=1}^{m} A_{ik} B_{kj}.$$

Consider the following example.

$$\begin{pmatrix} 1 & 2 & 3 \\ 4 & 5 & 6 \end{pmatrix} \begin{pmatrix} 7 \\ 8 \\ 9 \end{pmatrix}$$

The solution is found as follows.

$$\begin{pmatrix} 1 & 2 & 3 \\ 4 & 5 & 6 \end{pmatrix} \begin{pmatrix} 7 \\ 8 \\ 9 \end{pmatrix} = \begin{pmatrix} (1)(7) + (2)(8) + (3)(9) \\ (4)(7) + (5)(8) + (6)(9) \end{pmatrix} = \begin{pmatrix} 50 \\ 122 \end{pmatrix}$$

Matrix multiplication obeys the rules of associativity and distributivity, but not commutativity.

$$\overline{A}(\overline{BC}) = (\overline{AB})\overline{C}$$
$$\overline{A}(\overline{B} + \overline{C}) = \overline{AB} + \overline{AC}$$
$$(B + \overline{C})\overline{A} = \overline{BA} + \overline{CA}$$

Example: Determine the product $\overline{AB}$ of the following matrices.

$$\overline{A} = \begin{pmatrix} -1 & 2 & 8 \\ 4 & -3 & 7 \\ 0 & 1 & 4 \end{pmatrix} \quad \overline{B} = \begin{pmatrix} 0 & 5 & 0 \\ 7 & -2 & -1 \\ -8 & 0 & 3 \end{pmatrix}$$

The product $\overline{AB}$ is a 3×3 matrix. The first column of $\overline{AB}$ is the dot product of the first column of $\overline{B}$ with each row of $\overline{A}$.

$$\overline{AB} = \begin{pmatrix} -1 & 2 & 8 \\ 4 & -3 & 7 \\ 0 & 1 & 4 \end{pmatrix} \begin{pmatrix} 0 & 5 & 0 \\ 7 & -2 & -1 \\ -8 & 0 & 3 \end{pmatrix} = \begin{pmatrix} 0 + 14 - 64 & \cdot & \cdot \\ -21 - 56 & \cdot & \cdot \\ 7 - 32 & \cdot & \cdot \end{pmatrix}$$

The other columns of $\overline{AB}$ are found using the same approach for the other columns of $\overline{B}$.

$$\overline{AB} = \begin{pmatrix} -50 & -9 & 22 \\ -77 & 26 & 24 \\ -25 & -2 & 11 \end{pmatrix}$$

Determinants

Associated with every square matrix is a number called its determinant. The determinant of a matrix is typically denoted using straight brackets; thus, the determinant of matrix A is $|A|$. Use these formulas to calculate determinants.

$$\begin{vmatrix} a & b \\ c & d \end{vmatrix} = ad - bc$$

$$\begin{vmatrix} a_1 & b_1 & c_1 \\ a_2 & b_2 & c_2 \\ a_3 & b_3 & c_3 \end{vmatrix} = (a_1 b_2 c_3 + b_1 c_2 a_3 + c_1 a_2 b_3) - (a_3 b_2 c_1 + b_3 c_2 a_1 + c_3 a_2 b_1)$$

The second formula is found by repeating the first two columns and then using the diagonal lines to find the value of each expression shown below.

$$\begin{vmatrix} a_1 & b_1 & c_1 \\ a_2 & b_2 & c_2 \\ a_3 & b_3 & c_3 \end{vmatrix} \begin{matrix} a_1 & b_1 \\ a_2 & b_2 \\ a_3 & b_3 \end{matrix}$$
$$= (a_1 b_2 c_3 + b_1 c_2 a_3 + c_1 a_2 b_3) - (a_3 b_2 c_1 + b_3 c_2 a_1 + c_3 a_2 b_1)$$

Example: Find the value of the determinant of $\begin{pmatrix} 4 & -8 \\ 7 & 3 \end{pmatrix}$.

Use the formula for calculating the determinant.

$$\begin{vmatrix} 4 & -8 \\ 7 & 3 \end{vmatrix} = (4)(3) - (-8)(7) = 12 + 56 = 68$$

Applications of Matrices

Matrices are often used to solve systems of equations. They are also used by physicists, mathematicians, and biologists to organize and study data such as population growth, and they are used in finance for such purposes as investment growth and portfolio analysis. Matrices are easily translated into computer code in high-level programming languages and can be easily expressed in electronic spreadsheets.

The following is an example of using a matrix to solve a simple financial problem. A company has two stores. The incomes and expenses (in dollars) for the two stores, for three months, are shown in the matrices.

April	Income	Expenses		May	Income	Expenses		June	Income	Expenses
Store 1	190,000	170,000		Store 1	210,000	200,000		Store 1	220,000	215,000
Store 2	100,000	110,000		Store 2	125,000	120,000		Store 2	130,000	115,000

The owner wants to know what his first-quarter income and expenses were, so he adds the three matrices.

1st Quarter	Income	Expenses
Store 1	620,000	585,000
Store 2	355,000	345,000

Then, to find the profit for each store, subtract the total expenses from the total income.

Profit for Store 1 = $620,000 − $585,000 = $35,000
Profit for Store 2 = $355,000 − $345,000 = $10,000

Solving Systems of Equations Using Matrices

When given a system of equations, such as

$$ax + by = e$$
$$cx + dy = f,$$

the matrix equation is written in the following form.

$$\begin{pmatrix} a & b \\ c & d \end{pmatrix} \begin{pmatrix} x \\ y \end{pmatrix} = \begin{pmatrix} e \\ f \end{pmatrix}$$

The same general pattern follows for n equations in n variables. (The result is an $n \times n$ matrix with a variable vector and a constant vector, each with n entries.) The solution is found using the inverse of the matrix of coefficients. The inverse of a 2 $\times$ 2 matrix can be written as follows:

$$A^{-1} = \frac{1}{|A|} \begin{pmatrix} d & -b \\ -c & a \end{pmatrix}.$$

Then,

$$\begin{pmatrix} a & b \\ c & d \end{pmatrix}^{-1} \begin{pmatrix} a & b \\ c & d \end{pmatrix} \begin{pmatrix} x \\ y \end{pmatrix} = \begin{pmatrix} x \\ y \end{pmatrix} = \begin{pmatrix} a & b \\ c & d \end{pmatrix}^{-1} \begin{pmatrix} e \\ f \end{pmatrix}.$$

The solution set defined by the variable vector can then be found by performing the matrix multiplication on the right of the above equation.

$$\begin{pmatrix} x \\ y \end{pmatrix} = \frac{1}{|A|} \begin{pmatrix} d & -b \\ -c & a \end{pmatrix} \begin{pmatrix} e \\ f \end{pmatrix} = \frac{1}{|A|} \begin{pmatrix} ed - bf \\ af - ce \end{pmatrix}.$$

Solving systems of equations with many variables can involve the more complicated tasks of finding the determinant and the inverse of large matrices.

Note that if the determinant of a matrix is zero, then the matrix is called SINGULAR. In such cases, a unique solution to the system of equations does not exist.

> **SINGULAR:** occurs when the determinant of a matrix is zero

Gauss elimination

If a matrix larger than 2 $\times$ 2 must be inverted, then Gauss elimination can be used to find the solution. The approach for this technique first involves augmenting the matrix with the constant vector. Using the above example, the augmented matrix is

$$\left(\begin{array}{cc|c} a & b & e \\ c & d & f \end{array} \right).$$

The goal of Gauss elimination is to perform row operations such that the coefficient matrix becomes the identity matrix:

$$\begin{pmatrix} 1 & 0 & \cdots \\ 0 & 1 & \cdots \\ \vdots & \vdots & \ddots \end{pmatrix}$$

For the example matrix above, first divide the first row by a.

$$\left(\begin{array}{cc|c} 1 & \frac{b}{a} & \frac{e}{a} \\ c & d & f \end{array} \right)$$

Next, add c times the first row to the second row.

$$\begin{pmatrix} 1 & \frac{b}{a} & \Big| & \frac{e}{a} \\ 0 & d + \frac{cb}{a} & \Big| & f + \frac{ec}{a} \end{pmatrix}$$

The process can be continued until the result is found.

$$\begin{pmatrix} 1 & 0 & \Big| & \frac{ed - bf}{|A|} \\ 0 & 1 & \Big| & \frac{af - ce}{|A|} \end{pmatrix}$$

Example: Write the matrix equation of the following system of equations and solve for x and y.

$$3x - 4y = 2$$
$$2x + y = 5$$

$$\begin{pmatrix} 3 & -4 \\ 2 & 1 \end{pmatrix} \begin{pmatrix} x \\ y \end{pmatrix} = \begin{pmatrix} 2 \\ 5 \end{pmatrix} \qquad \text{Definition of matrix equation.}$$

$$\begin{pmatrix} x \\ y \end{pmatrix} = \frac{1}{11} \begin{pmatrix} 1 & 4 \\ -2 & 1 \end{pmatrix} \begin{pmatrix} 2 \\ 5 \end{pmatrix} \qquad \text{Multiply by the inverse of the coefficient matrix.}$$

$$\begin{pmatrix} x \\ y \end{pmatrix} = \frac{1}{11} \begin{pmatrix} 22 \\ 11 \end{pmatrix} \qquad \text{Matrix multiplication.}$$

$$\begin{pmatrix} x \\ y \end{pmatrix} = \begin{pmatrix} 2 \\ 1 \end{pmatrix} \qquad \text{Scalar multiplication.}$$

The solution is $x = 2$ and $y = 1$.

SKILL 13.4 **Applying a variety of models** *(e.g., vertex-edge graphs, trees, arrays)* **to solve problems**

Difference Equations

DIFFERENCE EQUA-TION: a discrete analog for a differential equation, with "differences" being analogous to derivatives

A **DIFFERENCE EQUATION** is a discrete analog for a differential equation, with "differences" being analogous to derivatives. For a sequence of numbers $\{a_n\}$, the first difference is defined as

$$d(a_n) = a_n - a_{n-1}$$

The second difference is given by

$$d^2(a_n) = d(a_n) - d(a_{n-1}) = a_n - 2a_{n-1} + a_{n-2}$$

Subsequent differences are defined in a similar fashion.

A difference equation is an equation composed of a discrete variable a_n and its differences of different orders. It is clear from the above definitions that a difference equation is nothing but a recurrence relation, and many people use the two terms interchangeably.

Graphs

A GRAPH is a set of points (or nodes) and lines (or edges) that connect some subset of these points. A FINITE GRAPH has a limited number of both nodes and edges. An example graph follows. Note that not all of the nodes in a graph need be connected to other nodes.

The edges of a graph may or may not have a specified direction or orientation; also, the edges (and nodes) may or may not have some assigned label or value. For instance, a graph representing airline flight paths might include nodes that represent cities and edges the represent the direction and distance of the paths between the cities.

Trees

A TREE is a graph that does not include any closed loops. In addition, a tree has no unconnected nodes (separate nodes or groups of connected nodes constitute a separate tree—groups of several trees are called a forest). In addition, the edges that connect the nodes of a tree do not have a direction or orientation. A FINITE TREE, like a finite graph, has a limited number of edges and nodes. The graph shown above is not a tree, but it takes the form of a tree with a few alterations:

Networks

A NETWORK is a graph (directed or undirected) in which each edge is assigned a positive real number in accordance with a specific function. The function may correspond to the distance between two points on a map, for instance.

GRAPH: a set of points (or nodes) and lines (or edges) that connect some subset of these points

FINITE GRAPH: a graph with a limited number of both nodes and edges

TREE: a graph that does not include any closed loops or unconnected nodes

FINITE TREE: a tree with a limited number of edges and nodes

NETWORK: a graph (directed or undirected) in which each edge is assigned a positive real number in accordance with a specific function

Solving Problems Using Trees and Graphs

Trees and graphs can be used to represent a wide variety of types of information. They can also be useful tools for solving problems that involve maps, hierarchies, directories, structures, communications networks, and a range of other objects.

Example: Find the shortest path between points A and B on the following directed graph.

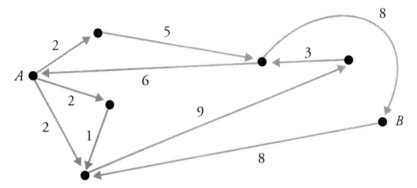

Taking careful note of the direction of the edges, find the possible routes through the graph from *A* to *B*. Only two paths are possible; choose the path with the smallest sum of the values along the associated edges.

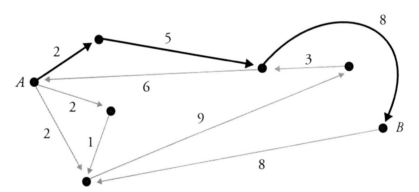

The total distance for the shortest path is 2 + 5 + 8 = 15.

DOMAIN V
MATHEMATICAL PROCESSES

PERSONALIZED STUDY PLAN

PAGE	COMPETENCY AND SKILL	KNOWN MATERIAL/ SKIP IT
249	**14: Understand mathematical connections and communication**	☐
	14.1: Identifying connections between concepts and procedures in mathematics	☐
	14.2: Identifying connections between mathematics and other disciplines	☐
	14.3: Expressing mathematical ideas in a variety of formats	☐
	14.4: Representing word problems algebraically	☐
	14.5: Identifying contributions to mathematics made by different individuals and cultures and the type of societal problems that gave rise to mathematical systems	☐
257	**15: Understand the content and methods for developing students' content-area reading skills to support their reading and learning in mathematics**	☐
	15.1: Demonstrating knowledge of key components and processes involved in reading	☐
	15.2: Demonstrating ability to plan instruction and select strategies to support all students' content-area reading	☐
	15.3: Demonstrating knowledge of explicit strategies for facilitating students' comprehension before, during, and after reading content-area texts and for promoting their use of comprehension strategies	☐
	15.4: Demonstrating knowledge of explicit strategies for promoting students' academic language and vocabulary development, including their knowledge of domain-specific vocabulary words	☐
	15.5: Demonstrating ability to plan instruction and select strategies that support students' reading and understanding of mathematics texts	☐

COMPETENCY 14
UNDERSTAND MATHEMATICAL CONNECTIONS AND COMMUNICATION

Identifying connections between concepts and procedures in mathematics

Recognition and understanding of the relationships between concepts and procedures is important to mathematical problem solving and the explanation of more complex processes. It becomes much easier for a student to retain information when it is presented from different viewpoints and linked to other familiar concepts. Ideally, a teacher will not present the information straight away but will let students think for themselves and discover the connections on their own with guidance from the teacher. Some examples of connections between familiar mathematical concepts and procedures are discussed below.

Recognition and understanding of the relationships between concepts and procedures is important to mathematical problem solving and the explanation of more complex processes.

- For instance, multiplication is simply repeated addition. This relationship explains the concept of variable addition. We can show that the expression $4x + 3x = 7x$ is true by rewriting 4 times x and 3 times x as repeated addition, yielding the expression $(x + x + x + x) + (x + x + x)$. Because of the relationship between multiplication and addition, variable addition is accomplished by coefficient addition.

- Addition and subtraction are really the same operation acting in opposite directions on the number line. Understanding this concept helps students in working with negative numbers, which are difficult for many students to grasp.

- The concept of rate appears in many different guises in mathematics such as in the speed of a vehicle, an interest rate, or the price per unit of an item. The concept of rate is also directly connected to the concept of slope of a straight line.

- Commonly used formulae such as $a^2 - b^2 = (a + b)(a - b)$ or $(a + b)^2 = a^2 + 2ab + b^2$ are not magical relationships that need to be memorized. They can simply be calculated by performing the familiar **FOIL** operation.

  Example: $(a + b)(a - b) = a^2 - ab + ba - b^2 = a^2 - b^2$

- In geometry, the perimeters, areas and volumes of different figures are usually presented as separate formulae. It is useful to point out that every area contains the product of two lengths (e.g. lw or πr^2) and every volume contains the product of three lengths (e.g. l^3, $\pi r^2 h$). This helps students understand the meaning of square and cubic units.

- The relationships between points, lines and planes become easier to visualize if one understands that a point is to a line as a line is to a plane. Just as two lines intersect in a point, two planes intersect in a line.

SKILL 14.2 Identifying connections between mathematics and other disciplines

Artists, musicians, scientists, social scientists, and business people use mathematical modeling to solve problems in their disciplines. These disciplines rely on the tools and symbols of mathematics to model natural events and manipulate data. Mathematics is a key aspect of visual art.

Artists use the geometric properties of shapes, ratios, and proportions in creating paintings and sculptures. For example, mathematics is essential to the concept of perspective. Artists must determine the appropriate lengths and heights of objects to portray three-dimensional distance in two dimensions.

Mathematics is also an important part of music. Many musical terms have mathematical connections. For example, the musical octave contains twelve notes and spans a factor of two in frequency. In other words, the frequency—the speed of vibration that determines tone and sound quality—doubles from the first note in an octave to the last. Thus, starting from any note we can determine the frequency of any other note using the following formula.

$$\text{Freq} = note \times 2^{\frac{N}{12}}$$

Here, N is the number of notes from the starting point and *note* is the frequency of the starting note. Mathematical understanding of frequency plays an important role in tuning musical instruments.

In addition to the visual and auditory arts, mathematics is an integral part of most scientific disciplines. The uses of mathematics in science are almost endless, and the following are but a few examples of how scientists use mathematics. Physical scientists use vectors, functions, derivatives, and integrals to describe and model the movement of objects. Biologists and ecologists use mathematics to model ecosystems and study DNA. Also, chemists use mathematics to study the interaction of molecules and to determine proper amounts and proportions of reactants.

Many social science disciplines use mathematics to model and solve problems. Economists, for example, use functions, graphs, and matrices to model the activities of producers, consumers, and firms. Political scientists use mathematics to model the behavior and opinions of the electorate. In addition, sociologists use mathematical functions to model the behavior of humans and human populations.

Finally, mathematical problem solving and modeling is essential to business planning and execution. For example, businesses rely on mathematical projections to plan business strategy. Additionally, stock market analysis and accounting rely on mathematical concepts.

SKILL 14.3 Expressing mathematical ideas in a variety of formats (e.g., verbally, graphically, symbolically)

Throughout this guide, mathematical operations and situations are represented through words, algebraic symbols, geometric diagrams, and graphs. A few commonly used representations are discussed below.

The basic mathematical operations are addition, subtraction, multiplication, and division. In word problems, these are represented by the following typical expressions.

Operation	Descriptive Words
Addition	plus, combine, sum, total, put together
Subtraction	minus, less, take away, difference
Multiplication	product, times, groups of
Division	quotient, into, split into equal groups

Symbolic representation is the basic language of mathematics. Converting data to symbols allows for easy manipulation and problem solving. Students should have the ability to recognize what the symbolic notation represents and to convert verbal information into symbolic form. For example, from the graph of a line, students should have the ability to determine the slope and intercepts and derive the line's equation from the observed data. Another possible application of symbolic representation is the formulation of algebraic expressions and relations from data presented in word-problem form.

Some verbal and symbolic representations of basic mathematical operations include the following:

Verbal	Symbolic
7 added to a number	$n + 7$
a number decreased by 8	$n - 8$
12 times a number divided by 7	$12n \div 7$
28 less than a number	$n - 28$
the ratio of a number to 55	$\frac{n}{55}$
4 times the sum of a number and 21	$4(n + 21)$

Multiplication can be shown using arrays. For instance, 3×4 can be expressed as 3 rows of 4 each.

□ □ □ □
□ □ □ □
□ □ □ □

In a similar manner, addition and subtraction can be demonstrated with symbols.

ψψψζζζ
$3 + 4 = 7$
$7 - 3 = 4$

Fractions can be represented using pattern blocks, fraction bars, or paper folding.

Diagrams of arithmetic operations can present mathematical data in visual form. For example, a number line can be used to add and subtract, as illustrated below.

Five added to negative four on the number line, or $-4 + 5 = 1$.

Pictorial representations can also be used to explain the arithmetic processes.

The diagram above shows that two groups of four equal eight, or $2 \times 4 = 8$. The next diagram illustrates the addition of two objects to three objects, resulting in five objects.

Concrete examples are real-world applications of mathematical concepts. For example, measuring the shadow produced by a tree or a building is a real-world application of trigonometric functions, the acceleration or velocity of a car is an application of derivatives, and finding the volume or the area of a swimming pool is a real-world application of geometric principles.

Pictorial illustrations of mathematic concepts help clarify difficult ideas and simplify problem solving. The following example illustrates the use of pictures.

Rectangle R represents the 300 students in School A. Circle P represents the 150 students that participate in band. Circle Q represents the 170 students that participate in a sport. 70 students participate in both band and a sport.

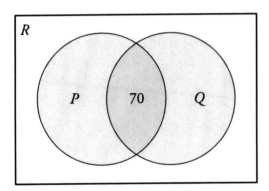

Although symbolic and verbal presentations of mathematical concepts and data can be both useful and informative, they are not always the most lucid representations of that information. The use of visual media can be helpful in numerous cases. Graphs and tables of data can, in many cases, provide a clearer representation of that data than can, for instance, a symbolic expression (for some form of regression, for example). Diagrams can also be extremely helpful, especially in problem-solving contexts. One of the chief rules of solving a problem is to draw a diagram (where appropriate) illustrating the problem; this approach helps organize information and it provides a perspective that often makes the information more accessible than it would be in words and mathematical expressions alone. Animations can also be helpful. Although animations generally require more technology (typically a computer) to construct than do diagrams, they provide an additional dimension to the visual presentation.

Throughout this guide, the concepts and examples that are presented often include graphs, tables, and diagrams to illustrate the information presented.

SKILL 14.4 **Representing word problems algebraically**

Representing word problems algebraically essentially involves identifying the variables and the relationships between them. The following is a systematic way to do this:

1. Read the problem carefully and identify which of the relevant numbers are known and which are unknown.

2. Assign a variable name to each unknown quantity. Make a clear note of this. For example, a student may assign variable x for the number of oranges and in the middle of solving the problem mistakenly assume that x is the price of an orange.

3. Write down the relationships between the variables in the form of equations or inequalities.

4. Make sure there are as many equations as there are unknown variables. If not, review the problem and see if any information has been missed.

Representing word problems algebraically requires translation of the words into symbols.

See Skill 14.3 for specific examples of correspondence between operations and verbal description and translation between words and symbols

SKILL 14.5 **Identifying contributions to mathematics made by different individuals and cultures and the type of societal problems that gave rise to mathematical systems**

Throughout the history of humanity, every culture, ethnicity, and gender has contributed to the field of mathematics and, thereby, to society in general.

The development of mathematics has been ongoing throughout history. The primary early uses of mathematics were for astronomy, architecture, trading and taxation. The early history of mathematics originated in Mesopotamia (Sumeria and Babylon), Egypt, Greece, and Rome.

The contributions of mathematics to such diverse fields as economics, physics, sociology, management, medicine, astronomy and psychology are manifold. Present-day contributions include development of algorithms that can ease Internet traffic congestion while increasing the rate at which data is transmitted, development of graph theory for applications in expanding the Internet, robotic vision systems and communication networks. High-level mathematics has revolutionized economics with set theory and axiomatic proofs. The documentation of a mathematical model of gasoline spray has been used to cut back on car emissions. For psychologists, mathematics (particularly statistics) has been and still is a crucial tool for quantifying and analyzing findings. Mathematics was also a crucial tool in creating the breakthrough in human genome research through the development of computational analysis.

Noted mathematicians from early times include Pythagoras (born 580 BCE) and Theano (the wife of Pythagoras who was born 546 BCE). Pythagoras was a mathematician and physician who wrote the significant piece on the principle of the "Golden Mean." Euclid (300 BCE) is considered the father of geometry; Archimedes (born 287 BCE) made the first real progress on the estimation of π, and Apollonius and Ptolemy (85 CE) also made significant contributions to the development of mathematics.

During the third century CE in China, Tsu Ch'ung-Chih estimated π as Archimedes did, using circumscribed and inscribed polygons. In India, Brahmagupta made valuable contributions to geometry during the sixth century CE, and the Arabs played an important role in preserving the work of the Greeks through translating and expanding that knowledge.

Archeological digs in Babylonia and Greece have uncovered counting boards. These include the Chinese abacus, whose current form dates from approximately 1200 CE. Prior to the development of the concept of zero, a counting board or abacus was the common method used for all types of calculations. In fact, the abacus is still taught in Asian schools and is used by some Asian proprietors. Blind children learn to use the abacus, which is an equivalent method of learning basic mathematical calculations.

Prior to the development of the concept of zero, a counting board or abacus was the common method used for all types of calculations.

Islamic culture from the sixth through twelfth centuries drew knowledge from areas ranging from Africa and Spain to India. Al-Khowarizmi introduced Hindu numerals to the West for the first time during the ninth century and wrote a significant article on algebra. At the beginning of the fifteenth century, notable Muslim mathematician Al-Kashi wrote the book Key to Arithmetic, in which he used decimals instead of fractions. Fibonacci made important contributions to algebra and geometry during the 1200s.

It was after the Renaissance era, however, that some of the most significant contributions were made. During the seventeenth century, Newton, along with Leibniz, developed calculus, and Descartes formulated analytical geometry. Maria Gaetana Agnesi is known for the "Witch of Agnesi": the modern version of the curve called the Cartesian equation. Also during this period, John Napier developed a theory of logarithms and Pascal and Fermat broadened knowledge of number theory.

The eighteenth century saw contributions by Gauss in arithmetic, algebra, and number theory. Gauss insisted that every area of mathematics must apply rigorous proofs, and this influenced Cauchy in the nineteenth century to develop a more comprehensible theory of limits, the definitive integral, continuity and the derivative. David Hilbert laid the foundations of geometry in the nineteenth century.

During the twentieth century, increased abstract mathematics broadened the definitions of the operations of systems so that areas of topology, algebra and geometry are connected. There are present-day individuals who have made significant contributions to the field of mathematics. David Blackwell was the first African-American to be named to the National Academy of Sciences, and he won the Von Neumann Theory Prize in 1979 for his contributions to the field of statistics. African-American Etta Falconer (1933–2002) received numerous awards and recognitions (from 1967 to 1995) during her lifetime for her contributions to furthering the opportunities for minorities and women in the fields of mathematics and science. Margaret Wright is well known in such fields as linear algebra and numerical and scientific computing. She has received several awards recognizing her contributions to mathematics. Sijue Wu received two awards in 2001 for her part in finding a solution to a long-standing problem in the water-wave equation.

This mix of cultures, genders, and ethnicities have culminated in substantial developments in many areas of mathematics, including algebra, our current numbering system, geometry, trigonometry, calculus, statistics and discrete mathematics.

COMPETENCY 15
UNDERSTAND THE CONTENT AND METHODS FOR DEVELOPING STUDENTS' CONTENT-AREA READING SKILLS TO SUPPORT THEIR READING AND LEARNING IN MATHEMATICS

SKILL Demonstrating knowledge of key components and processes
15.1 involved in reading *(e.g., vocabulary knowledge, including orthographic and morphological knowledge; background knowledge; knowledge of academic discourse, including the syntactic and organizational structures used in print and digital academic texts; print processing abilities, including decoding skills; use of cognitive and metacognitive skills and strategies)*

In 2000, the National Reading Panel released its now well-known report on teaching children to read. This report partially put to rest the debate between phonics and whole language. It essentially argued that word–letter recognition is as important as understanding what the text means. The report's "Big 5" critical areas of reading instruction are explained in the following sections.

Phonemic Awareness

PHONEMIC AWARENESS is the acknowledgement of sounds and words; for example, a child's realization that some words rhyme is one of the skills that fall under this category. *Onset* and *rhyme* are skills that might help students learn that the sound of the first letter "b" in the word "bad" can be changed with the sound "d" to make it "dad." The key in phonemic awareness is that it can be taught with the students' eyes closed; in other words, it's all about understanding sounds, not ascribing written letters to sounds.

PHONEMIC AWARENESS: the acknowledgement of sounds and words

Phonics

As opposed to phonemic awareness, the study of phonics must be done with the eyes open. PHONICS is the connection between sounds and the letters on a page. In other words, students learning phonics might see the word "bad" and sound each letter out slowly until they recognize that they just said the word.

PHONICS: the connection between sounds and the letters on a page

Fluency

FLUENCY: reading connected pieces of text

When students practice FLUENCY, they practice reading connected pieces of text. In other words, instead of looking at a word as just a word, they might read a sentence straight through. The point of fluency is for the student to comprehend what he or she is reading by putting words in a sentence together quickly. If a student is NOT fluent in reading, he or she would sound each letter or word out slowly and pay more attention to the phonics of each word. A fluent reader, on the other hand, might read a sentence out loud using appropriate intonations.

The best way to test for fluency is to have a student read something out loud, preferably a few sentences in a row. Most students just learning to read will not be very fluent right away, but with practice, they will increase their fluency. Even though fluency is not the same as comprehension, fluency is a good predictor of comprehension; when the student is freed from focusing on sounding out each word, he or she can shift attention to the meaning of the words.

Comprehension

COMPREHENSION: when the reader can ascribe meaning to text

COMPREHENSION simply means that the reader can ascribe meaning to text. Even though students may be good with phonics and may know what many words on a page mean, some of them are not able to demonstrate comprehension because they do not have the tools to help them comprehend. For example, students should know that stories often have structures (beginning, middle, and end). They should also know that when they are reading something and it does not make sense, they will need to employ "fix-up" strategies where they go back into the text they just read and look for clues. Teachers can use many strategies to teach comprehension, including questioning, asking students to paraphrase or summarize, utilizing graphic organizers, and focusing on mental images.

Vocabulary

Students will be better at comprehension if they have a stronger working vocabulary. Research has shown that students learn more vocabulary when it is presented in context, rather than in vocabulary lists, for example. Furthermore, the more students get to use particular words in context, the more they will remember each word and utilize the words in the comprehension of sentences that contain the words.

See also Skill 15.4

Reading Assessment

ASSESSMENT is the practice of collecting information about students' progress, and EVALUATION is the process of judging the students' responses to determine how well they are achieving particular goals or demonstrating reading skills.

Assessment and evaluation are intricately connected in the literacy classroom. Assessment is necessary because teachers need ways to determine what students are learning and how they are progressing. In addition, assessment is a tool that can also help students take ownership of their own learning and become partners in their ongoing development as readers and writers. In this day of public accountability, clear, definite, and reliable assessment creates confidence in public education. There are two broad categories of assessment.

FORMAL ASSESSMENT is composed of standardized tests and procedures carried out under prescribed conditions. Formal assessments include state tests, standardized achievement tests, NAEP tests, and the like.

INFORMAL ASSESSMENT is the use of observation and other nonstandardized procedures to compile anecdotal and observational data/evidence of students' progress. Informal assessment includes but is not limited to checklists, observations, and performance tasks.

Skills to be evaluated

- The ability to use syntactic cues when encountering an unknown word. Good readers will expect the word to fit the syntax they are familiar with. Poor readers may substitute a word that does not fit the syntax and will not correct themselves.

- The ability to use semantic cues to determine the meaning of an unknown word. Good readers will consider the meanings of all the known words in the sentence. Poor readers may read one word at a time with no regard for the other words.

ASSESSMENT: the practice of collecting information about students' progress

EVALUATION: the process of judging the students' responses to determine how well they are achieving particular goals or demonstrating reading skills

FORMAL ASSESSMENT: composed of standardized tests and procedures carried out under prescribed conditions

INFORMAL ASSESSMENT: the use of observation and other nonstandardized procedures to compile anecdotal and observational data/evidence of students' progress

- The ability to use schematic cues to connect words with prior knowledge. Good readers will incorporate what they know with what the text says or implies. Poor readers may think only of the word they are reading without associating it with prior knowledge.

- The ability to use phonics cues to improve ease and efficiency in reading. Good readers will apply letter and sound associations almost subconsciously. Poor readers may have one of two kinds of problems:

  A. They may have underdeveloped phonics skills, and use only an initial clue without analyzing vowel patterns before quickly guessing the word.

  B. They may use phonics skills in isolation, becoming so absorbed in the word "noises" that they ignore or forget the message of the text.

- The ability to process information from the text. Good readers should be able to get information from the text as well as store, retrieve, and integrate it for later use.

- The ability to use interpretive thinking to make logical predictions and inferences.

- The ability to use critical thinking to make decisions and insights about the text.

- The ability to use appreciative thinking to respond to the text, whether emotionally, mentally, or ideologically.

Methods of evaluation

- Assess students at the beginning of each year to determine grouping for instruction.

- Judge whether a student recognizes that a word does not make sense.

- Monitor whether the student knows when to ignore a reading mistake and read on or when to reread a sentence.

- Look for skills such as recognizing cause and effect, finding main ideas, and using comparison and contrast techniques.

- Keep dated records to follow individual progress. Focus on a few students each day. Grade them on a scale of one to five according to how well they perform certain reading abilities (such as making logical predictions). Include informal observations such as, "Ed was able to determine the meaning of the word 'immigrant' by examining the other words in the sentence."

- Remember that evaluation is important but fostering an enjoyment of reading is the ultimate goal. Keep reading pressure-free and fun so that students do not become intimidated by reading. Even if the students are not meeting standards, if they continue to want to read each day, that is a success!

Differentiation of Instruction

Teachers can differentiate instruction in order to address the needs of students with varying levels of reading proficiency.

DIFFERENTIATION OF INSTRUCTION occurs when the teacher will vary the content, process, or product used in instruction (Tomlinson, 1995).

> **DIFFERENTIATION OF INSTRUCTION**: when the teacher varies the content, process, or product used in instruction

There are three primary ways to differentiate:

- Content: The specifics of what is learned. This does not mean that whole units or concepts should be modified. However, within certain topics, specifics can be modified.

- Process: The route to learning the content. All students do not have to learn the content using exactly the same method.

- Product: The result of the learning. Usually, a product is the result or assessment of learning. For example, not all students are going to demonstrate complete learning on a quiz; likewise, not all students will demonstrate complete learning on a written paper.

There are two keys to successful differentiation:

- Knowing what is essential in the curriculum: Although certain things can be modified, other things must remain intact and in a specific order. Disrupting central components of a curriculum can actually damage a student's ability to learn something successfully.

- Knowing the needs of the students: While this can take quite some time to figure out, it is very important that teachers pay attention to the interests, tendencies, and abilities of their students so that they understand how each of their students will best learn.

Many students will need certain concepts explained in greater depth; others may pick up on concepts rather quickly. For this reason, teachers will want to adapt the curriculum in a way that gives students the opportunity to learn at their own pace while also keeping the class together as a community. Although this can be difficult, the more creative a teacher is with the ways in which students can demonstrate mastery, the more fun the experience will be for students and teachers. Furthermore, teachers will reach students more successfully if they tailor lesson plans, activities, groupings, and other elements of curriculum to each student's need. The reasons for differentiating instruction are based on two important differences in students: interest and ability.

Differentiating Reading Instruction

Differentiating reading instruction is a bit complex. When a teacher wants to ensure that each student in his class is getting the most out of the reading instruction, the teacher will need to consider the level at which the student is proficient in reading—as well as the specific areas in which each student struggles. It is first important to use a variety of sources of data to make decisions on differentiation, rather than rely on just one test, for example.

When teachers have proficient readers in their classrooms, they usually feel that these students need less attention and less work. This is a mistake. If these students are not provided appropriate instruction and challenging activities to increase their reading abilities further, they may become disengaged with school. These students benefit greatly from integrating classroom reading with other types of reading, perhaps complementing the whole-class novel with some additional short stories or nonfiction pieces.

When teachers have proficient readers in their classrooms, they usually feel that these students need less attention and less work. If these students are not provided appropriate instruction and challenging activities to increase their reading abilities further, they may become disengaged with school.

They also benefit from sustained silent reading, in which they can choose their own books and read independently. Discussion groups and teacher-led discussion activities are also very useful for these students. It is important, however, to ensure that these students do not feel that they have to do more work than everyone else. Remember, differentiation does not distinguish differences in quantity; it distinguishes differences in types of work.

Average readers may benefit from many of the things that highly proficient readers do; however, they may need more skill instruction. Most likely, they will not need as much skill instruction as weak readers, but they will benefit highly from having a teacher who knows which skills they are lacking and teaches them to use those skills in their own reading.

Weak readers need to focus highly on skills. Teachers will want to encourage them to make predictions, connect ideas, outline concepts, evaluate, and summarize. The activities that these students engage in should be developed to instill reading strategies that they can use in their independent reading and to propel them toward higher levels of reading.

Alternatives to Textbooks

There is a wide variety of materials available to today's teachers. Personal computers with Internet connections are becoming more common in classrooms, and teachers can bring the content of a reference book alive in text, motion, and sound. Textbook publishers often provide video, recordings, and software to accompany the text, as well as overhead transparencies and colorful posters to help students visualize what is being taught. To stay current in the field, teachers can scan the educational publishers' brochures that arrive at their principal's or department head's office or attend workshops, conferences, and presentations by educational publishers.

SKILL Demonstrating knowledge of explicit strategies for facilitating 15.3 students' comprehension before, during, and after reading content-area texts and for promoting their use of comprehension strategies

Content-area texts are usually nonfiction. Therefore, students can use specific strategies to better comprehend the text. Content area subjects often have texts with a great deal of information. More information is included than is necessary for students to know at one time. Therefore, it is necessary for students to develop specific skills to help them take in the important information while weeding out the less important.

- Highlighting: this is a difficult strategy for students to master. Even at the college level, it seems that students have a hard time determining what is most important. Students have a tendency to highlight too much information. Encourage students to highlight less: Key ideas and vocabulary are a good place to start.

- Outlining: this is a skill that many teachers use to help students understand the most important facts. Creating outlines can be difficult for some students, so teachers may want to provide the outline to the students to use as a guide when taking their own notes. In this way, the students know what to focus on when reading.

- Summarizing: this strategy helps students identify key information. To create a summary, a student should identify the main idea of a passage, and then find the details that support the main idea. Using this information, the student can then write a short summary.

- Textual features: these facilitate the location of pertinent information. Headings, bold text, text in boxes, diagrams, photos, and captions bring attention to important information and clarify key concepts and ideas. The table of contents and index allow students to search for information, and the glossary lists key terms and their definitions.

The point of comprehension instruction is not necessarily to focus just on the text(s) students are using at the very moment of instruction, but rather to help them learn the strategies that they can use independently with any other text.

COMMON METHODS OF TEACHING INSTRUCTION	
Summarization	Students go over the main point of the text, along with strategically chosen details that highlight the main point. This is not the same as paraphrasing, which is saying the same thing in different words. Teaching students how to summarize is very important because it will help them look for the most critical areas in a text and in nonfiction. For example, it will help them distinguish between main arguments and examples. In fiction, it helps students to learn how to focus on the main characters and events and distinguish those from the lesser characters and events.
Question Answering	While this tends to be overused in many classrooms, it is still a valid method of teaching students to comprehend. Students answer questions regarding a text, either out loud, in small groups, or individually on paper. The best questions are those that cause students to think about the text (rather than just find an answer within the text).
Question Generating	This is the opposite of question answering, although students can then be asked to answer their own questions or the questions of peers. In general, we want students to constantly question texts as they read. This is important because it causes students to become more critical readers. To teach students to generate questions helps them to learn the types of questions they can ask and it gets them thinking about how best to be critical of texts.
Graphic Organizers	Graphic organizers are graphical representations of content within a text. For example, Venn diagrams can be used to highlight the difference between two characters in a novel or two similar political concepts in a social studies textbook. Or, a teacher can use flow-charts with students to talk about the steps in a process, such as the steps of setting up a science experiment or the chronological events of a story. Semantic organizers are similar in that they graphically display information. The difference, usually, is that semantic organizers focus on words or concepts. For example, a word web can help students make sense of a word by mapping out from the central word all the similar and related concepts to that word.
Text Structure	Often in nonfiction—particularly in textbooks—and sometimes in fiction, text structures will give important clues to readers about what to look for. Students may not know how to make sense of all the types of headings in a textbook and do not realize that, for example, the side-bar story about a character in history is not the main text on a particular page in the history textbook. Teaching students how to interpret text structures gives them tools with which to tackle similar texts.
Monitoring Comprehension	Students need to be aware of their comprehension, or lack of it, in particular texts. So, it is important to teach students what to do when suddenly text stops making sense. For example, students can go back and reread the description of a character. Or, they can go back to the table of contents or the first paragraph of a chapter to see where they are headed.

Continued on next page

Textual Marking	This is where students interact with the text as they read. For example, armed with sticky notes, students can insert questions or comments regarding specific sentences or paragraphs within the text. This helps students focus on the importance of the small things, particularly when they are reading larger works (such as novels in high school). It also gives students a reference point on which to go back into the text when they need to review something.
Discussion	Small group or whole-class discussion stimulates thoughts about texts and gives students a larger picture of the impact of those texts. For example, teachers can strategically encourage students to discuss related concepts to the text. This helps students learn to consider texts within larger societal and social concepts. Or teachers can encourage students to provide personal opinions in discussion. By listening to various students' opinions, this will help all students in a class to see the wide range of possible interpretations and thoughts regarding one text.

SKILL 15.4 Demonstrating knowledge of explicit strategies for promoting students' academic language and vocabulary development, including their knowledge of domain-specific vocabulary words

Here are some strategies that teachers can use to increase the development of vocabulary skills in students:

Context clues help readers determine the meanings of words they are not familiar with. The CONTEXT of a word is the text that surrounds the word. Context clues can appear within the sentence itself, within the preceding and/or following sentences, or within the passage as a whole. Read the following sentences and attempt to determine the meaning of the word in bold print:

> CONTEXT: the text that surrounds the word

*The **luminosity** of the room was so incredible that there was no need for lights.*

If there was no need for lights, then one must assume that the word luminosity has something to do with giving off light. The definition of luminosity, therefore, is "the emission of light."

Word classification helps students draw comparisons between different types of words. Young children might begin by looking at parts of speech. Older students might begin by classifying the words in more specific categories based on the content area or other classification system.

ETYMOLOGY: the study of the history of words

ETYMOLOGY is the study of the history of words. Understanding the language basis of words can help in determining the meaning and in building comprehension. It is particularly useful to know the definitions of prefixes, suffixes, and root words; these can help determine the meaning of several other words. For example, the Latin root "bene" means "good" or "well." English words from this root include "benefit," "beneficial," and "beneficiary." In math, knowing Greek and Latin roots can help students learn the names of geometrical shapes and other mathematical terms.

Application of vocabulary words in new situations. Understanding what a word means in one context helps the student for that one reading passage. Learning to transfer that understanding to new and varied situations helps the student become a life-long learner and reader. This transfer of knowledge can be done by asking students to think of other situations where the word can be used, or by providing examples from other content areas.

CONTENT AREA VO-CABULARY: the specific vocabulary related to particular concepts of various academic disciplines (social science, science, math, art, etc.)

CONTENT AREA VOCABULARY is the specific vocabulary related to particular concepts of various academic disciplines (social science, science, math, art, etc).

While teachers tend to think of content area vocabulary as something that should be focused on just at the secondary level (middle and high school), even elementary school students studying various subjects will understand concepts better when the vocabulary used to describe them is explicitly explained. But it is true that in the secondary level, where students go to different teachers for each subject, content area vocabulary becomes more emphasized.

Often, educators believe that vocabulary should just be taught in a language arts class, not realizing that there is not enough time for students to learn the enormous vocabulary in only one class in order to be successful with a standards-based education and that the teaching of vocabulary related to a particular subject is a very good way to help students understand the subject better.

First and foremost, teachers should teach strategies to determine the meanings for difficult vocabulary when students encounter it on their own. Teachers can do this by teaching students how to identify the meanings of words in context (usually through activities where the word is taken out, and the students have to figure out a way to make sense of the sentence). In addition, dictionary skills must be taught in all subject areas. Teachers should also consider that teaching vocabulary is not just the teaching of words; rather, it is the teaching of complex concepts, each with histories and connotations.

When teachers explicitly teach vocabulary, it is best if they can connect new words to ideas, words, and experiences with which students are already familiar. This will help to reduce the strangeness of the new words. Furthermore, the more concrete the examples, the more likely students will be able to use the word in context.

Finally, students need plenty of exposure to the new words. They need to be able to hear and use the new words in many naturally produced sentences. The more one hears and uses a sentence in context, the more the word is solidified in the person's long-term vocabulary.

See also Skill 15.1

SKILL **Demonstrating ability to plan instruction and select strategies that**
15.5 **support students' reading and understanding of mathematics texts**
(e.g., asking students to translate between different mathematical representations, asking students to describe in words or sentences the relationship between symbols and the situation being modeled, matching mathematical representations to differences in learning styles)

According to Piaget, there are four primary cognitive structures or development stages: sensorimotor, preoperations, concrete operations, and formal operations. In the sensorimotor stage (0-2 years), intelligence takes the form of motor actions. In the preoperation stage (3-7 years), intelligence is intuitive in nature. Intelligence in the concrete operational stage (8-11 years) is logical but depends upon concrete referents. In the final stage of formal operations (12-15 years), thinking involves abstractions.

Even though middle-school students are typically ready to approach mathematics in abstract ways, some of them still require concrete referents such as manipulatives. It is useful to keep in mind that the developmental stages of individuals vary. In addition, different people have different learning styles, some tending more towards the visual and others relatively verbal. Research has shown that learning is most effective when information is presented through multiple modalities or representations. Most mathematics textbooks now use this multimodal approach.

Research has shown that learning is most effective when information is presented through multiple modalities or representations.

When introducing a new mathematical concept to students, teachers should utilize the concrete-to-representational-to-abstract sequence of instruction. The first step of the instructional progression is the introduction of a concept modeled with concrete materials. The second step is the translation of concrete models into representational diagrams or pictures. The third and final step is the translation of representational models into abstract models using only numbers and symbols.

Teachers should first use concrete models to introduce a mathematical concept because they are easiest to understand. For example, teachers can allow students to use counting blocks to learn basic arithmetic. Teachers should give students ample time and many opportunities to experiment, practice, and demonstrate mastery with the concrete materials.

The second step in the learning process is the translation of concrete materials to representational models. For example, students may use tally marks or pictures to represent the counting blocks they used in the previous stage. Once again, teachers should give students ample time to master the concept on the representational level.

The final step in the learning process is the translation of representational models into abstract numbers and symbols. For example, students represent the processes carried out in the previous stages using only numbers and arithmetic symbols.

To ease the transition, teachers should associate numbers and symbols with the concrete and representational models throughout the learning progression.

Throughout this guide, mathematical operations and situations are represented through words, algebraic symbols, geometric diagrams and graphs.

A few commonly used representations are discussed in Skill 14.3

SAMPLE TEST

SAMPLE TEST

Formulas

Formula	Description
$V = \frac{1}{3}Bh$	Volume of a right cone or a pyramid
$V = Bh$	Volume of a cylinder or a prism
$V = \frac{4}{3}\pi r^3$	Volume of a sphere
$A = 2\pi rh + 2\pi r^2$	Surface area of a cylinder
$A = 4\pi r^2$	Surface area of a sphere
$A = \pi r\sqrt{r^2 + h^2} = \pi rl$	Lateral surface area of a right cone
$S_n = \frac{n}{2}[2a_1 + (n - 1)d] = \frac{n(a_1 + a_n)}{2}$	Sum of an arithmetic series
$S_n = \frac{a(1 - r^n)}{1 - r}$	Sum of a finite geometric series
$\sum_{n=0}^{\infty} ar^n = \frac{a}{1 - r}, \ |r| < 1$	Sum of an infinite geometric series
$\frac{a}{\sin A} = \frac{b}{\sin B} = \frac{c}{\sin C}$	Law of sines
$c^2 = a^2 + b^2 - 2ab \cos C$	Law of cosines
$(x - h)^2 + (y - k)^2 = r^2$	Equation of a circle
$(y - k)^2 = 4c(x - h)^2$	Equation of a parabola
$\frac{(x - h)^2}{a^2} + \frac{(y - k)2}{b^2} = 1$	Equation of a ellipse
$\frac{(x - h)^2}{a^2} - \frac{(y - k)2}{b^2} = 1$	Equation of a hyperbola

Number Sense
(Skills 1.1 – 3.3)

(Easy) (Skill 1.1)

1. Mr. Brown feeds his cat premium cat food which costs $40 per month. Approximately how much will it cost to feed her for one year?

    A. $500

    B. $400

    C. $80

    D. $4800

(Average) (Skill 1.1)

2. The mass of a chocolate chip cookie is about:

    A. 1 kilogram

    B. 1 gram

    C. 15 grams

    D. 15 milligrams

(Average) (Skill 1.2)

3. Given W = whole numbers
    N = natural numbers
    Z = integers
    R = rational numbers
    I = irrational numbers

    which of the following is not true?

    A. $R \subset I$

    B. $W \subset Z$

    C. $Z \subset R$

    D. $N \subset W$

(Average) (Skill 1.2)

4. Which of the following is an irrational number?

    A. $.362626262...$

    B. $4\frac{1}{3}$

    C. $\sqrt{5}$

    D. $-\sqrt{16}$

(Easy) (Skill 1.2)

5. The conjugate of $4 + 5i$ is:

    A. $-4 + 5i$

    B. $4 - 5i$

    C. $4i + 5$

    D. $4i - 5$

(Easy) (Skill 1.2)

6. Simplify: $(6 + 3i) - (4 - 2i)$

    A. $2 + 5i$

    B. $2 + i$

    C. $10 + 5i$

    D. $2 - 2i$

(Skill 1.4) (Rigorous)

7. Express the complex number $1 + i$ in polar form.

    A. $\sqrt{2}(\cos\frac{\pi}{4} + i\sin\frac{\pi}{4})$

    B. $2(\cos\frac{\pi}{4} + i\sin\frac{\pi}{4})$

    C. $\sqrt{2}(\cos\frac{\pi}{2} + i\sin\frac{\pi}{2})$

    D. $\sqrt{2}(\sin\frac{\pi}{4} + i\cos\frac{\pi}{4})$

(Average) (Skill 2.1)

8. Find the LCM of 27, 90, and 84.

    A. 90

    B. 3,780

    C. 204,120

    D. 1,260

(Rigorous) (Skill 2.1)

9. What is the smallest number that is divisible by 3 and 5 and leaves a remainder of 3 when divided by 7?

    A. 15

    B. 18

    C. 25

    D. 45

(Average) (Skill 2.1)

10. Which of the following is always composite if x is odd, y is even, and both x and y are greater than or equal to 2?

    A. $x + y$

    B. $3x + 2y$

    C. $5xy$

    D. $5x + 3y$

(Average) (Skill 2.1)

11. Find the GCF of $2^2 \times 3^2 \times 5$ and $2^2 \times 3 \times 7$.

    A. $2^5 \times 3^3 \times 5 \times 7$

    B. $2 \times 3 \times 5 \times 7$

    C. $2^2 \times 3$

    D. $2^3 \times 3^2 \times 5 \times 7$

(Average) (Skill 2.2)

12. $24 - 3 \times 7 + 2 =$

    A. 5

    B. 149

    C. -3

    D. 189

(Average) (Skill 2.2)

13. $7t - 4 \times 2t + 3t \times 4 \div 2 =$

    A. $5t$

    B. 0

    C. $31t$

    D. $18t$

(Average) (Skill 2.3)

14. Which of the following illustrates an inverse property?

    A. $a + b = a - b$

    B. $a + b = b + a$

    C. $a + 0 = a$

    D. $a + (-a) = 0$

(Rigorous) (Skill 2.3)

15. Which of the following sets is closed under division?
    I) {1/2, 1, 2, 4}
    II) {−1, 1}
    III) {−1, 0, 1}

    A. I only

    B. II only

    C. III only

    D. I and II

(Rigorous) (Skill 2.3)

16. Which axiom is incorrectly applied?

$3x + 4 = 7$

Step a. $3x + 4 - 4 = 7 - 4$
additive equality

Step b. $3x + 4 - 4 = 3$
commutative axiom of addition

Step c. $3x + 0 = 3$
additive inverse

Step d. $3x = 3$
additive identity

A. Step a

B. Step b

C. Step c

D. Step d

(Rigorous) (Skill 2.3)

17. Which of the following sets is closed under division?

A. Integers

B. Rational numbers

C. Natural numbers

D. Whole numbers

(Average) (Skill 3.2)

18. Identify the correct sequence of sub-skills required for solving and graphing inequalities involving absolute value in one variable, such as $|x + 1| \le 6$.

A. Understanding absolute value, graphing inequalities, solving systems of equations

B. Graphing inequalities on a Cartesian plane, solving systems of equations, simplifying expressions with absolute value

C. Plotting points, graphing equations, graphing inequalities

D. Solving equations with absolute value, solving inequalities, graphing conjunctions and disjunctions

(Rigorous) (Skill 3.2)

19. Mr. Lacey is using problem solving to help students develop their math skills. He gives the class a box of pencils. He says that the pencils have to be divided so that each student has the same number of pencils. What step should come first in problem solving?

A. Find a strategy to solve the problem

B. Identify the problem

C. Count the number of pencils

D. Make basic calculations

(Rigorous) (Skill 3.3)

20. What is the total cost of the purchase of a suit for $295.99 and a pair of shoes for $69.95 including 6.5% sales tax?

A. $389.73

B. $398.37

C. $237.86

D. $315.23

(Average) (Skill 3.3)

21. The volume of water flowing through a pipe varies directly with the square of the radius of the pipe. If the water flows at a rate of 80 liters per minute through a pipe with a radius of 4 cm, at what rate would water flow through a pipe with a radius of 3 cm?

    A. 45 liters per minute

    B. 6.67 liters per minute

    C. 60 liters per minute

    D. 4.5 liters per minute

(Average) (Skill 3.3)

22. Express .0000456 in scientific notation.

    A. 4.56×10^{-4}

    B. 45.6×10^{-6}

    C. 4.56×10^{-6}

    D. 4.56×10^{-5}

Functions, Algebra, and Calculus (Skills 4.1 – 7.5)

(Average) (Skill 4.2)

23. State the domain of the function $f(x) = \dfrac{3x - 6}{x^2 - 25}$.

    A. $x \neq 2$

    B. $x \neq 5, -5$

    C. $x \neq 2, -2$

    D. $x \neq 5$

(Average) (Skill 4.2)

24. Find the domain of the function $\sqrt{6 - x^2}$.

    A. $x \geq \sqrt{6}$

    B. $-\sqrt{6} \leq x \leq \sqrt{6}$

    C. $0 \leq x \leq \sqrt{6}$

    D. $x \geq 0$

(Average) (Skill 4.4)

25. Given $f(x) = 3x - 2, f^{-1}(x) =$

    A. $3x + 2$

    B. $\dfrac{x}{6}$

    C. $2x - 3$

    D. $\dfrac{(x + 2)}{3}$

(Average) (Skill 4.4)

26. Given $f(x) = 3x - 2$ and $g(x) = x^2$, determine $g(f(x))$.

    A. $3x^2 - 2$

    B. $9x^2 + 4$

    C. $9x^2 - 12x + 4$

    D. $3x^3 - 2$

(Average) (Skill 5.2)

27. Solve $d = at(v_t - v_0)$ for v_0.

    A. $v_0 = atd - v_t$

    B. $v_0 = d - atv_t$

    C. $v_0 = atv_t - d$

    D. $v_0 = \dfrac{(atv_t - d)}{at}$

(Easy) (Skill 5.3)

28. Which of the following is equivalent to $\sqrt[b]{x^a}$?

    A. $x^{\frac{a}{b}}$

    B. $x^{\frac{b}{a}}$

    C. $a^{\frac{x}{b}}$

    D. $b^{\frac{x}{a}}$

(Rigorous) (Skill 5.3)

29. Evaluate $3^{\frac{1}{2}}(9^{\frac{1}{3}})$.

    A. $27^{\frac{5}{6}}$

    B. $9^{\frac{7}{12}}$

    C. $3^{\frac{5}{6}}$

    D. $3^{\frac{6}{7}}$

(Average) (Skill 5.3)

30. The exponential equation $2^5 = 32$ can be written as:

    A. $\log_2(5) = 32$

    B. $\log_{10}(32) = 5$

    C. $\log_5(32) = 2$

    D. $\log_2(32) = 5$

(Rigorous) (Skill 5.3)

31. Solve for x: $10^{x-3} + 5 = 105$.

    A. 3

    B. 10

    C. 2

    D. 5

(Easy) (Skill 5.4)

32. Given a vector with horizontal component 5 and vertical component 6, determine the length of the vector.

    A. 61

    B. $\sqrt{61}$

    C. 30

    D. $\sqrt{30}$

(Average) (Skill 6.1)

33. Which graph represents the equation of $y = x^2 + 3x$?

A.

B.

C.

D.

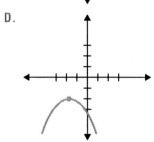

(Average) (Skill 6.1)

34. What is the equation of the graph shown below?

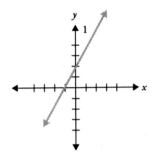

A. $2x + y = 2$

B. $2x - y = -2$

C. $2x - y = 2$

D. $2x + y = -2$

(Skill 6.2) (Rigorous)

35. What transformations have been applied to the function $f(x)$ shown below to obtain function $g(x)$?

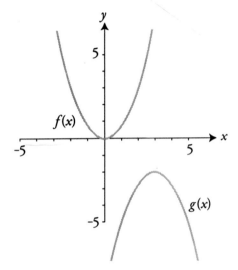

A. Reflection over x-axis, translation 3 units to the right, translation 2 units down

B. Translation 3 units to the right, translation 2 units down, reflection over x-axis

C. Translation 2 units down, translation 3 units to the right, reflection over x-axis

D. Reflection over y-axis, translation 3 units to the right, translation 2 units down

(Rigorous) (Skill 6.4)

36. The length of a picture frame is 2 inches greater than its width. If the area of the frame is 143 square inches, what is its width?

A. 11 inches

B. 13 inches

C. 12 inches

D. 10 inches

(Average) (Skill 6.4)

37. Find the height of a box with surface area of 94 sq. ft. with a width of 3 feet and a depth of 4 feet.

    A. 3 ft.

    B. 4 ft.

    C. 5 ft.

    D. 6 ft.

(Rigorous) (Skill 6.4)

38. Ralph and Rhonda can paint a barn together in 4 hours. If Ralph needs 6 more hours than Rhonda to paint the barn all by himself, how many hours does Rhonda need to paint the barn by herself?

    A. 5

    B. 6

    C. 7

    D. 8

(Easy) (Skill 7.1)

39. L'Hopital's rule provides a method to evaluate which of the following?

    A. Limit of a function

    B. Derivative of a function

    C. Sum of an arithmetic series

    D. Sum of a geometric series

(Average) (Skill 7.1)

40. Find the following limit: $\lim\limits_{x \to 2} \dfrac{x^2 - 4}{x - 2}$

    A. 0

    B. Infinity

    C. 2

    D. 4

(Rigorous) (Skill 7.1)

41. Find the following limit: $\lim\limits_{x \to 0} \dfrac{\sin 2x}{5x}$

    A. Infinity

    B. 0

    C. 1.4

    D. 1

(Average) (Skill 7.2)

42. Determine the measures of angles A and B.

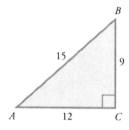

    A. $A = 30°, B = 60°$

    B. $A = 60°, B = 30°$

    C. $A = 53°, B = 37°$

    D. $A = 37°, B = 53°$

(Average) (Skill 7.2)

43. Which expression is not identical to $\sin x$?

    A. $\sqrt{1 - \cos^2 x}$

    B. $\tan x \cos x$

    C. $\dfrac{1}{\csc x}$

    D. $\dfrac{1}{\sec x}$

(Rigorous) (Skill 7.2)

44. Which expression is equivalent to $1 - \sin^2 x$?

 A. $1 - \cos^2 x$

 B. $1 + \cos^2 x$

 C. $\dfrac{1}{\sec x}$

 D. $\dfrac{1}{\sec^2 x}$

(Rigorous) (Skill 7.2)

45. For an acute angle x, $\sin x = 0.6$. What is $\cot x$?

 A. $\dfrac{5}{3}$

 B. 0.75

 C. 1.33

 D. 1

(Rigorous) (Skill 7.3)

46. Find the first derivative of the function: $f(x) = x^3 - 6x^2 + 5x + 4$.

 A. $3x^2 - 12x^2 + 5x$

 B. $3x^2 - 12x - 5$

 C. $3x^2 - 12x + 9$

 D. $3x^2 - 12x + 5$

(Rigorous) (Skill 7.4)

47. Evaluate: $\int_{0}^{2}(x^2 + x - 1)dx$.

 A. $\dfrac{11}{3}$

 B. $\dfrac{8}{3}$

 C. $-\dfrac{8}{3}$

 D. $-\dfrac{11}{3}$

(Rigorous) (Skill 7.4)

48. Find the antiderivative for the function $y = e^{3x}$.

 A. $3x(e^{3x}) + C$

 B. $3(e^{3x}) + C$

 C. $\dfrac{1}{3}(e^x) + C$

 D. $\dfrac{1}{3}(e^{3x}) + C$

(Rigorous) (Skill 7.4)

49. Find the area under the function $y = x^2 + 4$ from $x = 3$ to $x = 6$.

 A. 75

 B. 21

 C. 96

 D. 57

(Rigorous) (Skill 7.4)

50. If the velocity of a body is given by $v = 16 - t^2$, find the distance traveled from $t = 0$ until the body comes to a complete stop.

 A. 16

 B. 43

 C. 48

 D. 64

Measurement and Geometry (Skills 8.1 – 10.5)

(Average) (Skill 8.1)

51. The term "cubic feet" indicates which kind of measurement?

 A. Volume

 B. Mass

 C. Length

 D. Distance

(Rigorous) (Skill 8.1)

52. Given that M is a mass, V is a velocity, A is an acceleration and T is a time, what type of unit corresponds to the overall expression $\frac{AMT}{V}$?

   A. Mass

   B. Time

   C. Velocity

   D. Acceleration

(Average) (Skill 8.2)

53. Find the surface area of a box that is 3 feet wide, 5 feet tall, and 4 feet deep.

   A. 47 sq. ft.

   B. 60 sq. ft.

   C. 94 sq. ft.

   D. 188 sq. ft.

(Rigorous) (Skill 8.2)

54. Find the area of the figure pictured below.

   A. 136.47 m²

   B. 148.48 m²

   C. 293.86 m²

   D. 178.47 m²

(Rigorous) (Skill 8.2)

55. Compute the area of the shaded region, given a radius of 5 meters. Point O is the center.

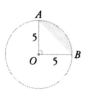

   A. 7.13 cm²

   B. 7.13 m²

   C. 78.5 m²

   D. 19.63 m²

(Rigorous) (Skill 8.2)

56. Determine the area of the shaded region of the trapezoid in terms of x and y.

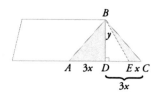

   A. $4xy$

   B. $2xy$

   C. $3x^2y$

   D. There is not enough information given

(Average) (Skill 8.3)

57. If a ship sails due south 6 miles, then due west 8 miles, how far is it from the starting point?

   A. 100 miles

   B. 10 miles

   C. 14 miles

   D. 48 miles

(Rigorous) (Skill 8.4)

58. If the area of the base of a cone is tripled, the volume will be:

    A. The same as the original

    B. 9 times the original

    C. 3 times the original

    D. 3π times the original

(Rigorous) (Skill 8.4)

59. If the radius of a right circular cylinder is doubled, how does its volume change?

    A. No change

    B. Also is doubled

    C. Four times the original

    D. Pi times the original

(Easy) (Skill 9.1)

60. Given that $QO \perp NP$ and $QO = NP$, quadrilateral $NOPQ$ can most accurately be described as a:

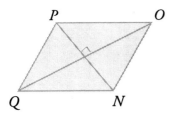

    A. Parallelogram

    B. Rectangle

    C. Square

    D. Rhombus

(Average) (Skill 9.1)

61. Which of the following statements about a trapezoid is incorrect?

    A. It has one pair of parallel sides

    B. The parallel sides are called bases

    C. If the two bases are the same length, the trapezoid is called isosceles

    D. The median is parallel to the bases

(Rigorous) (Skill 9.1)

62. What is the measure of minor arc AD, given the measure of arc PS is 40° and $m\angle K = 10°$?

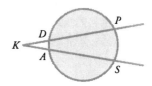

    A. 50°

    B. 20°

    C. 30°

    D. 25°

(Average) (Skill 9.1)

63. What is the degree measure of an interior angle of a regular 10-sided polygon?

    A. 18°

    B. 36°

    C. 144°

    D. 54°

(Average) (Skill 9.2)

64. Which theorem can be used to prove $\triangle BAK \cong \triangle MKA$?

A. SSS

B. ASA

C. SAS

D. AAS

(Easy) (Skill 9.3)

65. When you begin by assuming the conclusion of a theorem is false, then show that through a sequence of logically correct steps you contradict an accepted fact, this is known as:

A. Inductive reasoning

B. Direct proof

C. Indirect proof

D. Exhaustive proof

(Rigorous) (Skill 10.2)

66. Compute the distance from (-2, 7) to the line $x = 5$.

A. -9

B. -7

C. 5

D. 7

(Rigorous) (Skill 10.2)

67. Given $K(-4, y)$ and $L(2, -3)$ with midpoint $M(x, 1)$, determine the values of x and y.

A. $x = -1, y = 5$

B. $x = 3, y = 2$

C. $x = 5, y = -1$

D. $x = -1, y = -1$

(Easy) (Skill 10.3)

68. A glide reflection involves:

A. A translation and dilation

B. A reflection and dilation

C. A translation and a reflection

D. A reflection and a rotation

(Average) (Skill 10.3)

69. A point at (1, 2) on a Cartesian coordinate plane is translated two units to the left, reflected in the y-axis and then reflected in the x-axis. What is its final position?

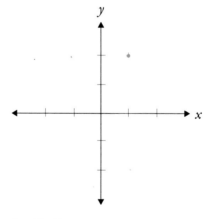

A. (3, 2)

B. (-1, 2)

C. (-2, 1)

D. (1, -2)

Data, Probability, and Discrete Math (Skills 11.1 – 13.4)

(Average) (Skill 11.1)

70. **Which of the following is not a valid method of collecting statistical data?**

    A. Random sampling

    B. Systematic sampling

    C. Cluster sampling

    D. Cylindrical sampling

(Easy) (Skill 11.1)

71. **Systematic random sampling involves:**

    A. Choosing items arbitrarily and in an unstructured manner

    B. Targeting a particular section of the population

    C. The collection of a sample at defined intervals

    D. Proportional sampling from subgroups

(Easy) (Skill 11.2)

72. **Which type of graph uses symbols to represent quantities?**

    A. Bar graph

    B. Line graph

    C. Pictograph

    D. Circle graph

(Average) (Skill 11.2)

73. **What conclusion can be drawn from the graph below?**

MLK Elementary School
Student Enrollment

A. The number of students in first grade exceeds the number in second grade

B. There are more boys than girls in the entire school

C. There are more girls than boys in the first grade

D. Third grade has the largest number of students

(Easy) (Skill 11.2)

74. The pie chart below shows sales at an automobile dealership for the first four months of a year. What percentage of the vehicles were sold in April?

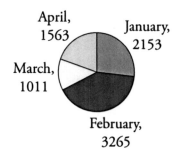

April, 1563

January, 2153

March, 1011

February, 3265

A. More than 50%

B. Less than 25%

C. Between 25% and 50%

D. None

(Easy) (Skill 11.4)

75. Compute the median for the following data set:

{12, 19, 13, 16, 17, 14}

A. 14.5

B. 15.17

C. 15

D. 16

(Rigorous) (Skill 11.4)

76. Compute the standard deviation for the following set of temperatures:
(37, 38, 35, 37, 38, 40, 36, 39)

A. 37.5

B. 1.5

C. 0.5

D. 2.5

(Rigorous) (Skill 11.4)

77. Half the students in a class scored 80% on an exam; most of the rest scored 85% except for one student who scored 10%. Which would be the best measure of central tendency for the test scores?

A. Mean

B. Median

C. Mode

D. Either the median or the mode because they are equal

(Average) (Skill 11.5)

78. To determine the odds for or against a given deviation from expected statistical distribution statisticians use:

A. The t-test

B. Linear regression

C. The chi-square test

D. Exponential regression

(Easy) (Skill 12.2)

79. A jar contains 3 red marbles, 5 white marbles, 1 green marble, and 15 blue marbles. If one marble is picked at random from the jar, what is the probability that it will be red?

A. $\frac{1}{3}$

B. $\frac{1}{8}$

C. $\frac{3}{8}$

D. $\frac{1}{24}$

(Rigorous) (Skill 12.2)

80. A die is rolled several times. What is the probability that a 3 will not appear before the third roll of the die?

    A. $\frac{1}{3}$

    B. $\frac{25}{216}$

    C. $\frac{25}{36}$

    D. $\frac{1}{216}$

(Rigorous) (Skill 12.2)

81. If there are three people in a room, what is the probability that at least two of them will share a birthday? (Assume a year has 365 days.)

    A. 0.67

    B. 0.05

    C. 0.008

    D. 0.33

(Rigorous) (Skill 12.4)

82. The probability density function for an exponential distribution is given by $f(x) = 2e^{-2x}$; $x \geq 0$. What is the median value for the variable x?

    A. 0.35

    B. 0.5

    C. 2.0

    D. 0.45

(Average) (Skill 13.1)

83. A school has 15 male teachers and 35 female teachers. In how many ways can they form a committee with 2 male teachers and 4 female teachers?

    A. 525

    B. 5497800

    C. 88

    D. 263894400

(Rigorous) (Skill 13.2)

84. What is the negation of a statement of the form "p and q"?

    A. not and not q

    B. not p and q

    C. not p or not q

    D. p or not q

(Average) (Skill 13.2)

85. The contrapositive of the statement "If I am hungry I eat" is:

    A. If I eat then I am hungry

    B. If I am not hungry I do not eat

    C. If I do not eat I am not hungry

    D. If I am hungry I do not eat

(Easy) (Skill 13.3)

86. The scalar multiplication of the number 3 with the matrix $\begin{pmatrix} 2 & 1 \\ 3 & 5 \end{pmatrix}$ yields:

    A. 33

    B. $\begin{pmatrix} 6 & 1 \\ 9 & 5 \end{pmatrix}$

    C. $\begin{pmatrix} 2 & 3 \\ 3 & 15 \end{pmatrix}$

    D. $\begin{pmatrix} 6 & 3 \\ 9 & 15 \end{pmatrix}$

(Rigorous) (Skill 13.3)

87. Evaluate the following matrix product:

$$\begin{pmatrix} 2 & 1 & 3 \\ 2 & 2 & 4 \end{pmatrix} \begin{pmatrix} 6 & 5 \\ 2 & 1 \\ 2 & 7 \end{pmatrix}$$

A. $\begin{pmatrix} 20 & 32 & 24 \\ 24 & 40 & 48 \end{pmatrix}$

B. $\begin{pmatrix} 20 & 32 \\ 40 & 24 \\ 24 & 48 \end{pmatrix}$

C. 116

D. $\begin{pmatrix} 20 & 32 \\ 24 & 40 \end{pmatrix}$

Mathematical Processes (Skills 14.1 – 15.5)

(Rigorous) (Skill 14.1)

88. What math principle is reinforced by matching numerals with number words?

   A. Sequencing

   B. Greater than and less than

   C. Number representations

   D. Rote counting

(Easy) (Skill 14.2)

89. Perspective in art is used to:

   A. Calculate proportions of the human body

   B. Measure the constituents of color

   C. Portray 3-dimensonal distances in 2 dimensions

   D. None of the above

(Rigorous) (Skill 14.3)

90. Cindy bought a package of cookies. She ate half of them and gave one-third of the remainder to a friend. She then had 20 fewer cookies than she did in the beginning. This information can be expressed symbolically in the following way:

   A. $\frac{n}{2} - \frac{n}{3} = n - 20$

   B. $\frac{n}{2} - \frac{n}{6} = n - 20$

   C. $\frac{n}{2}(1 - \frac{1}{3}) = n - 20$

   D. $\frac{n}{2} - \frac{n}{3} = n + 20$

(Average) (Skill 14.3)

91. Kindergarten students are doing a butterfly art project. They fold paper in half. On one half, they paint a design. Then they fold the paper closed and reopen. The resulting picture is a butterfly with matching sides. What math principle does this demonstrate?

   A. Slide

   B. Rotate

   C. Symmetry

   D. Transformation

(Average) (Skill 14.3)

92. Third grade students are looking at a circle graph. Most of the graph is yellow. A small wedge of the graph is blue. Each colored section also has a number followed by a symbol. What are the students most likely learning about?

   A. Addition

   B. Venn diagrams

   C. Percent

   D. Pictographs

(Easy) (Skill 14.4)

93. **When word problems are represented algebraically:**

    A. The number of equations should be more than the number of unknowns

    B. The number of equations should be equal to the number of unknowns

    C. The number of equations should be less than the number of unknowns

    D. There can be any number of equations

(Easy) (Skill 14.5)

94. **The "father of geometry" is:**

    A. Archimedes

    B. Euclid

    C. Pythagoras

    D. Apollonius

(Average) (Skill 15.1)

95. **Mr. Sanchez is having his students work with one-syllable words, removing the first consonant and substituting another, as in changing mats to hats. What reading skill are they working on?**

    A. Morphemic inflections

    B. Pronouncing short vowels

    C. Invented spelling

    D. Phonemic awareness

(Rigorous) (Skill 15.2)

96. **Which of the following is not a primary way to differentiate instruction?**

    A. Product

    B. Content

    C. Quantity

    D. Process

(Average) (Skill 15.3)

97. **To summarize a passage, a student should:**

    A. Answer the key questions raised in the passage

    B. Paraphrase the main idea

    C. Create a list of key words in the passage

    D. State the main idea and supporting details

(Easy) (Skill 15.3)

98. **A Venn diagram is an example of which type of comprehension strategy?**

    A. Text structure

    B. Graphic organizer

    C. Summarization

    D. Textual marking

(Easy) (Skill 15.4)

99. **Which of the following is true about content area vocabulary?**

    A. Content area vocabulary should be taught by connecting new words to familiar ideas, words, and experiences.

    B. Content area vocabulary should be taught beginning in middle school.

    C. Content area vocabulary should be taught primarily in language arts classes.

    D. Content area vocabulary should be introduced once and then used occasionally for review.

(Average) (Skill 15.5)

100. According to Piaget, at which developmental level would a child be able to learn formal algebra?

A. Pre-operational

B. Sensori-motor

C. formal operational

D. Concrete operational

Answer Key

ANSWER KEY						
1. A	16. B	31. D	46. D	61. C	76. B	91. C
2. C	17. B	32. B	47. B	62. B	77. B	92. C
3. A	18. D	33. C	48. D	63. C	78. C	93. B
4. C	19. B	34. B	49. A	64. C	79. B	94. B
5. B	20. A	35. A	50. B	65. C	80. C	95. C
6. A	21. A	36. A	51. A	66. D	81. C	96. A
7. A	22. D	37. C	52. A	67. A	82. A	97. C
8. B	23. B	38. B	53. C	68. C	83. B	98. D
9. D	24. B	39. A	54. B	69. D	84. C	99. D
10. C	25. D	40. D	55. B	70. D	85. C	100. B
11. C	26. C	41. C	56. B	71. C	86. D	
12. A	27. D	42. D	57. B	72. C	87. D	
13. A	28. A	43. D	58. C	73. B	88. C	
14. D	29. B	44. D	59. C	74. B	89. C	
15. B	30. D	45. C	60. C	75. C	90. B	

Rigor Table

RIGOR TABLE	
Rigor level	**Questions**
Easy 20%	1, 5, 6, 28, 32, 39, 60, 65, 68, 71, 72, 74, 75, 79, 86, 89, 93, 94, 96, 100
Average 41%	2, 3, 4, 8, 10, 12, 13, 14, 18, 21, 22, 23, 24, 25, 26, 27, 30, 33, 34, 37, 40, 42, 43, 51, 53, 57, 61, 63, 64, 69, 70, 73, 78, 83, 85, 91, 92, 95, 98, 99
Rigorous 39%	7, 9, 15, 16, 17, 19, 20, 29, 31, 35, 36, 38, 41, 44, 45, 46, 47, 48, 49, 50, 52, 54, 55, 56, 58, 59, 62, 66, 67, 76, 77, 80, 81, 82, 84, 87, 88, 90, 97

Sample Questions with Rationales

Formulas

Formula	Description
$V = \frac{1}{3}Bh$	Volume of a right cone or a pyramid
$V = Bh$	Volume of a cylinder or a prism
$V = \frac{4}{3}\pi r^3$	Volume of a sphere
$A = 2\pi rh + 2\pi r^2$	Surface area of a cylinder
$A = 4\pi r^2$	Surface area of a sphere
$A = \pi r\sqrt{r^2 + h^2} = \pi rl$	Lateral surface area of a right cone
$S_n = \frac{n}{2}[2a_1 + (n-1)d] = \frac{n(a_1 + a_n)}{2}$	Sum of an arithmetic series
$S_n = \frac{a(1 - r^n)}{1 - r}$	Sum of a finite geometric series
$\sum_{n=0}^{\infty} ar^n = \frac{a}{1-r}, \; \lvert r \rvert < 1$	Sum of an infinite geometric series
$\frac{a}{\sin A} = \frac{b}{\sin B} = \frac{c}{\sin C}$	Law of sines
$c^2 = a^2 + b^2 - 2ab\cos C$	Law of cosines
$(x - h)^2 + (y - k)^2 = r^2$	Equation of a circle
$(y - k)^2 = 4c(x - h)^2$	Equation of a parabola
$\frac{(x-h)^2}{a^2} + \frac{(y-k)2}{b^2} = 1$	Equation of a ellipse
$\frac{(x-h)^2}{a^2} - \frac{(y-k)2}{b^2} = 1$	Equation of a hyperbola

Number Sense
(Skills 1.1 – 3.3)

(Easy) (Skill 1.1)

1. Mr. Brown feeds his cat premium cat food which costs $40 per month. Approximately how much will it cost to feed her for one year?

   A. $500

   B. $400

   C. $80

   D. $4800

   Answer: A. $500

   12(40) = 480, which is closest to $500.

(Average) (Skill 1.1)

2. The mass of a chocolate chip cookie is about:

   A. 1 kilogram

   B. 1 gram

   C. 15 grams

   D. 15 milligrams

   Answer: C. 15 grams

   Since an ordinary cookie would not weigh as much as 1 kilogram or as little as 1 gram or 15 milligrams, the only reasonable answer is 15 grams.

(Average) (Skill 1.2)

3. Given W = whole numbers
   N = natural numbers
   Z = integers
   R = rational numbers
   I = irrational numbers

   which of the following is not true?

   A. $R \subset I$

   B. $W \subset Z$

   C. $Z \subset R$

   D. $N \subset W$

   Answer: A. $R \subset I$

   The rational numbers are not a subset of the irrational numbers. All of the other statements are true.

(Average) (Skill 1.2)

4. Which of the following is an irrational number?

   A. .362626262...

   B. $4\frac{1}{3}$

   C. $\sqrt{5}$

   D. $-\sqrt{16}$

   Answer: C. $\sqrt{5}$

   5 is an irrational number A and B can both be expressed as fractions. D can be simplified to -4, an integer and rational number.

(Easy) (Skill 1.2)

5. The conjugate of $4 + 5i$ is:

   A. $-4 + 5i$

   B. $4 - 5i$

   C. $4i + 5$

   D. $4i - 5$

   Answer: B. $4 - 5i$

   By definition, the conjugate of a complex number is obtained by changing the sign of its imaginary part.

(Easy) (Skill 1.2)

6. Simplify: $(6 + 3i) - (4 - 2i)$

   A. $2 + 5i$

   B. $2 + i$

   C. $10 + 5i$

   D. $2 - 2i$

   Answer: A. $2 + 5i$

   Use the rules of addition and subtraction for complex numbers. $(6 + 3i) - (4 - 2i)$ $= 6 + 3i - 4 + 2i = 2 + 5i$

(Skill 1.4) (Rigorous)

7. Express the complex number $1 + i$ in polar form.

   A. $\sqrt{2}(\cos \frac{\pi}{4} + i \sin \frac{\pi}{4})$

   B. $2(\cos \frac{\pi}{4} + i \sin \frac{\pi}{4})$

   C. $\sqrt{2}(\cos \frac{\pi}{2} + i \sin \frac{\pi}{2})$

   D. $\sqrt{2}(\sin \frac{\pi}{4} + i \cos \frac{\pi}{4})$

Answer: A. $\sqrt{2}(\cos \frac{\pi}{4} + i \sin \frac{\pi}{4})$

A complex number $a + bi$ can be represented using a vector of length r and an angle u measured in the counterclockwise direction from the x-axis. Using trigonometry, the complex number can be written as $a + bi$ 5 $r(\cos \theta + i \sin \theta)$ where $r = \sqrt{a^2 + b^2}$ and $\theta = \arctan\frac{b}{a}$. In this case, $a = b = 1$. Therefore $r = \sqrt{2}$ and $\theta = \frac{\pi}{4}$.

(Average) (Skill 2.1)

8. Find the LCM of 27, 90, and 84.

   A. 90

   B. 3,780

   C. 204,120

   D. 1,260

   Answer: B. 3,780

   To find the LCM of the above numbers, factor each into its prime factors and multiply each common factor the maximum number of times it occurs. Thus,

   $27 = 3 \times 3 \times 3$

   $90 = 2 \times 3 \times 3 \times 5$

   $84 = 2 \times 2 \times 3 \times 7$

   LCM $= 2 \times 2 \times 3 \times 3 \times 3 \times 5 \times 7 = 3,780$.

(Rigorous) (Skill 2.1)

9. What is the smallest number that is divisible by 3 and 5 and leaves a remainder of 3 when divided by 7?

   A. 15

   B. 18

   C. 25

   D. 45

Answer: D. 45

To be divisible by both 3 and 5, the number must be divisible by 15. Inspecting the first few multiples of 15, you will find that 45 is the first of the sequence that is 3 greater than a multiple of 7.

(Average) (Skill 2.1)

10. **Which of the following is always composite if x is odd, y is even, and both x and y are greater than or equal to 2?**

    A. $x + y$

    B. $3x + 2y$

    C. $5xy$

    D. $5x + 3y$

Answer: C. $5xy$

A composite number is a number that is not prime. The prime number sequence begins 2,3,5,7,11,13,17, …. To determine which of the expressions is *always* composite, experiment with different values of x and y, such as $x = 3$ and $y = 2$, or $x = 5$ and $y = 2$. It turns out that $5xy$ will always be an even number and is therefore composite if $y = 2$.

(Average) (Skill 2.1)

11. **Find the GCF of $2^2 \times 3^2 \times 5$ and $2^2 \times 3 \times 7$.**

    A. $2^5 \times 3^3 \times 5 \times 7$

    B. $2 \times 3 \times 5 \times 7$

    C. $2^2 \times 3$

    D. $2^3 \times 3^2 \times 5 \times 7$

Answer: C. $2^2 \times 3$

Choose the number of each prime factor that is in common.

(Average) (Skill 2.2)

12. $24 - 3 \times 7 + 2 =$

    A. 5

    B. 149

    C. -3

    D. 189

Answer: A. 5

According to the order of operations, multiplication is performed first, and then addition and subtraction from left to right.

(Average) (Skill 2.2)

13. $7t - 4 \times 2t + 3t \times 4 \div 2 =$

    A. $5t$

    B. 0

    C. $31t$

    D. $18t$

Answer: A. $5t$

First perform multiplication and division from left to right; $7t - 8t + 6t$, then add and subtract from left to right.

(Average) (Skill 2.3)

14. **Which of the following illustrates an inverse property?**

    A. $a + b = a - b$

    B. $a + b = b + a$

    C. $a + 0 = a$

    D. $a + (-a) = 0$

Answer: D. $a + (-a) = 0$

The correct answer is D because $a + (-a) = 0$ is a statement of the additive inverse property.

Answer: B. Step b

In simplifying from step a to step b, 3 replaced $7 - 4$, therefore the correct justification would be subtraction or substitution.

(Rigorous) (Skill 2.3)

15. Which of the following sets is closed under division?
    I) $\{1/2, 1, 2, 4\}$
    II) $\{-1, 1\}$
    III) $\{-1, 0, 1\}$

    A. I only

    B. II only

    C. III only

    D. I and II

Answer: B. II only

Set I is not closed because $\frac{4}{.5} = 8$ and 8 is not in the set. Set III is not closed because $\frac{1}{0}$ is undefined. Set II is closed because $\frac{-1}{1} = -1, \frac{1}{-1} = -1, \frac{1}{1} = 1, \frac{-1}{-1} = 1$, and all the quotients are in the set.

(Rigorous) (Skill 2.3)

16. Which axiom is incorrectly applied?
    $3x + 4 = 7$

    Step a. $3x + 4 - 4 = 7 - 4$
    additive equality

    Step b. $3x + 4 - 4 = 3$
    commutative axiom of addition

    Step c. $3x + 0 = 3$
    additive inverse

    Step d. $3x = 3$
    additive identity

    A. Step a

    B. Step b

    C. Step c

    D. Step d

(Rigorous) (Skill 2.3)

17. Which of the following sets is closed under division?

    A. Integers

    B. Rational numbers

    C. Natural numbers

    D. Whole numbers

Answer: B. Rational numbers

In order to be closed under division, when any two members of the set are divided, the answer must be contained in the set. This is not true for integers, natural, or whole numbers as illustrated by the counter example $\frac{11}{2} = 5.5$.

(Average) (Skill 3.2)

18. Identify the correct sequence of sub-skills required for solving and graphing inequalities involving absolute value in one variable, such as $|x + 1| \le 6$.

    A. Understanding absolute value, graphing inequalities, solving systems of equations

    B. Graphing inequalities on a Cartesian plane, solving systems of equations, simplifying expressions with absolute value

    C. Plotting points, graphing equations, graphing inequalities

    D. Solving equations with absolute value, solving inequalities, graphing conjunctions and disjunctions

Answer: D. Solving equations with absolute value, solving inequalities, graphing conjunctions and disjunctions

The steps listed in answer D would look like this for the given example:

If $|x + 1| \leq 6$, then $-6 \leq x + 1 \leq 6$, which means $-7 \leq x \leq 5$. Then the inequality would be graphed on a number line and would show that the solution set is all real numbers between -7 and 5, including -7 and 5.

(Rigorous) (Skill 3.2)

19. Mr. Lacey is using problem solving to help students develop their math skills. He gives the class a box of pencils. He says that the pencils have to be divided so that each student has the same number of pencils. What step should come first in problem solving?

    A. Find a strategy to solve the problem

    B. Identify the problem

    C. Count the number of pencils

    D. Make basic calculations

Answer: B. Identify the problem

The first step in problem solving is always to identify the problem.

(Rigorous) (Skill 3.3)

20. What is the total cost of the purchase of a suit for $295.99 and a pair of shoes for $69.95 including 6.5% sales tax?

    A. $389.73

    B. $398.37

    C. $237.86

    D. $315.23

Answer: A. $389.73

Before the tax, the total comes to $365.94. Then, the tax is .065($365.94) = $23.79. With the tax added on, the total bill is $365.94 + $23.79 = $389.73. (The same answer can be found in a quicker way: 1.065($365.94) = $389.73.)

(Average) (Skill 3.3)

21. The volume of water flowing through a pipe varies directly with the square of the radius of the pipe. If the water flows at a rate of 80 liters per minute through a pipe with a radius of 4 cm, at what rate would water flow through a pipe with a radius of 3 cm?

    A. 45 liters per minute

    B. 6.67 liters per minute

    C. 60 liters per minute

    D. 4.5 liters per minute

Answer: A. 45 liters per minute

Set up the direct variation: $\frac{V}{r^2} = \frac{V}{r^2}$. Substitution yields $\frac{80}{16} = \frac{V}{9}$. Solve for V to get 45 liters per minute.

(Average) (Skill 3.3)

22. Express .0000456 in scientific notation.

    A. 4.56×10^{-4}

    B. 45.6×10^{-6}

    C. 4.56×10^{-6}

    D. 4.56×10^{-5}

Answer: D. 4.56×10^{-5}

In scientific notation, the decimal point belongs to the right of the 4, the first significant digit. To get from 4.56×10^{-5} back to 0.0000456, we would move the decimal point 5 places to the left.

Functions, Algebra, and Calculus (Skills 4.1 – 7.5)

(Average) (Skill 4.2)

23. State the domain of the function $f(x) = \frac{3x - 6}{x^2 - 25}$.

    A. $x \neq 2$

    B. $x \neq 5, -5$

    C. $x \neq 2, -2$

    D. $x \neq 5$

Answer: B. $x \neq 5, -5$

The values of 5 and –5 must be omitted from the domain of all real numbers because if x took on either of those values, the denominator of the fraction would have a value of 0, and therefore the fraction would be undefined.

(Average) (Skill 4.2)

24. Find the domain of the function $\sqrt{6 - x^2}$.

    A. $x \geq \sqrt{6}$

    B. $-\sqrt{6} \leq x \leq \sqrt{6}$

    C. $0 \leq x \leq \sqrt{6}$

    D. $x \geq 0$

Answer: B. $-\sqrt{6} \leq x \leq \sqrt{6}$

The expression under the square root sign cannot be negative. Hence we must have $6 - x^2 \geq 0; \rightarrow x^2 \leq 6; \rightarrow x \leq \sqrt{6}$ and $x \geq -\sqrt{6}$

(Average) (Skill 4.4)

25. Given $f(x) = 3x - 2, f^{-1}(x) =$

    A. $3x + 2$

    B. $\frac{x}{6}$

    C. $2x - 3$

    D. $\frac{(x + 2)}{3}$

Answer: D. $\frac{(x + 2)}{3}$

To find the inverse, $f^{-1}(x)$, of the given function, reverse the variables in the given equation, $y = 3x - 2$, to get $x = 3y - 2$. Then solve for y as follows: $x + 2 = 3y$, and $y = \frac{x + 2}{3}$.

(Average) (Skill 4.4)

26. Given $f(x) = 3x - 2$ and $g(x) = x^2$, determine $g(f(x))$.

    A. $3x^2 - 2$

    B. $9x^2 + 4$

    C. $9x^2 - 12x + 4$

    D. $3x^3 - 2$

Answer: C. $9x^2 - 12x + 4$

The composite function $g(f(x))$ is $g(f(x)) = (3x - 2)^2 = 9x^2 - 12x + 4$.

(Average) (Skill 5.2)

27. Solve $d = at(v_t - v_0)$ for v_0.

    A. $v_0 = atd - v_t$

    B. $v_0 = d - atv_t$

    C. $v_0 = atv_t - d$

    D. $v_0 = \dfrac{(atv_t - d)}{at}$

    Answer: D. $v_0 = \dfrac{(atv_t - d)}{at}$

    Using the distributive property and other properties of equality to isolate v_0 yields
    $$d = atv_t - atv_0$$
    $$atv_0 = atv_t - d$$
    $$v_0 = \frac{atv_t - d}{at}.$$

(Easy) (Skill 5.3)

28. **Which of the following is equivalent to $\sqrt[b]{x^a}$?**

    A. $x^{\frac{a}{b}}$

    B. $x^{\frac{b}{a}}$

    C. $a^{\frac{x}{b}}$

    D. $b^{\frac{x}{a}}$

    Answer: A. $x^{\frac{a}{b}}$

    The bth root, expressed in the form $\sqrt[b]{}$, can also be written as an exponential, $\frac{1}{b}$. Writing the expression in this form, $(x^a)^{\frac{1}{b}}$, and then multiplying exponents yields $x^{\frac{a}{b}}$.

(Rigorous) (Skill 5.3)

29. **Evaluate $3^{\frac{1}{2}}(9^{\frac{1}{3}})$.**

    A. $27^{\frac{5}{6}}$

    B. $9^{\frac{7}{12}}$

    C. $3^{\frac{5}{6}}$

    D. $3^{\frac{6}{7}}$

Answer: B. $9^{\frac{7}{12}}$

Getting the bases the same yields $3^{\frac{1}{2}} 3^{\frac{2}{3}}$. Adding exponents yields $3^{\frac{7}{6}}$. Additional manipulation of exponents produces $3^{\frac{7}{6}} = 3^{\frac{14}{12}} = (3^2)^{\frac{7}{12}} = 9^{\frac{7}{12}}$.

(Average) (Skill 5.3)

30. **The exponential equation $2^5 = 32$ can be written as:**

    A. $\log_2(5) = 32$

    B. $\log_{10}(32) = 5$

    C. $\log_5(32) = 2$

    D. $\log_2(32) = 5$

Answer: D. $\log_2(32) = 5$

By definition, $\log_2(32) = 5$ corresponds to $2^5 = 32$. Answer D is thus correct.

(Rigorous) (Skill 5.3)

31. **Solve for x: $10^{x-3} + 5 = 105$.**

    A. 3

    B. 10

    C. 2

    D. 5

Answer: D. 5

Simplify: $10^{x-3} = 100$. Taking the logarithm to base 10 of both sides yields $(x - 3)\log_{10} 10 = \log_{10} 100$. Thus, $x - 3 = 2$ and $x = 5$. Answer D is correct.

(Easy) (Skill 5.4)

32. Given a vector with horizontal component 5 and vertical component 6, determine the length of the vector.

   A. 61

   B. $\sqrt{61}$

   C. 30

   D. $\sqrt{30}$

   Answer: B. $\sqrt{61}$

   Using the Pythagorean Theorem, we get a length of $\sqrt{36 + 25} = \sqrt{61}$.

(Average) (Skill 6.1)

33. Which graph represents the equation of $y = x^2 + 3x$?

   A.

   B.

   C.

   D.

   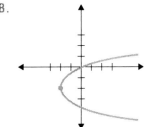

Answer: C.

Answer B is not the graph of a function. Answer D is the graph of a parabola where the coefficient of x^2 is negative. Answer A appears to be the graph of $y = x^2$. To find the x-intercepts of $y = x^2 + 3x$, set $y = 0$ and solve for x: $0 = x^2 + 3x = x(x + 3)$ to get $x = 0$ or $x = -3$. Therefore, the graph of the function intersects the x-axis at $x = 0$ and $x = -3$. The correct answer is C.

(Average) (Skill 6.1)

34. **What is the equation of the graph shown below?**

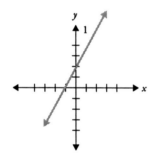

A. $2x + y = 2$

B. $2x - y = -2$

C. $2x - y = 2$

D. $2x + y = -2$

Answer: B

By observation, we see that the graph has a y-intercept of 2 and a slope of $\frac{2}{1} = 2$. Therefore, its equation is $y = mx + b = 2x + 2$. Rearranging the terms yields $2x - y = -2$.

(Skill 6.2) (Rigorous)

35. **What transformations have been applied to the function $f(x)$ shown below to obtain function $g(x)$?**

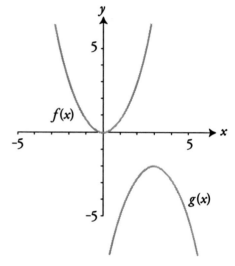

A. Reflection over x-axis, translation 3 units to the right, translation 2 units down

B. Translation 3 units to the right, translation 2 units down, reflection over x-axis

C. Translation 2 units down, translation 3 units to the right, reflection over x-axis

D. Reflection over y-axis, translation 3 units to the right, translation 2 units down

Answer: A. Reflection over *x*-axis, translation 3 units to the right, translation 2 units down

Notice that choices A, B and C have the same transformations but in a different order. Only A produces the correct answer. First, reflection over the *x*-axis leaves the vertex at the origin but has the parabola opening downwards. The translations 3 units to the right and 2 units down bring the vertex to the point (3, –2) which is the vertex of *g*(*x*) as shown in the figure.

(Rigorous) (Skill 6.4)

36. The length of a picture frame is 2 inches greater than its width. If the area of the frame is 143 square inches, what is its width?

   A. 11 inches

   B. 13 inches

   C. 12 inches

   D. 10 inches

Answer: A. 11 inches

First set up the equation for the problem. If the width of the picture frame is *w*, then $w(w + 2) = 143$. Next, solve the equation to obtain *w*. Using the method of completing squares we have
$w^2 + 2w + 1 = 144$
$(w + 1)^2 = 144$
$w + 1 = \pm 12.$
Thus *w* is 11 or –13. Since the width cannot be negative, the correct answer is 11 inches.

(Average) (Skill 6.4)

37. Find the height of a box with surface area of 94 sq. ft. with a width of 3 feet and a depth of 4 feet.

   A. 3 ft.

   B. 4 ft.

   C. 5 ft.

   D. 6 ft.

Answer: C. 5 ft.

Use the expression for surface area and solve for the unknown value *h*.

$94 = 2(3h) + 2(4h) + 2(12)$
$94 = 6h + 8h + 24$
$94 = 14h + 24$
$70 = 14h$
$5 = h$
Thus, the height of the box is 5 feet.

(Rigorous) (Skill 6.4)

38. Ralph and Rhonda can paint a barn together in 4 hours. If Ralph needs 6 more hours than Rhonda to paint the barn all by himself, how many hours does Rhonda need to paint the barn by herself?

   A. 5

   B. 6

   C. 7

   D. 8

Answer: B. 6

Let the number of hours Rhonda needs to paint the barn by herself be x. Then Ralph needs $x + 6$ hours to paint the barn by himself.

In 1 hour Rhonda paints $\frac{1}{x}$ of the barn and Ralph paints $\frac{1}{(x + 6)}$ of the barn.

In 4 hours Rhonda paints $\frac{4}{x}$ of the barn and Ralph paints $\frac{4}{(x + 6)}$ of the barn.

Since both of them together paint the whole barn in 4 hours, we can write

$$\frac{4}{x} + \frac{4}{x} + 6 = 1$$
$$\rightarrow \frac{4x + 24 + 4x}{x(x + 6)} = 1$$
$$\rightarrow 8x + 24 = x^2 + 6x$$
$$\rightarrow x^2 - 2x - 24 = 0$$
$$\rightarrow (x - 6)(x + 4) = 0$$

The solutions to the above equation are $x = 6$, and $x = -4$. Since in this case we cannot have a negative answer, the number of hours Rhonda needs to paint the barn by herself is 6.

(Easy) (Skill 7.1)

39. **L'Hopital's rule provides a method to evaluate which of the following?**

    A. Limit of a function

    B. Derivative of a function

    C. Sum of an arithmetic series

    D. Sum of a geometric series

Answer: A. Limit of a function

L'Hopital's rule is used to find the limit of a function by taking the derivatives of the numerator and denominator. Since the primary purpose of the rule is to find the limit, A is the correct answer.

(Average) (Skill 7.1)

40. **Find the following limit: $\lim\limits_{x \to 2} \frac{x^2 - 4}{x - 2}$**

    A. 0

    B. Infinity

    C. 2

    D. 4

Answer: D. 4

First, factor the numerator and cancel the common factor to get the limit.

$$\lim\limits_{x \to 2} \frac{x^2 - 4}{x - 2} = \lim\limits_{x \to 2} \frac{(x - 2)(x + 2)}{(x - 2)} = \lim\limits_{x \to 2} (x + 2) = 4$$

(Rigorous) (Skill 7.1)

41. **Find the following limit: $\lim\limits_{x \to 0} \frac{\sin 2x}{5x}$**

    A. Infinity

    B. 0

    C. 1.4

    D. 1

Answer: C. 1.4

Since substituting $x = 0$ will give an undefined answer, we can use L'Hospital's rule and take derivatives of both the numerator and denominator to find the limit.

$$\lim\limits_{x \to 0} \frac{\sin 2x}{5x} = \lim\limits_{x \to 0} \frac{2\cos 2x}{5}$$

Now substitute $x = 0$:

$$\lim\limits_{x \to 0} \frac{2\cos 2x}{5} = \frac{2}{5} = 1.4$$

(Average) (Skill 7.2)

42. Determine the measures of angles A and B.

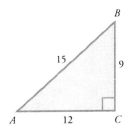

A. $A = 30°, B = 60°$

B. $A = 60°, B = 30°$

C. $A = 53°, B = 37°$

D. $A = 37°, B = 53°$

Answer: D. $A = 37°, B = 53°$

Using the diagram, note that
$\tan A = \frac{9}{12} = 0.75$
$\arctan 0.75 = 37°$.
Since angle B is complementary to angle A, the measure of angle B is therefore 53 degrees.

(Average) (Skill 7.2)

43. Which expression is not identical to $\sin x$?

A. $\sqrt{1 - \cos^2 x}$

B. $\tan x \cos x$

C. $\frac{1}{\csc x}$

D. $\frac{1}{\sec x}$

Answer: D. $\frac{1}{\sec x}$

Using the basic definitions of the trigonometric functions and the Pythagorean identity, it can be seen that the first three options are all identical to $\sin x$.
$\sec x = \frac{1}{\cos x}$ is not the same as $\sin x$.

(Rigorous) (Skill 7.2)

44. Which expression is equivalent to $1 - \sin^2 x$?

A. $1 - \cos^2 x$

B. $1 + \cos^2 x$

C. $\frac{1}{\sec x}$

D. $\frac{1}{\sec^2 x}$

Answer: D. $\frac{1}{\sec^2 x}$

Using the Pythagorean Identity, it is apparent that $\sin^2 x + \cos^2 x = 1$. Thus, $1 - \sin^2 x = \cos^2 x$, which by definition is equal to $\frac{1}{\sec^2 x}$. The correct answer is D.

(Rigorous) (Skill 7.2)

45. For an acute angle x, $\sin x = 0.6$. What is $\cot x$?

A. $\frac{5}{3}$

B. 0.75

C. 1.33

D. 1

Answer: C. 1.33

Using the Pythagorean Identity, it is apparent that $\sin^2 x + \cos^2 x = 1$. Thus, $\cos x = \sqrt{1 - \frac{9}{25}} = \frac{4}{5}$ and $\cot x = \frac{\cos x}{\sin x} = \left(\frac{4}{5}\right)\left(\frac{5}{3}\right) = \frac{4}{3}$.

(Rigorous) (Skill 7.3)

46. Find the first derivative of the function:
$f(x) = x^3 - 6x^2 + 5x + 4.$

A. $3x^2 - 12x^2 + 5x$

B. $3x^2 - 12x - 5$

C. $3x^2 - 12x + 9$

D. $3x^2 - 12x + 5$

Answer: D. $3x^2 - 12x + 5$

Use the Power Rule for polynomial differentiation: if $y = ax^n$, then $y' = nax^{n-1}$. Then, $f'(x) = 3x^2 - 12x + 5$

(Rigorous) (Skill 7.4)

47. Evaluate: $\int_0^2 (x^2 + x - 1)dx$.

    A. $\frac{11}{3}$

    B. $\frac{8}{3}$

    C. $-\frac{8}{3}$

    D. $-\frac{11}{3}$

Answer: B. $\frac{8}{3}$

Use the Fundamental Theorem of Calculus to find the definite integral: given a continuous function f on an interval $[a, b]$, then $\int_a^b f(x)dx = F(b) - F(a)$, where F is an antiderivative of f. $\int_0^2 (x^2 + x - 1)dx = (\frac{x^3}{3} + \frac{x^2}{2} - x)$ Evaluate the expression at $x = 2$, at $x = 0$, and then subtract to get $\frac{8}{3} + \frac{4}{2} - 2 - 0 = \frac{8}{3}$.

(Rigorous) (Skill 7.4)

48. Find the antiderivative for the function $y = e^{3x}$.

    A. $3x(e^{3x}) + C$

    B. $3(e^{3x}) + C$

    C. $\frac{1}{3}(e^x) + C$

    D. $\frac{1}{3}(e^{3x}) + C$

Answer: D. $\frac{1}{3}(e^{3x}) + C$

Use the rule for integration of functions of e: $\int e^x dx = e^x + C$ $\int e^{3x} dx = \frac{1}{3} \int e^u du = \frac{1}{3}e^u + C = \frac{1}{3}e^{3x} + C$.

(Rigorous) (Skill 7.4)

49. Find the area under the function $y = x^2 + 4$ from $x = 3$ to $x = 6$.

    A. 75

    B. 21

    C. 96

    D. 57

Answer: A. 75

To find the area, set up the definite integral: $\int_3^6 (x^2 + 4)dx = (\frac{x^3}{3} + 4x)_3^6$. Evaluate the expression at $x = 6$ and $x = 3$ to get $(\frac{x^3}{3} + 4x)_3^6 = \frac{6^3}{3} + 4(6) - [\frac{3^3}{3} + 4(3)] = 72 + 24 - 9 - 12 = 75$. The correct answer is A.

(Rigorous) (Skill 7.4)

50. If the velocity of a body is given by $v = 16 - t^2$, find the distance traveled from $t = 0$ until the body comes to a complete stop.

    A. 16

    B. 43

    C. 48

    D. 64

Answer: B. 43

Recall that the derivative of the distance function is the velocity function. Conversely, the integral of the velocity function is the distance function. To find the time needed for the body to come to a stop when $v = 0$, solve for t:

$v(t) = 16 - t^2 = 0$

$t = 4$

Thus, the body travels from time $t = 0$ to time $t = 4$. The distance function (excluding the constant of integration, which is unneeded here) is

$s\,(t) = \int v(t)\,dt = 16t - \frac{t^3}{3}$.

At $t = 4$,

$s(4) = 16(4) - \frac{4^3}{3} = \frac{128}{3} \approx 42.7$.

The body travels approximately 42.7 units.

Measurement and Geometry (Skills 8.1 – 10.5)

(Average) (Skill 8.1)

51. The term "cubic feet" indicates which kind of measurement?

A. Volume

B. Mass

C. Length

D. Distance

Answer: A. Volume

The word *cubic* indicates that this is a term describing volume.

(Rigorous) (Skill 8.1)

52. Given that M is a mass, V is a velocity, A is an acceleration and T is a time, what type of unit corresponds to the overall expression $\frac{AMT}{V}$?

A. Mass

B. Time

C. Velocity

D. Acceleration

Answer: A. Mass

Use unit analysis to find the simplest expression for the units associated with the expression. Choose any unit system: for example, the metric system.

$$\frac{AMT}{V} - \frac{\left(\frac{m}{s^2}\right)(kg)\,(s)}{\left(\frac{m}{s}\right)}$$

Simplify the units in the expression

$$\frac{AMT}{V} - \frac{\left(\frac{m}{s}\right)(kg)}{\left(\frac{m}{s}\right)} = kg$$

Kilograms is a unit of mass, and thus the correct answer is A.

(Average) (Skill 8.2)

53. Find the surface area of a box that is 3 feet wide, 5 feet tall, and 4 feet deep.

A. 47 sq. ft.

B. 60 sq. ft.

C. 94 sq. ft.

D. 188 sq. ft.

Answer: C. 94 sq. ft.

Let's assume the base of the rectangular solid (box) is 3 by 4 and the height is 5. Then, the surface area of the top and bottom together is 2(12) = 24. The sum of the areas of the front and back are 2(15) = 30, and the sum of the areas of the sides are 2(20) = 40. The total surface area is therefore 94 square feet.

(Rigorous) (Skill 8.2)

54. Find the area of the figure pictured below.

A. 136.47 m²

B. 148.48 m²

C. 293.86 m²

D. 178.47 m²

Answer: B. 148.48 m²

Divide the figure into two rectangles and one quarter circle. The tall rectangle on the left has dimensions 10m by 4m and, thus, an area of 40m². The center rectangle has dimensions 7m by 10m and, thus, an area of 70m². The quarter circle has an area of .25(π) (7m)² = 38.48m². The total area is therefore approximately 148.48m².

(Rigorous) (Skill 8.2)

55. Compute the area of the shaded region, given a radius of 5 meters. Point *O* is the center.

A. 7.13 cm²

B. 7.13 m²

C. 78.5 m²

D. 19.63 m²

Answer: B. 7.13 m²

The area of triangle *AOB* is .5(5) (5) = 12.5 square meters. Since $\frac{90}{360}$ = .25, the area of sector *AOB* (the pie-shaped piece) is approximately .25(π)5² = 19.63. Subtracting the triangle area from the sector area to get the area of segment *AB* yields approximately 19.63 − 12.5 = 7.13 square meters.

(Rigorous) (Skill 8.2)

56. Determine the area of the shaded region of the trapezoid in terms of *x* and *y*.

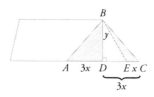

A. 4*xy*

B. 2*xy*

C. 3*x²y*

D. There is not enough information given

Answer: B. 2*xy*

To find the area of the shaded region, find the area of triangle *ABC* and then subtract the area of triangle *DBE*. The area of triangle *ABC* is $.5(6x)(y) = 3xy$. The area of triangle *DBE* is $.5(2x)(y) = xy$. The difference is $2xy$.

(Average) (Skill 8.3)

57. If a ship sails due south 6 miles, then due west 8 miles, how far is it from the starting point?

   A. 100 miles

   B. 10 miles

   C. 14 miles

   D. 48 miles

Answer: B. 10 miles

Draw a right triangle with legs of 6 and 8. Find the hypotenuse using the Pythagorean Theorem:
$6^2 + 8^2 = c^2 = 36 + 64 = 100$
Therefore, $c = 10$ miles.

(Rigorous) (Skill 8.4)

58. If the area of the base of a cone is tripled, the volume will be:

   A. The same as the original

   B. 9 times the original

   C. 3 times the original

   D. 3π times the original

Answer: C. 3 times the original

The formula for the volume of a cone is $V = \frac{1}{3}Bh$, where *B* is the area of the circular base and *h* is the height. If the area of the base is tripled, the volume becomes $V = \frac{1}{3}(3B)h = Bh$, or three times the original area.

(Rigorous) (Skill 8.4)

59. If the radius of a right circular cylinder is doubled, how does its volume change?

   A. No change

   B. Also is doubled

   C. Four times the original

   D. Pi times the original

Answer: C. Four times the original

If the radius of a right circular cylinder is doubled, the volume is multiplied by four because in the formula, the radius is squared, therefore the new volume is 2 × 2 or four times the original.

(Easy) (Skill 9.1)

60. Given that $QO \perp NP$ and $QO = NP$, quadrilateral *NOPQ* can most accurately be described as a:

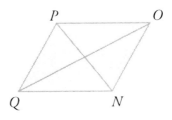

   A. Parallelogram

   B. Rectangle

   C. Square

   D. Rhombus

Answer: C. Square

In an ordinary parallelogram, the diagonals are not perpendicular or equal in length. In a rectangle, the diagonals are not necessarily perpendicular. In a rhombus, the diagonals are not equal in length. In a square, the diagonals are both perpendicular and congruent.

(Average) (Skill 9.1)

61. **Which of the following statements about a trapezoid is incorrect?**

    A. It has one pair of parallel sides

    B. The parallel sides are called bases

    C. If the two bases are the same length, the trapezoid is called isosceles

    D. The median is parallel to the bases

    Answer: C. If the two bases are the same length, the trapezoid is called isosceles

    A trapezoid is isosceles if the two legs (not bases) are the same length.

(Rigorous) (Skill 9.1)

62. **What is the measure of minor arc AD, given the measure of arc PS is 40° and $m\angle K = 10°$?**

    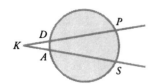

    A. 50°

    B. 20°

    C. 30°

    D. 25°

Answer: B. 20°

The formula relating the measure of angle K and the two arcs it intercepts is $m\angle K = \frac{1}{2}(mPS - mAD)$ Substituting the known values yields $10 = \frac{1}{2}(40 - mAD)$. Solving for mAD gives an answer of 20 degrees.

(Average) (Skill 9.1)

63. **What is the degree measure of an interior angle of a regular 10-sided polygon?**

    A. 18°

    B. 36°

    C. 144°

    D. 54°

Answer: C. 144°

The formula for finding the measure of each interior angle of a regular polygon with n sides is $\frac{(n-2)180}{n}$. For $n = 10$, $\frac{8(180)}{10} = 144$.

(Average) (Skill 9.2)

64. **Which theorem can be used to prove $\triangle BAK \cong \triangle MKA$?**

    A. SSS

    B. ASA

    C. SAS

    D. AAS

Answer: C. SAS

Since side *AK* is common to both triangles, the triangles can be proved congruent by using the Side-Angle-Side Postulate.

(Easy) (Skill 9.3)

65. When you begin by assuming the conclusion of a theorem is false, then show that through a sequence of logically correct steps you contradict an accepted fact, this is known as:

A. Inductive reasoning

B. Direct proof

C. Indirect proof

D. Exhaustive proof

Answer: C. Indirect proof

By definition this describes the procedure of an indirect proof.

(Rigorous) (Skill 10.2)

66. Compute the distance from (-2, 7) to the line $x = 5$.

A. -9

B. -7

C. 5

D. 7

Answer: D. 7

The line $x = 5$ is a vertical line passing through (5, 0) on the Cartesian plane. By observation, the distance along the horizontal line from the point (-2, 7) to the line $x = 5$ is 7 units.

(Rigorous) (Skill 10.2)

67. Given $K(-4, y)$ and $L(2, -3)$ with midpoint $M(x, 1)$, determine the values of x and y.

A. $x = -1, y = 5$

B. $x = 3, y = 2$

C. $x = 5, y = -1$

D. $x = -1, y = -1$

Answer: A. $x = -1, y = 5$

The formula for finding the midpoint (a, b) of a segment passing through the points (x_1, y_1) and (x_2, y_2) is $(a, b) = (\frac{x_1 + x_2}{2}, \frac{y_1 + y_2}{2})$. Setting up the corresponding equations from this information yields $x = \frac{-4 + 2}{2}$ and $1 = \frac{y - 3}{2}$. Solving for x and y yields $x = -1$ and $y = 5$.

(Easy) (Skill 10.3)

68. A glide reflection involves:

A. A translation and dilation

B. A reflection and dilation

C. A translation and a reflection

D. A reflection and a rotation

Answer: C. A translation and a reflection

A glide reflection involves a combined translation along and a reflection across a single specified line. The characteristic that defines a glide reflection as opposed to a simple combination of an arbitrary translation and arbitrary reflection is that the direction of translation is parallel with the line of reflection.

(Average) (Skill 10.3)

69. A point at (1, 2) on a Cartesian coordinate plane is translated two units to the left, reflected in the *y*-axis and then reflected in the *x*-axis. What is its final position?

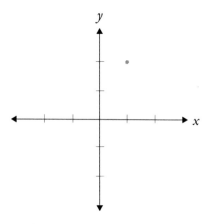

A. (3, 2)

B. (-1, 2)

C. (-2, 1)

D. (1, -2)

Answer: D. (1, -2)

After translation 2 units to the left, the point is at (-1, 2). After reflection in the *y*-axis, it is back in its original position (1, 2). After reflection in the *x*-axis it is at (1, -2).

Data, Probability, and Discrete Math (Skills 11.1 – 13.4)

(Average) (Skill 11.1)

70. Which of the following is not a valid method of collecting statistical data?

A. Random sampling

B. Systematic sampling

C. Cluster sampling

D. Cylindrical sampling

Answer: D. Cylindrical sampling

There is no such method as cylindrical sampling.

(Easy) (Skill 11.1)

71. **Systematic random sampling involves:**

A. Choosing items arbitrarily and in an unstructured manner

B. Targeting a particular section of the population

C. The collection of a sample at defined intervals

D. Proportional sampling from subgroups

Answer: C. The collection of a sample at defined intervals

Systematic random sampling involves the collection of a sample at defined intervals (for instance, every tenth part to come off a manufacturing line). Here, it is assumed that the population is ordered randomly and there is no hidden pattern that may compromise the randomness of the sampling.

(Easy) (Skill 11.2)

72. **Which type of graph uses symbols to represent quantities?**

    A. Bar graph

    B. Line graph

    C. Pictograph

    D. Circle graph

Answer: C. Pictograph

A pictograph shows comparison of quantities using symbols. Each symbol represents a number of items.

(Average) (Skill 11.2)

73. **What conclusion can be drawn from the graph below?**

    MLK Elementary School
    Student Enrollment

    A. The number of students in first grade exceeds the number in second grade

    B. There are more boys than girls in the entire school

    C. There are more girls than boys in the first grade

    D. Third grade has the largest number of students

Answer: B. There are more boys than girls in the entire school

In Kindergarten, first grade and third grade, there are more boys than girls. The number of extra girls in grade two is more than compensated by the extra boys in all the other grades put together.

(Easy) (Skill 11.2)

74. **The pie chart below shows sales at an automobile dealership for the first four months of a year. What percentage of the vehicles were sold in April?**

    A. More than 50%

    B. Less than 25%

    C. Between 25% and 50%

    D. None

Answer: B. Less than 25%

It is clear from the chart that the April segment covers less than a quarter of the pie.

(Easy) (Skill 11.4)

75. Compute the median for the following data set:

    {12, 19, 13, 16, 17, 14}

    A. 14.5

    B. 15.17

    C. 15

    D. 16

Answer: C. 15

Arrange the data in ascending order: 12, 13, 14, 16, 17, 19. The median is the middle value in a list with an odd number of entries. When there is an even number of entries, the median is the mean of the two center entries. Here the average of 14 and 16 is 15.

(Rigorous) (Skill 11.4)

76. Compute the standard deviation for the following set of temperatures:
    (37, 38, 35, 37, 38, 40, 36, 39)

    A. 37.5

    B. 1.5

    C. 0.5

    D. 2.5

Answer: B. 1.5

First find the mean: $\frac{300}{8} = 37.5$. Then, using the formula for standard deviation yields

$$\sqrt{\frac{2(37.5-37)^2 + 2(37.5-38)^2 + (37.5-35)^2 + (37.5-40)^2 + (37.5-36)^2 + (37.5-39)^2}{8}}.$$

This expression has a value of 1.5.

(Rigorous) (Skill 11.4)

77. Half the students in a class scored 80% on an exam; most of the rest scored 85% except for one student who scored 10%. Which would be the best measure of central tendency for the test scores?

    A. Mean

    B. Median

    C. Mode

    D. Either the median or the mode because they are equal

Answer: B. Median

In this set of data, the median would be the most representative measure of central tendency because the median is independent of extreme values. Because of the 10% outlier, the mean (average) would be disproportionately skewed. In this data set, it is true that the median and the mode (number which occurs most often) are the same, but the median remains the best choice because of its special properties.

(Average) (Skill 11.5)

78. **To determine the odds for or against a given deviation from expected statistical distribution statisticians use:**

 A. The t-test

 B. Linear regression

 C. The chi-square test

 D. Exponential regression

 Answer: C. The chi-square test

 The chi-square test is a method of determining the odds for or against a given deviation from expected statistical distribution.

(Easy) (Skill 12.2)

79. **A jar contains 3 red marbles, 5 white marbles, 1 green marble, and 15 blue marbles. If one marble is picked at random from the jar, what is the probability that it will be red?**

 A. $\frac{1}{3}$

 B. $\frac{1}{8}$

 C. $\frac{3}{8}$

 D. $\frac{1}{24}$

 Answer: B. $\frac{1}{8}$

 The total number of marbles is 24 and the number of red marbles is 3. Thus the probability of picking a red marble from the jar is $\frac{3}{24} = \frac{1}{8}$.

(Rigorous) (Skill 12.2)

80. **A die is rolled several times. What is the probability that a 3 will not appear before the third roll of the die?**

 A. $\frac{1}{3}$

 B. $\frac{25}{216}$

 C. $\frac{25}{36}$

 D. $\frac{1}{216}$

 Answer: C. $\frac{25}{36}$

 The probability that a 3 will not appear before the third roll is the same as the probability that the first two rolls will consist of numbers other than 3. Since the probability of any one roll resulting in a number other than 3 is $\frac{5}{6}$, the probability of the first two rolls resulting in a number other than 3 is $\left(\frac{5}{6}\right) \times \left(\frac{5}{6}\right) = \frac{25}{36}$.

(Rigorous) (Skill 12.2)

81. **If there are three people in a room, what is the probability that at least two of them will share a birthday? (Assume a year has 365 days.)**

 A. 0.67

 B. 0.05

 C. 0.008

 D. 0.33

Answer: C. 0.008

The best way to approach this problem is to use the fact that the probability of an event plus the probability of the event not happening is unity. First, find the probability that no two people will share a birthday and then subtract the result from 1. The probability that two of the people will not share a birthday is $\frac{364}{365}$ (since the second person's birthday can be one of the 364 days other than the birthday of the first person). The probability that the third person will also not share either of the first two birthdays is $\left(\frac{364}{365}\right)\left(\frac{363}{365}\right) = 0.992$. Therefore, the probability that at least two people will share a birthday is $1 - 0.992 = 0.008$.

(Rigorous) (Skill 12.4)

82. **The probability density function for an exponential distribution is given by $f(x) = 2e^{-2x}$; $x \geq 0$. What is the median value for the variable x?**

    A. 0.35

    B. 0.5

    C. 2.0

    D. 0.45

Answer: A. 0.35

The integral of the probability distribution function to the upper limit of the median value is equal to $\frac{1}{2}$.

If the median value is $x = a$,

$$\int_0^a 2e^{-2x}\,dx = \frac{1}{2}$$
$$\rightarrow -[e^{-2x}]_0^a = \frac{1}{2}$$
$$\rightarrow 1 - e^{-2a} = \frac{1}{2}$$
$$\rightarrow e^{-2a} = \frac{1}{2}$$
$$\rightarrow -2a = \ln\left(\frac{1}{2}\right)$$
$$\rightarrow a = 0.35$$

(Average) (Skill 13.1)

83. **A school has 15 male teachers and 35 female teachers. In how many ways can they form a committee with 2 male teachers and 4 female teachers?**

    A. 525

    B. 5497800

    C. 88

    D. 263894400

Answer: B. 5497800

The number of ways one can pick 2 male teachers out of 15 = $^{15}_2C = \frac{15!}{13!2!} = \frac{14 \times 15}{2} = 102$

The number of ways one can pick 4 female teachers out of 35 = $^{35}_4C = \frac{35!}{31!4!} = \frac{32 \times 33 \times 34 \times 35}{2 \times 3 \times 4} = 52360$

Hence, the total number of ways the committee can be chosen = $105 \times 52360 = 5497800$

(Rigorous) (Skill 13.2)

84. What is the negation of a statement of the form "*p* and *q*"?

A. not and not *q*

B. not *p* and *q*

C. not *p* or not *q*

D. *p* or not *q*

Answer: C. not *p* or not *q*

The negation of *p* is (not *p*) and the negation of *q* is (not *q*). Since (*p* and *q*) is true only when both *p* and *q* are true, negating either *p* or q negates (*p* and *q*). Hence the negation of (*p* and *q*) is (not *p*) or (not *q*).

(Average) (Skill 13.2)

85. The contrapositive of the statement "If I am hungry I eat" is:

A. If I eat then I am hungry

B. If I am not hungry I do not eat

C. If I do not eat I am not hungry

D. If I am hungry I do not eat

Answer: C. If I do not eat I am not hungry

The contrapositive of the statement "if *p* then *q*" is given by "if not *q* then not *p*".

(Easy) (Skill 13.3)

86. The scalar multiplication of the number 3 with the matrix $\begin{pmatrix} 2 & 1 \\ 3 & 5 \end{pmatrix}$ yields:

A. 33

B. $\begin{pmatrix} 6 & 1 \\ 9 & 5 \end{pmatrix}$

C. $\begin{pmatrix} 2 & 3 \\ 3 & 15 \end{pmatrix}$

D. $\begin{pmatrix} 6 & 3 \\ 9 & 15 \end{pmatrix}$

Answer: D. $\begin{pmatrix} 6 & 3 \\ 9 & 15 \end{pmatrix}$

In scalar multiplication of a matrix by a number, each element of the matrix is multiplied by that number.

(Rigorous) (Skill 13.3)

87. Evaluate the following matrix product:

$$\begin{pmatrix} 2 & 1 & 3 \\ 2 & 2 & 4 \end{pmatrix} \begin{pmatrix} 6 & 5 \\ 2 & 1 \\ 2 & 7 \end{pmatrix}$$

A. $\begin{pmatrix} 20 & 32 & 24 \\ 24 & 40 & 48 \end{pmatrix}$

B. $\begin{pmatrix} 20 & 32 \\ 40 & 24 \\ 24 & 48 \end{pmatrix}$

C. 116

D. $\begin{pmatrix} 20 & 32 \\ 24 & 40 \end{pmatrix}$

Answer: D. $\begin{pmatrix} 20 & 32 \\ 24 & 40 \end{pmatrix}$

The product of a 2 × 3 matrix with a 3 × 2 matrix is a 2 × 2 matrix. This alone should be enough to identify the correct answer. Each term in the 2 × 2 matrix is calculated as described below.

Matrix 1, row 1 multiplied by matrix 2, column 1 yields entry 1, 1: $2 \times 6 + 1 \times 2 + 3 \times 2 = 12 + 2 + 6 = 20$.

Matrix 1, row 1 multiplied by matrix 2, column 2 yields entry 1, 2: $2 \times 5 + 1 \times 1 + 3 \times 7 = 10 + 1 + 21 = 32$.

Matrix 1, row 2 multiplied by matrix 2, column 1 yields entry 2, 1: $2 \times 6 + 2 \times 2 + 4 \times 2 = 12 + 4 + 8 = 24$.

Matrix 1, row 2 multiplied by matrix 2, column 2 yields entry 2, 2: $2 \times 5 + 2 \times 1 + 4 \times 7 = 10 + 2 + 28 = 40$.

Mathematical Processes (Skills 14.1 – 15.5)

(Rigorous) (Skill 14.1)

88. What math principle is reinforced by matching numerals with number words?

    A. Sequencing

    B. Greater than and less than

    C. Number representations

    D. Rote counting

Answer: C. Number representations

When matching numerals with number words, students are recognizing that a numeral (such as 5) has a corresponding number word (five). The numeral 5 and the word five are two representations of the same number.

(Easy) (Skill 14.2)

89. Perspective in art is used to:

    A. Calculate proportions of the human body

    B. Measure the constituents of color

    C. Portray 3-dimensonal distances in 2 dimensions

    D. None of the above

Answer: C. Portray 3-dimensonal distances in 2 dimensions

Artists use perspective to determine the appropriate lengths and heights of objects to portray three-dimensional distance in two dimensions.

(Rigorous) (Skill 14.3)

90. Cindy bought a package of cookies. She ate half of them and gave one-third of the remainder to a friend. She then had 20 fewer cookies than she did in the beginning. This information can be expressed symbolically in the following way:

    A. $\frac{n}{2} - \frac{n}{3} = n - 20$

    B. $\frac{n}{2} - \frac{n}{6} = n - 20$

    C. $\frac{n}{2}(1 - \frac{1}{3}) = n - 20$

    D. $\frac{n}{2} - \frac{n}{3} = n + 20$

Answer: B. $\frac{n}{2} - \frac{n}{6} = n - 20$

If Cindy started out with n cookies, she ate $\frac{n}{2}$ and had $\frac{n}{2}$ left. Of these, she gave her friend $\frac{1}{3} \times \frac{n}{2} = \frac{n}{2}$ cookies.

(Average) (Skill 14.3)

91. Kindergarten students are doing a butterfly art project. They fold paper in half. On one half, they paint a design. Then they fold the paper closed and reopen. The resulting picture is a butterfly with matching sides. What math principle does this demonstrate?

    A. Slide

    B. Rotate

    C. Symmetry

    D. Transformation

Answer: C. Symmetry

By folding the painted paper in half, the design is mirrored on the other side, creating symmetry and reflection. The butterfly design is symmetrical about the center.

(Average) (Skill 14.3)

92. Third grade students are looking at a circle graph. Most of the graph is yellow. A small wedge of the graph is blue. Each colored section also has a number followed by a symbol. What are the students most likely learning about?

    A. Addition

    B. Venn diagrams

    C. Percent

    D. Pictographs

Answer: C. Percent

The symbol after the numbers of the sections indicates that students are learning about percents instead of an exact number.

(Easy) (Skill 14.4)

93. When word problems are represented algebraically:

    A. The number of equations should be more than the number of unknowns

    B. The number of equations should be equal to the number of unknowns

    C. The number of equations should be less than the number of unknowns

    D. There can be any number of equations

Answer: B. The number of equations should be equal to the number of unknowns

In order to solve a system of equations for several unknown variables, the number of equations must be equal to the number of variables.

(Easy) (Skill 14.5)

94. The "father of geometry" is:

    A. Archimedes

    B. Euclid

    C. Pythagoras

    D. Apollonius

Answer: B. Euclid

Euclid wrote a set of thirteen books around 330 BCE called the *Elements*. He outlined ten axioms and then deduced 465 theorems. This was the inception of formalized geometry.

(Average) (Skill 15.1)

95. Mr. Sanchez is having his students work with one-syllable words, removing the first consonant and substituting another, as in changing mats to hats. What reading skill are they working on?

A. Morphemic inflections

B. Pronouncing short vowels

C. Invented spelling

D. Phonemic awareness

Answer: D. Phonemic awareness

Phonemic awareness is the acknowledgement of sounds and words; a child's realization that some words rhyme is one of the skills that fall under this category.

(Rigorous) (Skill 15.2)

96. Which of the following is not a primary way to differentiate instruction?

A. Product

B. Content

C. Quantity

D. Process

Answer: C. Quantity

Teachers can differentiate instruction by modifying content, process, or product. Differentiation does not distinguish differences in quantity of work for different students; it distinguishes differences in types of work.

(Average) (Skill 15.3)

97. To summarize a passage, a student should:

A. Answer the key questions raised in the passage

B. Paraphrase the main idea

C. Create a list of key words in the passage

D. State the main idea and supporting details

Answer: D. State the main idea and supporting details

To create a summary, a student should identify the main idea of a passage and the details that support the main idea.

(Easy) (Skill 15.3)

98. A Venn diagram is an example of which type of comprehension strategy?

A. Text structure

B. Graphic organizer

C. Summarization

D. Textual marking

Answer: B. Graphic organizer

Graphic organizers are graphical representations of content. Venn diagrams, a type of graphic organizer, show the similarities and differences between two concepts.

(Easy) (Skill 15.4)

99. **Which of the following is true about content area vocabulary?**

   A. Content area vocabulary should be taught by connecting new words to familiar ideas, words, and experiences.

   B. Content area vocabulary should be taught beginning in middle school.

   C. Content area vocabulary should be taught primarily in language arts classes.

   D. Content area vocabulary should be introduced once and then used occasionally for review.

   Answer: A. Content area vocabulary should be taught by connecting new words to familiar ideas, words, and experiences.

   When teachers explicitly teach vocabulary, it is best if they can connect new words to ideas, words, and experiences with which students are already familiar. This will help to reduce the strangeness of the new words.

(Average) (Skill 15.5)

100. **According to Piaget, at which developmental level would a child be able to learn formal algebra?**

   A. Pre-operational

   B. Sensori-motor

   C. Formal operational

   D. Concrete operational

Answer: C. Formal operational

According to Piaget, it is only at the formal operational stage beyond age twelve that a child is able to understand abstract symbolic concepts required in formal algebra. Basic algebraic ideas using concrete representations may be introduced in the previous stage.

CPSIA information can be obtained at www.ICGtesting.com
Printed in the USA
BVOW04s1257180815

413857BV00005B/152/P